100 best
Decorated
Cookies

Hope you enjoy
making cookies all
year long! Use your own
ideas too! —

Love,
Grandma + Grandpa Essy
from Iowa

100 best Decorated Cookies

Featuring 750 step-by-step photos

Julie Anne Hession

Robert ROSE

For complete cataloguing information, see page 254.

Disclaimer

The recipes in this book have been carefully tested by our kitchen and our tasters. To the best of our knowledge, they are safe and nutritious for ordinary use and users. For those people with food or other allergies, or who have special food requirements or health issues, please read the suggested contents of each recipe carefully and determine whether or not they may create a problem for you. All recipes are used at the risk of the consumer.

We cannot be responsible for any hazards, loss or damage that may occur as a result of any recipe use.

For those with special needs, allergies, requirements or health problems, in the event of any doubt, please contact your medical adviser prior to the use of any recipe.

Design and production: Joseph Gisini and Daniella Zanchetta/PageWave Graphics Inc.
Editor: Sue Sumeraj
Cover image:
  Photographer: Colin Erricson
  Associate photographer: Matt Johannsson
  Food styling: Kathryn Roberston
Interior images:
  Photography: Jeff Green
  Food styling: Suzy Eaton and Julie Anne Hession
  Food styling assistant: Danni Skadburg
  Hand model: Suzy Eaton
  Playing card (page 240): ©istockphoto.com/omergenc

Cover image: Flip-flops (page 68) and Swimming Trunks (page 66)

We acknowledge the financial support of the Government of Canada through the Book Publishing Industry Development Program (BPIDP) for our publishing activities.

Published by Robert Rose Inc.
120 Eglinton Avenue East, Suite 800, Toronto, Ontario, Canada M4P 1E2
Tel: (416) 322-6552 Fax: (416) 322-6936
www.robertrose.ca

Printed and bound in China

1 2 3 4 5 6 7 8 9 PPLS 21 20 19 18 17 16 15 14 13

Contents

For Mom and Dad. One of you gave me my first rolling pin and taught me how to bake cookies. The other always gobbles them up, making me feel like the best baker in the world.

Acknowledgments

This book would never have come together without the help of many talented and supportive people. Some worked to make the 750(+) photos accurate and clear — no small feat. Some focused on the manuscript to ensure a neat and logical layout. Some simply encouraged me with their enthusiastic feedback as I created each design. Some did all three (and much more). Thank you to each and every one of you — you all deserve several dozen cookies!

To my editor, Sue Sumeraj, it has been a great pleasure working with you. Despite the fact that I am an early bird and you are a night owl, our communication always felt completely in sync. (The three-hour time difference helped!) Your expertise and perspective helped to create a user-friendly manuscript from a large amount of information, and I learned so much from you throughout the process. I'm looking forward to that game of pool during my next trip to Toronto!

Bob Dees, thank you for having faith in my abilities as a cookie decorator when I first proposed this idea and for valuing my input throughout the course of this project. Thank you also for giving me the freedom, flexibility and extra time to turn my own ideas into the 100 final designs. I think we picked the right ones!

Joseph Gisini, I hope you have finally gotten some well-deserved sleep after the countless hours you spent working on this book's photos. My thanks to you and the team at PageWave Graphics for coordinating the project's many moving parts and working closely with everyone to make sure we achieved the best possible outcome.

Thanks to Suzy Eaton and her team for their dedicated work on styling in both Salt Lake City and over several long days in Las Vegas. Thank you to Jeff Green and his team for doing such a great job on both the step-by-step and "hero" photographs — we were very fortunate to find you!

Thank you to Marian Jarkovich for your support on the book's marketing and production, and to Martine Quibell for managing the press and public relations. It has been a pleasure to work with you both.

Brett, Lisa, Tina and Camilla, thank you for serving as my cookie "focus group" and for your honest and helpful feedback. I feel so fortunate to have met such a talented group through our crazy little cooking contest hobby.

Thank you to Brandi Farra at Brandi Marketing for continuing to create beautiful, creative and thoughtful content for my websites and social media outlets (and for being a good friend!).

Thank you to my friends, former customers and readers of my blog, *Peanut Butter and Julie*. Your delighted reactions when I opened a bakery box full of decorated cookies or posted a new design on the blog gave me confidence to propose this idea for a book. Thank you to all of the other baking bloggers and cookie decorators out there who continue to inspire me every day with their gorgeous, adorable and perfectly piped creations, and who continue to teach me with helpful tips and techniques.

Mom, thank you for sparking my interest in cookie decorating through our annual holiday tradition of making cookies for Santa. Jay, since you were always decorating right next to me, I guess you could take credit for teaching me everything I know about icing and sprinkles. Dad, thank you for being so enthusiastic about the sample designs I showed you while working on this project — and for always being willing to taste-test those samples!

Finally, thank you to my husband, Eric, for supporting and encouraging me throughout this project and allowing me to (once again!) turn the kitchen into my "office." Just when you thought that constant film of flour in the kitchen from my first cookbook was a thing of the past, it returned for book number two... along with a dining room table covered with stacks of decorated cookies! The fact that you would often enjoy two or three of my sample cookies — even though you don't eat sweets — gave me the ultimate motivation to keep creating.

Introduction

My very first memory of decorating cookies is from when I was about three years old, right around Christmastime. Each Christmas, my mother would cover our dining room table with an easy-to-clean cloth, then top it with trays of baked sugar cookies shaped like stockings, Christmas trees, snowmen and angels. Next to the trays would be bowls of her traditional confectioners' sugar and milk frosting, colored red, green, blue, yellow and white, which my brother, Jay, and I would smear onto the cookies in thick layers using a blunt butter knife. The finishing touch for our "designs" was a selection of colored sprinkles, jimmies and sugars, half of which inevitably ended up on the floor. While the results of our efforts were by no means works of art (although a yellow and green snowman was definitely unique!), our main motivation was to eat our cookies… and perhaps save a few for Santa and his reindeer.

Although I dabbled in it here and there through the years, cookie decorating as I now know it really didn't catch my attention until I opened up a bakery and specialty foods store in Las Vegas called Julie Anne's. One of my managers, Meredith, was classically trained and very skilled in all areas of baking. Since I was completely self-taught, I often picked up new techniques by observing her work. Meredith used to make beautifully decorated butterfly and flower cookies, which we sold at the store, and it was through her that I learned the basic skill of decorating cookies using royal icing. Meredith, I'm not even sure if you know all of this, but thank you!

I would love to say I was a talented cookie decorator from the get-go. I would love to say this, but I can't. My piping technique started out shaky at best, and my icing consistencies left a lot to be desired. Despite this, I still loved experimenting with cookie designs, and I saw my skill level improving with every batch. I loved the creativity involved in coming up with a new shape idea and figuring out how I could bring it to life in the form of a cookie. Eventually, friends started to ask me to make Baby Onesie cookies (page 208) for their baby showers or Sparkly Tutus (page 116) for their daughter's birthday party, which was the ultimate compliment!

I can't tell you how many times I have presented some of my decorated cookies to someone whose reaction has been, "Wow! Those must have taken forever to make. I could never do that." I always say that it really isn't that hard and just requires a bit of time, practice and organization — which is always met with a dubious "Yeah, right!" expression. But it's true! I promise.

My goal for *100 Best Decorated Cookies* is to take the intimidation factor out of royal icing, pastry bags, fondant and disco dust (I mean, really, something called disco dust should never be intimidating!) and turn everyone, whether a first-time decorator or a long-time baker, into a cookie decorating star. Instead of being "off limits," I want people to see that all of the designs in this collection, from a simple basketball (page 162) to a fancy French painter (page 231) are not only attainable but fun to make. And you can't beat the "Hey! I did that!" feeling of accomplishment when you are showing off your completed work.

Along with the 100 different cookie designs, you will also find a wide array of cookie dough recipes, from whole wheat and peanut butter varieties to gluten-free and vegan options. Mix and match cookie shapes and dough as you please, pairing them with icing in a complementary flavor. For example, you might decorate Dark Chocolate Sugar Cookies (page 40) with Peppermint Royal Icing (variation, page 47).

Equipped with a set of tools and techniques, all of which I have detailed in chapter 1, and the instructional step-by-step photos that accompany each and every design, you will be amazed by how easily these creations come together. Make them as a thoughtful personalized gift, a fun addition to your party spread, a scene-stealing contribution to your school's bake sale or simply an extra-special treat to have at home.

You'll think they're almost too pretty to eat… almost.

Part 1

Getting Started

1

Equipment, Ingredients & Techniques

Equipment and Tools

The process of decorating cookies is much easier with a little help from the following tools and supplies. Some of the items may require a trip to your local craft or baking supply store, while others may already be found in your kitchen (or elsewhere in your house). You can also refer to the Source Guide (page 253) for some of my favorite online resources.

Electric Mixer

I prefer to use my trusty stand mixer for making cookie dough and royal icing. It's powerful enough for a double batch of dough when I want to make a lot of cookies, and its handy whisk attachment whips up fluffy icing while I stand there and watch it work! If you don't have a stand mixer, a handheld mixer will work well for the icing, although it will likely take a few minutes longer to reach the proper consistency.

Cookie Cutters

Once you start collecting cookie cutters, it can be difficult to stop (trust me, I know). Fortunately, cutters are now available in a mind-bogglingly wide variety of shapes, sizes and even price points. If you can dream up a cookie theme, chances are pretty good that a cutter already exists. Refer to the Source Guide (page 253) for my favorite cutter merchants.

Most cookie cutters are constructed from one of three materials: copper, tin or plastic. Copper cutters tend to be the sturdiest but are also the most expensive. If you plan to invest in copper cutters, I suggest selecting shapes you'll use more frequently, such as gingerbread people, hearts or rectangles. Tin and plastic cutters can cost as little as $1 apiece. Of the two, I prefer tin cutters because they have sharper sides and, as a result, make more precise cuts. But plastic cutters are great to have on hand when you're working with children on designs such as A-B-C Cookie Pops (page 184).

Several designs in this book require round cutters in various sizes, so it is helpful to have a set of graduated circular cutters on hand. That said, you can also get creative with what you already have on hand in the kitchen! Round drinking glasses, biscuit cutters and even jar lids can all serve as substitutes.

Mini cutters are used in some designs to add dimension and detail, usually with rolled fondant. You can find inexpensive themed sets of these cutters (fall-themed, Christmas-themed, baby-themed) at your local craft store or online. In addition to decorating cookies, these cutters are useful for making decorative pie crusts.

After you use your cutters, wash them with soapy water and make sure they are thoroughly dry before putting them away, so they do not rust. If you only have a few cutters, a simple storage bin or a designated drawer should suffice for storage, but if your collection grows into the hundreds (as mine has), you might need a better way to organize it. Otherwise, finding that *one* cutter you need becomes next to impossible. I created a section in my garage just for my cutters, dividing them into categories and hanging them on a set of long metal rods, much like a display you would see in a retail store.

Using a Handheld Mixer to Make Cookie Dough

If you don't have a stand mixer, you can use a handheld electric mixer to mix the liquids for your cookie dough (step 2 for most of my recipes), but the flour mixture should be stirred into the liquids by hand, using a sturdy wooden spoon.

Pastry Bags

Pastry bags, also called piping bags, are used for almost every design in this book. They are available in two forms — disposable and non-disposable — and in a variety of sizes. For the purpose of decorating cookies, I always use disposable 12-inch (30 cm) bags, as they make it easier to clean up. If you are planning to do a fair amount of decorating, buy a set of 100 bags to get the most bang for your buck.

In a pinch, a large zip-top bag can serve as a decent substitute for a pastry bag, but they are not as sturdy, so I don't recommend using them on a regular basis. Simply snip off one corner of the zip-top bag as you would the tip of the pastry bag (see "Filling a Pastry Bag," page 24).

Couplers

Couplers are two-piece plastic tools that connect decorating tips to pastry bags. While they are not required for piping, I find them useful for two reasons. First, if you plan to change the tip while decorating, a coupler makes doing so both easier and neater. Second, bags fitted with couplers tend to leak less than bags fitted only with tips. Couplers are very inexpensive and are usually packaged in sets of four. I recommend having eight to twelve couplers on hand in your cookie "kit."

Decorating Tips

Decorating tips are available in both metal and plastic. I only use metal tips (except in the case of squeeze bottles), as they seem to retain their shape better than plastic tips. Decorating tips are used in all aspects of cookie decorating, from outlining to flooding to fine detail work. Some even serve double duty as cutters for fondant pieces, as with the Party Hat design (page 106). While tips come in a wide selection of sizes and shapes, for the designs in this book you'll only need the following:

- **#1 round tip:** Creates very thin lines for piping and fine detail work.
- **#2 round tip:** Used most often for piping, detail work and squeeze bottles.
- **#3 round tip:** Creates larger piped lines.
- **#5 round tip:** Used to cut fondant for the Mouse and Cheese design (page 124).
- **#10 round tip:** A 1/4-inch (0.5 cm) tip used to cut out detail pieces.
- **#13:** A small star tip, used in detail work for the Piece of Cake design (page 108).
- **#66 or #67:** A small leaf tip.

Squeeze Bottles

I used to decorate cookies using a set of pastry bags for outlining and a set of bowls for flooding. Then I invested in a set of plastic squeeze bottles and started using two-step icing (see page 24). Squeeze bottles and two-step icing enable you to outline and flood shapes without switching tools.

I prefer (and recommend) buying squeeze bottles that are specifically manufactured for decorating, differentiated by the fact that they come with an attached coupler and a plastic decorating tip (which is interchangeable

Templates

For a few designs in the collection, such as Painter's Palette (page 234), templates are used in place of cutters. Some templates are for the cookie itself, while others are for detail pieces. If I have a cookie design in mind for which I cannot find a cutter (rare, but it happens), I create my own template to trace, either by using clip art or by drawing it freehand. You'll find my templates on pages 251–252 and details about working with them on page 32.

with other metal tips). You can use generic squeeze bottles, like those you might find in a restaurant supply store, but their tips are generally better for flooding than for piping straight lines. I have an assortment of both 6-inch (15 cm) and 8-inch (20 cm) bottles to use, depending on how much icing I need.

Parchment Paper

I always line my cookie sheets with parchment paper, rather than using Silpat or lightly greasing them, as I find that this results in the most even baking. A few years ago, I purchased a large box of parchment paper (1,000 sheets!) at my kitchen supply store, because the small boxes available at grocery stores are always so expensive. I don't recommend that you do this unless you are a frequent baker (or can split a box with friends), but it's a great money-saving tip if you are.

Small Bowls

Keep a collection of small, dishwasher-safe bowls on hand for mixing various icing colors. I found mine at a dollar store. If you can find bowls with a small spout, it will be easier to transfer icing to squeeze bottles. My bowls do not have spouts, and I get by just fine — but I am always on the lookout for an inexpensive spouted variety!

Damp Towels

Keep a few damp towels on hand when decorating cookies — it can be a messy process! You will find that you are constantly wiping down surfaces, bowls and your hands to keep colors and embellishments from transferring to the wrong places. Damp towels are also great for covering large bowls of royal icing to keep it from crusting.

Scissors

I keep a small, sharp pair of scissors with my decorating tools. It is useful for snipping off the corners of pastry bags.

Rubber Bands

I've developed a sixth sense for locating stray rubber bands around my house, as I never seem to have any when I need them for decorating! Rubber bands are used to secure the non-piping end of a pastry bag so that the icing stays in the bag (rather than squirting all over your hands). Wrap the rubber band several times around the end of the bag, forming a tight seal. You can also use twist-ties for this purpose, but I find that rubber bands work better.

Disposable Gloves

Disposable gloves will be your new best friend when you start coloring fondant. Gel paste can stain your hands and is difficult to remove, so purchase a box of gloves for when you are kneading in the color. I found inexpensive gloves at a restaurant supply store, but they are also available in the cleaning supply section of most grocery stores.

Handy Uses for Parchment Paper

Parchment paper can be used to line your work surface when you are adding sparkle to cookies. It will catch any excess sparkle, which you can funnel back into the bottle. I also store my decorated, or partially decorated, cookies on parchment-lined cookie sheets during the various phases of decorating, rather than placing them directly on the cookie sheets.

Rolling Pins

I suggest having two rolling pins on hand. One should be a standard rolling pin, used to roll out cookie dough. My version is a thin, tapered pin, which I've found the easiest to work with and store. It is also helpful to have a smaller (8- to 9-inch/20 to 23 cm) silicone or wooden rolling pin, which makes rolling out small pieces of fondant much easier. Look for these small pins in the cake decorating section of your craft or baking supply store.

Cookie Sheets

If you are planning to bake a large number of cookies, it is helpful to have three or four standard cookie sheets on hand. That way, you can have two sheets in the oven while you're cutting out cookies and adding them to two others, for a seamless baking cycle. That said, two cookie sheets will work just fine. Any cookie sheets you have on hand are fine for these recipes, but I prefer rimless heavy-duty aluminum half-sheet pans. Aluminum pans conduct heat quickly and uniformly, whereas darker sheets can cause cookies to brown too quickly.

Wire Racks

Standard wire cooling racks allow cookies to cool faster than if they remain on cookie sheets. Racks are also useful during the decorating process. Place iced cookies on a wire rack set over a sheet of parchment paper. Sprinkle cookies with sanding sugar or disco dust, shaking excess off onto the parchment. This is a great way to save valuable decorating resources!

Tweezers

I recommend buying a pair of tweezers to keep with your other decorating tools. They will help you add small embellishments, such as silver nonpareils, white edible pearls or petite fondant bows, to wet icing. Fingers are usually too big to accomplish this task neatly and precisely.

Toothpicks

Toothpicks are used to make feathered designs in wet icing (see page 29). Their fine tips make it easy to work even within small areas. I keep a box of toothpicks with my decorating kit.

X-acto Knife

While a small, sharp knife will often do, X-acto knives are even smaller and sharper (razor sharp!), so they are a better choice for cutting fondant pieces and tracing templates. An X-acto knife consists of a small, slanted, razor-like blade mounted on a body the size and shape of a standard ballpoint pen. X-acto knives can be found in the baking aisle of well-stocked craft stores. If you don't see them there, look near the sewing supplies or in the scrapbooking section. They are not recommended for use by children, and should always be stored with their caps on (you don't want to learn that the hard way).

Plastic Wrap

I purchased an industrial-sized roll of plastic wrap at a kitchen supply store so I'd always have it handy. I use it to wrap dough, cover bowls of royal icing and wrap fondant so that it doesn't dry out.

Ruler

I use a standard 6- to 12-inch (15 to 30 cm) ruler along with an X-acto knife to cut straight sides on pieces of fondant and to draw templates for straight lines onto cookies. It's amazing how much better decorated cookies look when the piped lines are straight!

Edible Markers

Did you know that edible markers exist? They do, and they are fantastic! The name is a bit misleading — you can't actually eat the marker — but the ink is indeed edible and can be drawn right onto cookies or dried royal icing. I use these markers for detail where piping isn't necessary, such as for bags for the Mummy Trick-or-Treaters (page 76). They are also an alternative to using an X-acto knife for tracing a template; simply pipe over the marker line as you would a line drawn by an X-acto knife.

Paintbrushes

Small food-safe paintbrushes come in handy when you are adding sparkle (see page 28) to your cookies. (You will learn that I am a big fan of adding sparkle!) I recommend having two to four brushes of various sizes — at least two, because one should remain dry for applying dry luster dust, while the other may get wet dabbing surfaces with water or applying wet luster dust.

Cookie Pop Sticks

This collection only has one cookie pop design (page 184), but you could certainly apply the technique to any of the basic designs in the book (such as the "Just Married" Cars on page 203). Cookie pop sticks, also used for cake and pie pops, are generally about 6 inches (15 cm) long and are made from paper. Look for them in the baking aisle of craft stores or well-stocked grocery stores.

Texture Set

A texture set, used for the Wedding Cake design (page 200), is used to emboss fondant with a textured design before attaching it to a cookie. A plastic textured mat is lightly misted with nonstick spray and then placed on top of the fondant. Light pressure from a rolling pin transfers the mat's design to the fondant. The sets are available in a variety of designs and can be found in the baking aisle of well-stocked craft stores or online (see the Source Guide, page 253). While a texture set is indeed a specialty tool, it's fun to have for creating special-occasion cookies!

Key Ingredients

Once you've gotten your feet wet decorating cookies, you'll find that having a supply kit full of decorating ingredients allows you to be a bit more flexible with your creativity. What color should I make this dress cookie? Should I add luster dust shimmer or disco dust glitter? How about a pink fondant belt? That said, you certainly don't need to feel like you are required to run out and spend a fortune on every item listed below in order to create show-stopping designs. My collection has amassed over several years, as I add one or two items at a time (okay, I might have had a few baking supply sprees in there too), until I had to create a designated cookie decorating section in my kitchen!

Cookie Dough Basics

- **Flour:** All of the cookies in this book, except for Gluten-Free Sugar Cookies (page 37), are made using standard all-purpose flour.
- **Butter:** Unsalted butter is used for all cookies in this book except Vegan Sugar Cookies (page 38), which use whipped vegan butter. I prefer to use unsalted butter because it allows you to control the amount of salt in your recipes (salted butter can have a varying amount of salt). In addition, unsalted butter tends to be fresher, with a shorter shelf life, because salt acts as a preservative. Butter should be at room temperature when it is added to these recipes.
- **Eggs:** All of the cookie recipes (except Vegan Sugar Cookies) use large eggs and egg yolks.
- **Zest:** Several of the recipes use either orange zest or lemon zest in the dough. I like to add zest to many of my creations because it really brightens up the flavor of both sweet and savory recipes. In all cases, if you prefer, zest can be omitted from recipes.

Confectioners' (Icing) Sugar

You will become very familiar with confectioners' (icing) sugar when creating the designs in this book! It is the main ingredient used to make both Classic Royal Icing (page 47) and Vegan Royal Glaze (page 48). Classic Royal Icing calls for 2 lbs (1 kg) of sugar, which is the same as two standard boxes or one standard bag. Vegan Royal Glaze uses double this amount.

Meringue Powder

Meringue powder consists of powdered egg whites, cornstarch and stabilizers, and it is the key ingredient for getting your royal icing to set and dry. Although some people make royal icing using egg whites or powdered egg whites, I only use meringue powder because I find the results to be most consistent (and many people don't like the idea of using raw egg whites). You can find meringue powder in the baking aisle of most craft stores, but I tend to buy it in bulk online or at a baking supply store, as it saves me money over time.

Grating Citrus Zest

The best way to grate zest is with a rasp grater (such as a Microplane) — one of my favorite kitchen tools and a great investment if you don't have one.

Flavorings

Plain old royal icing has a reputation for being kind of, well, *blah*, so I like to add flavor to brighten up its blank canvas. My favorite flavoring is freshly squeezed lemon juice, which I substitute for some of the water called for in the recipe (see tip, page 47), depending on my desired level of tart/sweet contrast. Create other flavors by adding extracts, such as pure vanilla, almond or mint. Use extracts that contain oil sparingly, as too much oil can affect how long it takes for royal icing to set, and it can cause the icing to separate. Clear extracts are best for keeping your icing bright white.

Food Colorings: Liquids vs. Gels

Having a wide array of food colors for your royal icing and fondant not only makes decorating easier, but also makes it more fun, as the various shades will spark your creativity. You can also use a basic set of colors to mix new hues (e.g., red plus blue = purple).

As with other decorating tools, you have a choice when it comes to the type of food coloring you use: liquid food coloring or gel paste. Both will stain your hands and clothing, so be careful when mixing!

Adding Coloring

Whether you use liquid food coloring or gel paste, add only a small amount of coloring at a time. A little can go a long way. Colors tend to dry a bit darker than their shade when wet, so keep this in mind when mixing. See page 22 for more tips on tinting icing, and page 30 for tips on coloring fondant.

- **Liquid food coloring:** Liquid food coloring is the standard coloring found in the grocery store, either in the baking section or next to the extracts. I almost never use liquid coloring for decorating, as it affects the consistency of the royal icing.
- **Gel paste:** I almost exclusively use gel paste to color my royal icing and fondant because the color is more concentrated and the paste's thicker texture does not alter the icing's consistency. You can buy gel paste in small jars or in squeeze bottles (both small and large). I keep larger amounts of the colors I use most often, such as black and red, and smaller portions of "specialty colors," such as avocado green. I currently have a mix of both jars and squeeze bottles, but am starting to gravitate toward squeeze bottles, as the colors seem to have the best concentration and don't dry out as easily. There are many good brands of gel paste available, but my favorite is AmeriColor, mainly because its red and black gels were the first I found that actually turned out red and black! Some black gels never seem to get past the dark gray stage; AmeriColor's gel requires only a small squeeze for a jet black color.

Fondant

I often describe fondant as "sugar-based decorating play dough," as it reminds me of the malleable, colorful product I used as a kid. Some people are intimidated by fondant, but it is really quite easy to use and, once you get the hang of it, it opens up the world of decorating possibilities! Fondant detail is great for giving your cookies a layer of texture and, because it dries hard, it's ideal for adding a shape to the top of a cookie (as with the Baby Onesie cookies on page 208). Be sure to keep fondant tightly wrapped when you're not working with it, as it can dry out quickly — a costly mistake! Fondant used to be a challenge to find, but its recent surge in popularity has made it readily available in craft stores and some grocery store baking aisles. For tips on working with fondant, see page 30.

Sanding Sugars

Decorative sanding sugars are now available in just about every color imaginable and in a variety of textures. For the designs in this book, I opted for fine sanding sugars, as I think they provide a cleaner, more even finish. Sanding sugars are a good way to add some sparkle to your cookies while the icing is still wet, without being overly glittery. You can find these sugars in basic colors in most baking aisles, but refer to the Source Guide (page 253) for a wider variety of shades. See "Adding Sparkle" (page 28) for details on how to apply sanding sugars to your cookies.

Disco Dust

After using disco dust over and over again, I have come to believe it earned its name because you end up looking like a human disco ball when you use it. No matter how careful you are, this glittering substance seems to end up *everywhere!* Disco dust is what you should use when you want to give your cookies the most sparkle or want to make a certain part of a cookie really stand out. Although disco dust usually comes in a small jar, a little bit goes a long way. See "Adding Sparkle" (page 28) for details on how to apply disco dust to your cookies.

Luster Dust

Luster dust is much finer than either disco dust or sanding sugar, and it serves two purposes for the designs in this book. First, it's an easy way to add a bit of shimmer to a cookie that needs a finishing touch. When I look at a cookie and think, "Hmmm… it needs *something*," luster dust always does the trick! Second, mixed with a few drops of vodka or lemon juice, luster dust can be painted onto cookies to give them gold or silver metallic detailing.

Dragées

Dragées are small edible balls, sometimes covered in a metallic coat. They are an easy way to add bits of detail work to a cookie, such as a "pearl necklace" or other decorative accents. The designs in this book use silver and white "pearl" dragées, both of which are readily available in baking aisles.

Royal Icing Decorations

Some of the designs in this book call for royal icing decorations, which are premade decorations you can attach directly to your cookies. I often use royal icing eyes for animals, and one design (the Snowman on page 85) uses a premade royal icing flower. The eyes can be found in the baking aisle of most craft stores, but in all cases you can pipe the decorations with royal icing instead of using a premade variety.

Candies, Jimmies and Nonpareils

Explore your grocery store's baking and candy aisles to find new embellishments for your cookies. You never know when inspiration may strike! Round red hots, M&Ms, jelly beans, gumdrops, colored jimmies, nonpareils and licorice strings are just a few of your many options.

Metallic Embellishments

Metallic embellishments such as disco dust and dragées are labeled "non-toxic," but keep in mind that the U.S. Food and Drug Administration has approved them *only as decorations*. That said, they are perfectly fine to eat in small doses — but I don't recommend handfuls!

Cookie Decorating Techniques

Storing Dough

Cookie dough can be stored in the refrigerator, tightly wrapped in plastic, for about 3 days. Or it can be frozen for up to 6 months. When freezing dough, I like to double-wrap it in plastic and then seal it in a large zip-top bag. Thaw dough overnight in the refrigerator before use.

Successful cookie decorating involves certain key techniques, some of which are used in every single design. Following is a comprehensive list of the techniques used in this book, from rolling out cookie dough to adding that final touch of sparkle. You might find yourself referring to this section often in the beginning, but soon these techniques will become second nature and you will only need an occasional refresher!

Rolling and Cutting Dough

For all of the cookie dough recipes in this book, the dough must be cold before you roll it out, as cold dough retains its shape better when baking. The minimum refrigeration time is usually 1 to 2 hours, but you can also prepare dough several days in advance (see "Storing Dough," at left).

The easiest way to roll out dough is on a lightly floured, cold work surface. Too much flour will affect the final texture of your cookies, so use restraint when coating your surface. Many bakers like to roll out dough between two sheets of parchment paper or waxed paper, thus eliminating the need for extra flour. I have never taken to this method because I like to see my dough as it is rolled out so that I can gauge its evenness.

When rolling out dough, I use the "turn" method for best results. This means I roll across the dough once, applying even pressure, then give the disk a one-eighth turn and roll it again. I keep repeating the one-eighth turn and roll until my dough has reached the desired thickness (about $1/4$ inch/0.5 cm). Cut as many cookies as possible from the dough, then reroll scraps as necessary. If at any time during the rolling process the dough becomes too soft, simply rewrap it and return it to the refrigerator for 15 minutes to firm up.

When transferring cut-outs to cookie sheets (especially cookies with odd or delicate shapes), I use a thin, flat spatula with a large surface area so that it catches all parts of the cookie. You certainly don't want your French Painter (page 231) to lose an arm! The recipes in this book generally produce between 24 and 48 cookies, depending on the size and shape of your cutter.

Baking Cookies

The cookies in this book have a baking time of 11 to 15 minutes in a conventional oven, but they could take a few minutes longer if you are using more than one cookie sheet. Be sure to switch the positions of your cookie sheets halfway through the baking process to ensure even browning. I like to have at least three (and preferably four) cookie sheets on hand for baking larger batches of cookies, so that I can roll and position one set while the other set is baking. Once cookies are baked, transfer them to wire racks to cool completely.

Tinting Icing

First, plan your palette. Before I start working on a cookie design, I make a list of the different icing colors I will need. Then I divide the royal icing based on an estimate of how much of each color is required. For most colors, I have the appropriate gel paste in supply, but occasionally I need to create a new color (e.g., for Piece of Cake, page 108) using a combination of colors from my collection.

To tint icing, add the desired amount of gel to the icing and stir with a spoon or a rubber spatula until the gel is completely incorporated. Always tint icing gradually. Gel pastes, especially those that come in squeeze bottles, are highly concentrated, so just a small squeeze may yield your desired color. If you are not sure about a particular combination of colors, test out your theory using a small amount of royal icing.

Royal icing tends to dry a bit darker than it looks when first mixed, so keep this in mind when creating your colors.

Adjusting Icing Consistency

When you're using royal icing for the designs in this book, it will be one of three consistencies: piping icing, flooding icing or two-step icing (my personal favorite).

Piping Icing

Piping icing is the thickest of the three. Shiny and similar in texture to toothpaste, piping icing holds its shape without spreading when it is placed on a cookie. This consistency should squeeze out of a pastry bag with light pressure (if your hands are straining, it's too thick). It is used to outline shapes and to add details such as eyes, lettering and accent marks. The recipe for Classic Royal Icing (page 47) creates icing that is ready to pipe.

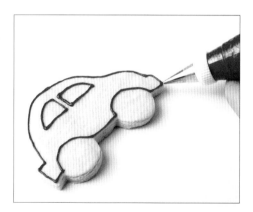

Flooding Icing

"Flooding" refers to the technique of filling cookies or sections of cookies that have been outlined with piping icing. Flooding icing is thinned enough that it spreads easily, using very little guidance from a toothpick or the tip of a squeeze bottle. I rarely use flooding icing, as I prefer two-step icing.

To reach flooding consistency, add liquid (either water or lemon juice) to piping icing 1 teaspoon (5 mL) at a time, stirring after each addition. If you are working with a large amount of icing, you can add a couple of teaspoons (10 mL) or even a tablespoon (15 mL) at a time, but trust me, a little goes a long way, so be conservative! The final result should resemble syrup that is room temperature or cool, as opposed to resembling water. One good test for this is the "ribbon test," also used for two-step icing. Using a spoon, drizzle a ribbon of icing across the top of your icing bowl. If the ribbon completely disappears in 2 to 3 seconds, leaving a glossy flat surface, you have reached flooding consistency.

A cookie outlined with piping icing, then flooded with flooding icing.

Two-Step Icing

When I discovered this icing, it changed my cookie decorating life. I know, that's a strong statement, but it's true. This icing not only saves time, it saves on cleanup, which we can all agree is a great quality!

A cookie outlined and flooded with two-step icing.

The name "two-step icing" may be a bit misleading. It does not take just two steps to make it; rather, it allows you to both outline and flood without switching tools. Sound good? Read on!

Two-step icing has the texture of hair gel or cool honey, slightly thicker than flooding icing. It is thick enough to hold its shape when piped, but thin enough to create a smooth surface when used for flooding. It also results in a more fluid overall finish. When cookies are outlined with piping icing, then flooded with flooding icing, you can sometimes detect the separation between the outline and the filling because of the different textures. Two-step icing looks completely smooth.

I almost always use two-step icing, placing it in a squeeze bottle for both outlining and flooding, but if you prefer to use the alternative method, you can outline using a pastry bag and flood using a squeeze bottle (see "Piping," page 27, and "Flooding," page 28).

To reach two-step icing consistency, add liquid (either water or lemon juice) to piping icing 1 teaspoon (5 mL) at a time, stirring after each addition, until the icing has the texture of hair gel. Use the "ribbon test," as for flooding consistency (see page 23), but this time, your ribbon should disappear in about 15 seconds.

Filling a Pastry Bag

To fill a pastry bag for piping, you can use one of two methods: the traditional method, which you may have seen in other cookie decorating books or online, or the easy cleanup method, which I recently discovered. If you have spent any time with a pastry bag, you know that the process of cleaning the bag is the worst part, and it's almost impossible not to end up with icing all over your hands and under your fingernails. Thanks to the creativity of Karen at KarensCookies.net, this new method not only makes cleanup a breeze, it also eliminates the leakage that sometimes occurs from your coupler when icing squeezes through small holes. I almost exclusively use the easy cleanup method now — thanks, Karen!

For either method, you will need a disposable or reusable pastry bag, piping consistency icing (see page 23), a coupler, a decorating tip, scissors and a rubber band or twist-tie. See page 25 for step-by-step instructions on the traditional method, and page 26 for step-by-step instructions on the easy cleanup method.

Filling a Squeeze Bottle

Squeeze bottles are used for both flooding icing and two-step icing. The best way to fill one is to pour the icing directly from its bowl into the bottle. This might feel a bit awkward at first, but you will get the hang of it! If your hand is too shaky and you are ending up with more icing on the counter than in the bottle, try using a bowl with a spout or even a funnel to make the transfer.

Filling a Pastry Bag: The Traditional Method

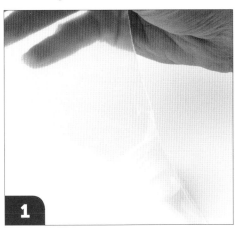

1 Separate the coupler so that you have a tube-shaped piece and a screw-top. ■ Place the tube-shaped piece inside the pastry bag so that the smaller opening faces the bag's tip.

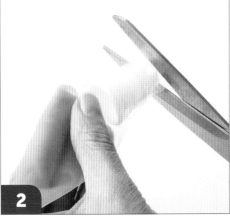

2 Using scissors, snip off the tip of the bag so that the hole is just large enough for the coupler tube to peek through. ■ (If the hole is too large, pressure will push the whole coupler through the bag or the icing will leak.)

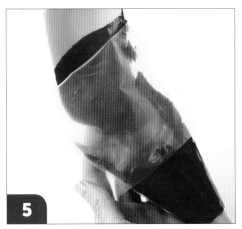

3 Place the desired decorating tip over the coupler tube so that it covers the end of the bag.

4 Place the coupler's screw-top over the tip and twist to secure tightly.

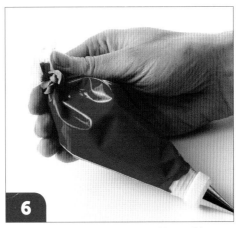

5 Fold the wide end of the bag out over itself, about halfway down. ■ Using a large spoon or spatula, transfer icing to the bag, filling it only about halfway (refill if necessary).

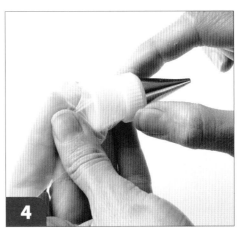

6 Unfold the bag and secure it with a rubber band or twist-tie positioned at the top of the icing.

Storing Icing

Royal icing can be stored for up to 1 week, very tightly covered in bowls, either at room temperature on in the refrigerator. If the icing separates during this time, which is likely, simply stir it until it returns to the desired consistency. Icing can also be stored in squeeze bottles for a few days, but if you see evidence of separation, you will need to transfer it to a bowl, stir it, then return it to the bottle. (I tried simply shaking the bottle vigorously, but that didn't work. Maybe you are stronger than I am!)

Filling a Pastry Bag:
The Easy Cleanup Method

1 Line your work surface with a large square of plastic wrap. ■ Using a large spoon or spatula, transfer icing to the center of the upper third of the plastic wrap.

2 Starting from the top, roll the icing up in the plastic wrap, leaving the ends on both sides extended.

3 Holding both ends of the plastic wrap, spin the plastic "rope" several times, as if you were twirling a jump rope, until the packet of icing is snug between the two twisted ends.

4 Using scissors, cut off one end of the rope, about 3 inches (7.5 cm) from the packet.

5 Pull the cut end of the rope through a pastry bag fitted with a coupler.

6 Snip off any excess plastic.

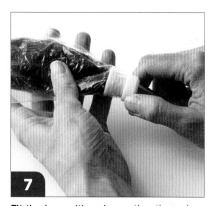

7 Fit the bag with a decorating tip and the coupler's screw-top.

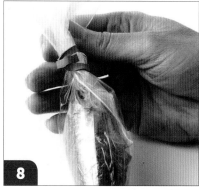

8 Secure the bag with a rubber band or twist-tie.

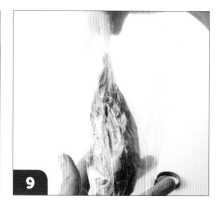

9 When you are done with the pastry bag, simply undo the rubber band and pull out the plastic packet — no messy hands!

Adapted from KarensCookies.net. Used with permission.

Piping

The best advice I can give about piping royal icing is this: practice, practice, practice. While piping outlines, detail and especially lettering onto cookies may be one of the more intimidating parts of cookie decorating, the more you practice the more those somewhat shaky lines will turn into perfectly steady, straight lines.

Holding the Pastry Bag

When piping, hold the pastry bag with both hands. One hand should be positioned around the base to guide the piping, and the other should be around the top of the bag, near the rubber band or twist-tie. I always have my right hand at the bottom, but do whatever feels natural for you.

The bag should be held at a 45-degree angle just above the cookie's surface. Squeeze the bag with your top hand, applying just enough pressure so that the icing emerges from the tip in a steady stream. Guide the icing using your bottom hand to move the tip along the cookie.

Piping an Outline

Every cookie in this book has an outline piped around the outside border. The cookie might be outlined in one icing color or several. When piping an outline, you will either use a pastry bag, holding it as described above, or a plastic squeeze bottle (see sidebar, page 28). Either way, while applying pressure, move along the border at a steady pace until your outline is completed, trying to stay close to the edge of the cookie.

Piping Straight Lines

Piping a perfectly straight line without any sort of guidance is a gift. Unfortunately, I do not possess this particular gift, so I enlist a little bit of help (which is nothing to be ashamed of!). To create a guide for my straight lines, I use a ruler and an X-acto knife to make a template over which I pipe the line.

Piping Words and Letters

Even more than piping a straight line, piping perfectly uniform, straight letters and words can be a challenge. Words can end up positioned on a slant, poorly proportioned or, worst of all, misspelled! To avoid this, I use edible markers to write templates for my words, over which I pipe the icing. I often draw a straight line with an X-acto knife as a base for writing the letters.

Keeping Your Pastry Bag Upright

If you have filled a pastry bag with icing but are not using it right away, set it upright in a tall drinking glass until you're ready for it.

Piping a Leopard Print

Three of the cookies in this book — Little Black Dress (page 188), Leopard-Print Purse (page 190) and Leopard-Print Pumps (page 192) — instruct you to use black and brown icing to pipe a leopard print onto the cookies. Here's a close-up of what this leopard print should look like.

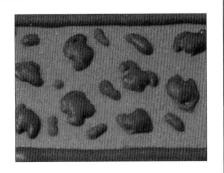

Wet-on-Dry Detailing

Detail work adds another layer of texture to a cookie when more icing is piped on top of icing that has already set. It can be as simple as piping around the edges of a cookie for a finished look, or you might be creating a face for an animal or adding pockets and a lapel to a coat. Most often, detail work is done using a very fine line from a #1 or a #2 decorating tip.

Flooding

Once your cookie has been outlined, it is ready to be flooded. When flooding the interior of a cookie, you have two choices. You can either use a squeeze bottle, which is my preferred alternative — and certainly less messy — or you can use a spoon and a toothpick.

Using a Squeeze Bottle

Hold your squeeze bottle over the center of the section that needs to be filled. Squeeze some icing onto the cookie, letting it flow into the space. Use the tip of your squeeze bottle to move the icing into any blank areas, squeezing a bit more if necessary, until the entire surface is evenly filled.

Using a Spoon and a Toothpick

If you do not have a squeeze bottle, you can use this method. It's definitely not as streamlined, but it still does the trick! Using a small spoon, transfer a small amount of flooding icing from its bowl to the center of the cookie. As the icing spreads, use the tip of a toothpick to move it into any blank areas, adding a bit more icing if necessary, until the entire surface is evenly filled.

Wet-on-Wet Detailing

When you add details or a design in a different color on top of wet icing, the new icing "settles" into the base color, making one flat layer (as with the Polka-Dot Bonnet design on page 60) rather than the added texture you get with wet-on-dry detailing (above). In this case, you need to work fairly quickly when adding the design to make sure the base color is still wet. It is best to use two-step icing or flooding icing for a wet-on-wet design, as piping icing is generally too thick for the design to settle correctly. If you are adding a polka-dot design, hold your squeeze bottle straight up and down over the cookie instead of at an angle.

Feathering

Feathering is a variation of wet-on-wet detailing that can make an impressive patterned design (seen in Mittens, page 90, and in the Sailboat design, page 114) using only a squeeze bottle and a toothpick. The consistency of the two icings you use should be the same, whether flooding consistency or two-step consistency. For step-by-step instructions, see page 29.

Adding Sparkle

As you look through the designs in this collection, you will see that I like to add a little pizzazz to my cookies whenever I can. A bit of sparkle can accent an area of a cookie that you want to highlight, such as a cheerleader's hair bow (page 163), or it can take a design, such as a glass of champagne (page 198), from very simple to extra-special. Sparkle can be added to wet icing or dry icing (see page 30).

Feathering

1

Outline and flood the cookie using one color.

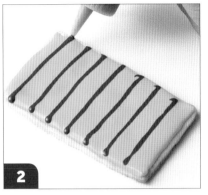

2

Vertical feathering: Working quickly while the icing is still wet, use a squeeze bottle filled with a contrasting color to pipe straight parallel lines horizontally across the cookie, spacing them an equal distance apart.

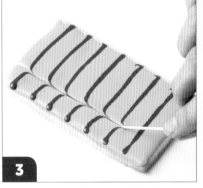

3

Position the tip of a toothpick near the left edge of the parallel lines, just above the top line. ■ Quickly drag the toothpick down through all the lines, creating a feathered design.

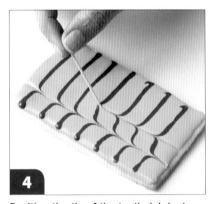

4

Position the tip of the toothpick just below the bottom line and a little to the right of the first feathered design. ■ Quickly drag the toothpick up through all the lines, creating a feathered design in the opposite direction.

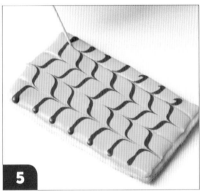

5

Continue moving the toothpick an equal distance to the right and making alternating downward and upward strokes until you have reached the right edge of the parallel lines. ■ Let icing set for at least 6 hours or overnight.

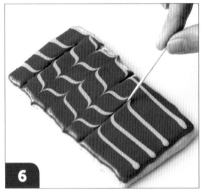

6

Horizontal feathering: Make your parallel lines (step 2) vertical and, starting at the top of the vertical lines, drag the toothpick from left to right, then right to left, for steps 3 through 5, working your way down to the bottom of the lines.

Marbling

For some cookies in this book, a technique called marbling is used. Marbling is similar to feathering in that it involves dragging the tip of a toothpick through multiple colors of wet icing, but marbling can create a wider variety of designs, such as swirls, spirals and loops. Examples of marbling can be seen in Butterfly (page 62), Autumn Leaves (page 84), Peppermint Candy (page 98) and Slice of Lemon (page 216).

Adding Sparkle On Wet Icing

Disco dust and sanding sugar are sprinkled on top of wet icing. Do your sprinkling over a piece of parchment paper or a paper plate. That way, you can catch excess sparkle that doesn't stick to the icing, then funnel it back into the jar (so you won't need to buy a new one as quickly!). Sprinkle disco dust or sanding sugar generously over the cookie so that it is evenly coated. If some dust or sugar remains on unwanted areas of the cookie even after you shake off excess, wait for the icing to dry completely, then use a small food-safe paintbrush or a cotton swab to brush off stray crystals.

Adding Sparkle On Dry Icing

Luster dust can be added to dry icing surfaces either to add shimmer or to give them a metallic finish. For some simple sparkle, use a dry food-safe paintbrush to lightly coat the surface in luster dust, brushing off excess. To add a solid coat of metallic color (as for the Champagne Glass design, page 198):

1. Outline and flood (if necessary) the target area with white icing or a color similar to that of the luster dust (e.g., yellow for gold dust or gray for silver dust). Let the icing dry completely.
2. In a small bowl, mix $1/4$ to $1/2$ tsp (1 to 2 mL) luster dust with a few drops of vodka (preferable) or lemon juice (see sidebar, at left). The mixture should not be overly runny.
3. Use a small food-safe paintbrush to coat the target area with the liquid luster. Let dry.

Working with Fondant

When many people hear the word "fondant," they immediately think, "Oh, working with fondant is *much* too difficult. That's for experts only. I can't do that!" True, there are some examples of fondant work where the skill level is dazzling, but these are usually elaborate, multi-tiered wedding cakes that a team of trained bakers has worked on for days. These are cookies, and yes, you *can* create every single one of these designs. Just think of fondant as that play dough or modeling clay you so adeptly mastered back in elementary school.

Coloring Fondant

I have one word for you when it comes to coloring fondant: gloves. Wear disposable gloves or your hands will be the same color as the fondant. To color fondant, add a small amount of gel paste, then knead it in with your hands until the color is evenly distributed throughout the fondant. If at any time during the kneading the fondant becomes sticky, simply add a bit of cornstarch, which will eventually disappear as you continue kneading.

Rolling Out Fondant

Because of its sticky nature, fondant should be rolled out on a surface lightly dusted with cornstarch. Although you can use a standard rolling pin, it is easier to roll out smaller pieces with a small silicone or wooden pin. Most fondant is rolled out to a thickness of either $1/16$ or $1/8$ inch (2 or 3 mm).

Cutting Shapes

You can cut shapes from rolled fondant using small cutters, which you can find in the baking aisle of your craft store. Some shapes for the designs in this book, such as the belts for the Little Black Dress cookies (page 188), are cut freehand using an X-acto knife and a ruler. Once the shapes are cut, you can use a pointed modeling tool to add detail, such as veins on a leaf, if desired. Some finished fondant pieces are applied to cookies while they are still malleable; others are set aside to dry completely before they are attached to cookies.

Forming Shapes by Hand

Some of the fondant pieces in my designs are molded by hand. Don't expect your version to look exactly like mine. Since this work is freehand, allow yourself a bit of creative flexibility. Just mold the fondant with your fingers as you would clay, adding bits of cornstarch if it becomes too sticky.

Attaching Fondant

Fondant can be attached to a cookie with either a dab of royal icing or a dab of water. Fondant is best applied to more fondant (as with the Giraffe horns on page 134) with a dab of water and light pressure. After attaching fondant, set the cookies aside to dry.

Adding Embellishments

One thing you can do to give your cookies more "personality" is to add textural and colorful embellishments, such as metallic dragées, edible white pearls and royal icing decorations like eyes and flowers. You can find these decorations in baking supply stores or well-stocked craft stores, or you can order them from one of the sources listed on page 253.

Although embellishments can be added by hand, where small spheres are concerned this method can prove both difficult and frustrating (and you usually end up with several balls rolling off your counter and onto the floor). I like to apply small decorations using a pair of tweezers that I keep solely for cookie decorating purposes. While you might at first feel like you're playing a game of Operation, you will soon find that your tweezers save you a lot of aggravation!

Embellishments can be applied directly to wet royal icing or, for a "cleaner" look, you can apply most decorations by brushing the target surface with a dab of warm water.

Using an X-acto Knife

For tracing templates, cutting fondant and making lines to guide piping, nothing works as well as an X-acto knife. Place the cookie dough or fondant on a cutting board before cutting so that you don't harm your work surface. Hold an X-acto knife as you would a pen, applying enough pressure to the intended surface (fondant or cookie dough) to cut all the way through (unless otherwise instructed). Be careful to keep your other hand out of the way of the knife's path! If you are using a ruler to draw a straight line to use as a guide, simply run the X-acto knife gently along the length of the ruler.

Be careful to store your X-acto knife with its cap on, so that you don't injure yourself when reaching for it, and keep it out of reach of children.

Storing Fondant

Fondant can be expensive, and it dries out very quickly. When you're done using it, be sure to tightly wrap fondant in plastic wrap and place it in a sealed zip-top bag. Store fondant at room temperature.

Several designs in this book use templates, either for the cookie shape itself or for a fondant piece that is attached to the cookie. I've included a template if I felt a shape might be too challenging for you to draw freehand. (I want to make your life as easy as possible!) Look for my templates on pages 251–252.

It is best to transfer templates to waxed or parchment paper, which are both food-friendly. Copy the template from the book onto regular white paper, then place the waxed or parchment paper over the copy and trace the design.

Cut out your template and use an X-acto knife to cut around it on the cookie dough or fondant. With fondant, it is sometimes easier to wait about 15 minutes between rolling out and tracing. This lets the fondant firm up a bit, as soft fondant can tear easily.

Getting Ready to Decorate

As a "type A" personality, I can't start a cookie decorating session without all of my tools ready and in the correct place. Yes, setting everything up takes a bit of extra time, but it is so much better than having to stop and look for something once you have entered cookie decorating mode! Here are some tips for setting up your cookie studio:

1. **Read through the instructions.** I know, I know. You're excited to get going. But trust me, this step is important. Take a few minutes and read through all the instructions in the design — and read the recipes for the cookie dough and the icing too — so that there are no surprises along the way. This will also help you picture the process as you move from start to finish.

2. **Make a list (and check it twice!)** Whether it's a mental list or a written list, go through all of the steps you need to accomplish and make sure you have every tool and ingredient needed to get the job done. Are you out of any gel paste colors? Where is the meringue powder? Do you have enough clean small bowls? Yes, yes and yes? Good! You're ready!

3. **Create a timeline.** Again, this could be mental or written. Do you need the cookies for this evening? Many cookies are a two-day project, though some have a shorter timeline. It helps to give yourself at least one full day to complete a design, but two days is optimal. If you can make your cookie dough and bake the cookies in advance, that's even better.

4. **Set out spoons and bowls.** Have several spoons and small bowls on hand for mixing icing colors.

Storing Decorated Cookies

Once decorated cookies have dried, they will keep for 1 to 2 weeks, although their flavor is best if they are eaten within 1 week. The best way to store cookies is in a tightly sealed container, such as a large rectangular food-safe plastic container or a metal tin. Carefully place cookies in layers, separated with waxed or parchment paper. Be careful not to overcrowd cookies or layers of decoration may loosen and fall off. You worked much too hard on these pieces of art!

5. **Have towels and parchment paper handy.** Keep plenty of paper towels and damp kitchen towels nearby for easy cleanup. You will need them! You'll also want to have a ready supply of parchment paper with which to line work surfaces and catch stray embellishments.

6. **Wear an apron.** I never remember to wear an apron, but I have more than one stained T-shirt that makes me wish I would. Here's hoping your memory is better than mine!

7. **Prepare the icing.** This task probably takes the most time of all the set-up steps, but once it's done, your decorating will be much easier. Get all of your icing colored, thinned to the correct consistency and transferred to either pastry bags or squeeze bottles (unless the instructions say to keep it covered in a bowl).

8. **Give yourself space.** There are lots of moving parts involved in decorating cookies: icings, cookie sheets, pastry bags… Clear away any items you are not currently using so you can focus on the task at hand. If you are outlining and flooding cookies, move the rolling pin and fondant so that you can work without knocking something onto a freshly flooded cookie. (I learned this the hard way!)

Keep Icing Covered

While I am preparing each color of icing, I cover the main bowl with a damp towel to keep it from crusting, which will affect your piping, flooding — just about everything!

Packaging and Shipping Cookies

Not much beats receiving a package containing custom-decorated sugar cookies! Once you have mastered these 100 designs, you will never need to worry about what to send your friends and family for holidays, birthdays or any other cookie-worthy celebrations.

- **Packaging:** For party favors and for shipping, I like to individually wrap cookies in clear cellophane favor bags tied at the top with a matching ribbon. You can find these inexpensive bags at craft stores, sold in sets of 10 to 100. You can also bag two cookies in a set, such as the Easter Bunny (page 52) and his Carrot (page 54)!

- **Shipping:** When shipping cookies, do not overcrowd the box. Package cookies in layers and separate them with tissue paper for cushioning. Make sure the box is sturdy enough to withstand any accidental bang-ups!

Troubleshooting Tips

Here are a few extra tips that might help you along in your decorating adventures.

- The least efficient way to decorate three dozen cookies is one at a time, especially if they are very detailed. If your design is mostly red, with blue and yellow accents, outline and flood the red portion of all the cookies first, then add all the blue accents, then all the yellow accents. The process will have a bit of an assembly line feel to it. There are some cookies, such as those that require wet-on-wet detailing or feathering (see page 28), that must be done one at a time, but this is always noted in the instructions.
- If you have a heavy hand with the water or lemon juice, your icing may be too thin. Watery icing can be fixed by stirring in sifted confectioners' (icing) sugar in small amounts until the desired consistency is reached.
- On the contrary, if your icing is too thick, thin it by adding water or lemon juice, 1 tsp (5 mL) at a time, until the desired consistency is reached.
- I used to occasionally deal with colors on my cookies bleeding as they dried, which frustrated me to no end. It turned my lovingly piped lines into a blurry mess! I never had this problem when using icing made with meringue powder, only when using icing made with egg whites. Whether or not this is a coincidence, I now only use meringue powder for my royal icing. I also prefer to use gel paste coloring instead of liquid food coloring. If your icing is too runny, there is a better chance that it is going to bleed.
- If icing is stored for more than a day or two, it often starts to separate. To fix this, stir it until it has returned to the desired consistency. Don't store icing in a pastry bag for more than a day, as it is very hard to reblend it in the bag.
- Tiny air bubbles are common in freshly mixed icing because of the whipping motion used to make it. To prevent these little critters from infesting your beautifully smooth and flat cookie surface with craters, let freshly mixed icing rest for a few minutes so that bubbles can settle. If bubbles are visible on the surface of your cookie after flooding, pop them with the tip of a needle or a toothpick. *Bubbles, be gone!*

Expect Casualties

There will be casualty cookies. This happens to cookie decorating professionals just as often as it happens to newbies. A cookie drops on the floor, or your hand jerks when piping a design, and that particular cookie is removed from the mix. Give yourself a bit of flexibility to make some mistakes by baking more cookies than you need. (The good news: you get to eat your mistakes!)

2
Cookie Dough & Icing Recipes

Julie Anne's Classic Vanilla-Orange Sugar Cookies

Makes 24 to 40 cookies

Tips

If you don't have a stand mixer, you can use a handheld electric mixer for step 2, but in step 3, use a wooden spoon to stir in the flour mixture.

It's easier to bake these cookies using 4 cookie sheets, rather than 2. While the first batch of cookies is baking, you can roll and cut shapes for the second batch so that they are ready to bake as soon as the first batch is done.

While working with one disk of dough, keep the other disks in the refrigerator until ready to use. Chilled dough retains its shape better.

Variation

Use lemon or lime zest instead of orange zest, or omit the zest altogether for a more traditional vanilla sugar cookie.

I first created this sugar cookie recipe when I owned a bakery/café called Julie Anne's. The vanilla-orange flavor was inspired by the Creamsicle, one of my favorite childhood treats. These cookies were a hit with our customers, as were the fun decorated shapes we would create with the dough.

- **Stand mixer (see tip, at left), fitted with paddle attachment**
- **Cookie cutter of choice**
- **2 to 4 cookie sheets, lined with parchment paper (see tip, at left)**

3¼ cups	all-purpose flour	800 mL
½ tsp	salt	2 mL
1 cup	granulated sugar	250 mL
1¼ cups	unsalted butter, at room temperature	300 mL
1	large egg	1
1	large egg yolk	1
1 tbsp	grated orange zest	15 mL
2 tsp	vanilla extract	10 mL

1. In a medium bowl, whisk together flour and salt.

2. In bowl of stand mixer, beat sugar and butter on medium speed until light and fluffy, about 3 minutes. Beat in egg, egg yolk, orange zest and vanilla until well combined.

3. With the mixer on low speed, gradually add flour mixture to the bowl, mixing until combined.

4. Turn dough out onto a work surface and divide into three equal pieces. Shape each piece into a flat disk. Wrap each disk tightly in plastic wrap. Refrigerate for at least 1 hour, until cold, or for up to 3 days.

5. Preheat oven to 350°F (180°C), placing racks in the upper and lower thirds.

6. On a lightly floured work surface, roll out one disk of dough to a thickness of ¼ inch (0.5 cm). Using cookie cutter, cut out shapes and carefully transfer them to 2 prepared cookie sheets, spacing them about 1 inch (2.5 cm) apart. Reroll scraps as necessary. Repeat process with more dough until both cookie sheets are full.

7. Bake for 11 to 15 minutes, switching positions of cookie sheets halfway through, until cookies are set and very lightly browned. Let cookies cool on cookie sheets for 10 minutes, then carefully transfer cookies to wire racks to cool completely before decorating.

8. Repeat steps 6 and 7 with the remaining dough.

Gluten-Free Sugar Cookies

The formula for these cookies is based on the recipe for my gluten-free pie crust. When I first created it, I had little experience with gluten-free baking, and I was concerned that my attempts would lack flavor and be difficult to work with. I could not have been more wrong! Like my pie dough (which has become one of my favorites), this cookie dough rolls out beautifully, holds its shape in the oven and bakes up crisp, buttery and delicious.

- Stand mixer (see tip, page 36), fitted with paddle attachment
- Cookie cutter of choice
- 2 to 4 cookie sheets, lined with parchment paper (see tip, page 36)

1½ cups	brown rice flour	375 mL
1 cup	sweet rice flour	250 mL
½ cup	potato starch	125 mL
¼ cup	tapioca starch	60 mL
½ tsp	xanthan gum	2 mL
½ tsp	salt	2 mL
1¼ cups	granulated sugar	300 mL
1¼ cups	unsalted butter, at room temperature	300 mL
1	large egg	1
1	large egg yolk	1
2 tsp	grated lemon zest (optional)	10 mL
2 tsp	vanilla extract	10 mL

1. In a medium bowl, whisk together brown rice flour, sweet rice flour, potato starch, tapioca starch, xanthan gum and salt.

2. In bowl of stand mixer, beat sugar and butter on medium speed until light and fluffy, about 3 minutes. Beat in egg, egg yolk, lemon zest (if using) and vanilla until well combined.

3. With the mixer on low speed, gradually add flour mixture to the bowl, mixing until combined.

4. Turn dough out onto a work surface and divide into three equal pieces. Shape each piece into a flat disk. Wrap each disk tightly in plastic wrap. Refrigerate for at least 1 hour, until cold, or for up to 3 days.

5. Preheat oven to 350°F (180°C), placing racks in the upper and lower thirds.

6. On a surface lightly dusted with cornstarch (see tip, at right), roll out one disk of dough to a thickness of ¼ inch (0.5 cm). Using cookie cutter, cut out shapes and carefully transfer them to 2 prepared cookie sheets, spacing them about 1 inch (2.5 cm) apart. Reroll scraps as necessary. Repeat process with more dough until both cookie sheets are full.

7. Bake for 11 to 15 minutes, switching positions of cookie sheets halfway through, until cookies are set and very lightly browned. Let cookies cool on cookie sheets for 10 minutes, then carefully transfer cookies to wire racks to cool completely before decorating.

8. Repeat steps 6 and 7 with the remaining dough.

Makes 24 to 40 cookies

Tips

Lemon zest brightens up the flavor of the dough, but feel free to replace it with orange zest or omit it altogether.

Instead of using cornstarch, you may roll out the dough using one of the other gluten-free ingredients, such as brown rice flour or potato starch.

Vegan Sugar Cookies

Makes 24 to
40 cookies

Tips

Egg substitutes, such as Ener-G Egg Replacer, can be found in the vegan section of well-stocked grocery stores.

Whipped vegan butter, such as Earth Balance, comes in a tub as opposed to a stick. It is easier to mix into dough when softened.

This dough tends to be a bit stickier than other cookie dough, so you will likely need extra flour when dividing it and rolling it out, to prevent it from sticking to the work surface.

If the dough starts to soften too much when you are rerolling scraps, wrap it and return it to the refrigerator for 20 minutes to firm up. Meanwhile, work with one of the other chilled disks.

Variation

Substitute soy milk or almond milk for the coconut milk.

Vegan baking can be a challenge, as many of the standard baking ingredients — butter, eggs and milk — are not allowed. Fortunately, there is now a wide variety of non-dairy substitutes for these key ingredients, allowing vegans everywhere to join in on the cookie decorating fun. A bit of almond extract in this dough rounds out the flavor perfectly (and smells heavenly when baking!)

- **Stand mixer (see tip, page 36), fitted with paddle attachment**
- **Cookie cutter of choice**
- **2 to 4 cookie sheets, lined with parchment paper (see tip, page 36)**

3½ cups	all-purpose flour	875 mL
1 tbsp	powdered egg replacer (see tip, at left)	15 mL
½ tsp	salt	2 mL
¼ tsp	baking powder	1 mL
1 cup	granulated sugar	250 mL
1 cup	whipped vegan butter (see tip, at left), at room temperature	250 mL
2 tsp	vanilla extract	10 mL
1 tsp	almond extract	5 mL
¼ cup	unsweetened coconut milk	60 mL

1. In a medium bowl, whisk together flour, egg replacer, salt and baking powder.

2. In bowl of stand mixer, beat sugar and vegan butter on medium speed until light and fluffy, about 4 minutes. Beat in vanilla and almond extract until well combined.

3. With the mixer on low speed, add flour mixture alternately with coconut milk, making three additions of flour and two of milk and beating until combined.

4. Turn dough out onto a lightly floured work surface and divide into three equal pieces. Shape each piece into a flat disk. Wrap each disk tightly in plastic wrap. Refrigerate for at least 2 hours, until cold, or for up to 3 days.

5. Preheat oven to 350°F (180°C), placing racks in the upper and lower thirds.

6. On a generously floured work surface, roll out one disk of dough to a thickness of ¼ inch (0.5 cm). Using cookie cutter, cut out shapes and carefully transfer them to 2 prepared cookie sheets, spacing them about 1 inch (2.5 cm) apart. Reroll scraps as necessary. Repeat process with remaining disks of dough.

7. Bake for 11 to 15 minutes, switching positions of cookie sheets halfway through, until cookies are set and very lightly browned. Let cookies cool on cookie sheets for 10 minutes, then carefully transfer cookies to wire racks to cool completely before decorating.

8. Repeat steps 6 and 7 with the remaining dough.

Whole Wheat Sugar Cookies

When attached to the title of a baked good, the term "whole wheat" is often associated with a grainy texture or lack of flavor. These cookies take that misconception and throw it right out the window! The winning combination of cinnamon, orange and honey makes this recipe an easy and delicious way to sneak a few extra whole grains into your diet.

- Stand mixer (see tip, page 36), fitted with paddle attachment
- Cookie cutter of choice
- 2 to 4 cookie sheets, lined with parchment paper (see tip, page 36)

2½ cups	whole wheat flour	625 mL
1 cup	all-purpose flour	250 mL
½ tsp	ground cinnamon	2 mL
½ tsp	salt	2 mL
¼ tsp	baking powder	1 mL
1 cup	granulated sugar	250 mL
1 cup	unsalted butter, at room temperature	250 mL
1	large egg	1
½ cup	liquid honey	125 mL
2 tsp	grated orange zest	10 mL
1 tsp	vanilla extract	5 mL

1. In a medium bowl, whisk together whole wheat flour, all-purpose flour, cinnamon, salt and baking powder.

2. In bowl of stand mixer, beat sugar and butter on medium speed until light and fluffy, about 3 minutes. Beat in egg, honey, orange zest and vanilla until well combined.

3. With the mixer on low speed, gradually add flour mixture to the bowl, mixing until combined.

4. Turn dough out onto a work surface and divide into three equal pieces. Shape each piece into a flat disk. Wrap each disk tightly in plastic wrap. Refrigerate for at least 1 hour, until cold, or for up to 3 days.

5. Preheat oven to 350°F (180°C), placing racks in the upper and lower thirds.

6. On a lightly floured work surface, roll out one disk of dough to a thickness of ¼ inch (0.5 cm). Using cookie cutter, cut out shapes and carefully transfer them to 2 prepared cookie sheets, spacing them about 1 inch (2.5 cm) apart. Reroll scraps as necessary. Repeat process with remaining disks of dough.

7. Bake for 11 to 15 minutes, switching positions of cookie sheets halfway through, until cookies are set and very lightly browned. Let cookies cool on cookie sheets for 10 minutes, then carefully transfer cookies to wire racks to cool completely before decorating.

8. Repeat steps 6 and 7 with the remaining dough.

Tip

If the dough starts to soften too much when you are rerolling scraps, wrap it and return it to the refrigerator for 20 minutes to firm up. Meanwhile, work with one of the other chilled disks.

Variation

You can make these cookies 100% whole wheat by replacing the all-purpose flour with whole wheat flour.

Dark Chocolate Sugar Cookies

Makes 24 to 40 cookies

Tips

It's easier to bake these cookies using 4 cookie sheets, rather than 2. While the first batch of cookies is baking, you can roll and cut shapes for the second batch so that they are ready to bake as soon as the first batch is done.

Sometimes cocoa powder can be lumpy. If that's the case, it is better to sift the ingredients in step 1 rather than whisk, as whisking is less likely to break up the lumps.

This recipe was inspired by the dark chocolate wafer cookies that my mom used make into a chocolate pie crust. I can't seem to find those cookies in the store anymore, so I decided to create my own. These deep chocolate cookies hold their shape beautifully when they bake, and their rich flavor is a nice complement to sweet royal icing.

- **Stand mixer (see tip, page 36), fitted with paddle attachment**
- **Cookie cutter of choice**
- **2 to 4 cookie sheets, lined with parchment paper (see tip, at left)**

3¼ cups	all-purpose flour	800 mL
1 cup	unsweetened cocoa powder	250 mL
½ tsp	salt	2 mL
1¾ cups	granulated sugar	425 mL
1¼ cups	unsalted butter, at room temperature	300 mL
2	large eggs	2
1 tbsp	vanilla extract	15 mL

1. In a medium bowl, whisk together flour, cocoa powder and salt (see tip, at left).

2. In bowl of stand mixer, beat sugar and butter on medium speed until light and fluffy, about 3 minutes. Beat in eggs, one at a time, beating well after each addition. Beat in vanilla.

3. With the mixer on low speed, gradually add flour mixture to the bowl, mixing until combined.

4. Turn dough out onto a work surface and divide into three equal pieces. Shape each piece into a flat disk. Wrap each disk tightly in plastic wrap. Refrigerate for at least 1 hour, until cold, or for up to 3 days.

5. Preheat oven to 350°F (180°C), placing racks in the upper and lower thirds.

6. On a lightly floured work surface, roll out one disk of dough to a thickness of ¼ inch (0.5 cm). Using cookie cutter, cut out shapes and carefully transfer them to 2 prepared cookie sheets, spacing them about 1 inch (2.5 cm) apart. Reroll scraps as necessary. Repeat process with remaining disks of dough.

7. Bake for 11 to 15 minutes, switching positions of cookie sheets halfway through, until cookies are set and very lightly browned. Let cookies cool on cookie sheets for 10 minutes, then carefully transfer cookies to wire racks to cool completely before decorating.

8. Repeat steps 6 and 7 with the remaining dough.

Peanut Butter Sugar Cookies

Makes 24 to 40 cookies

I have a blog called *Peanut Butter and Julie,* so it should come as no surprise that I love all things peanut butter. Creating a peanut butter–flavored sugar cookie for this book was a must! These not-too-sweet cookies have a toasty, subtle peanut buttery flavor, and they pair perfectly with a glass of ice cold milk.

- Stand mixer (see tip, at right), fitted with paddle attachment
- Cookie cutter of choice
- 2 to 4 cookie sheets, lined with parchment paper (see tip, page 40)

3½ cups	all-purpose flour	875 mL
½ tsp	salt	2 mL
¼ tsp	baking soda	1 mL
1 cup	creamy peanut butter (see tip, at right), at room temperature	250 mL
¾ cup	unsalted butter, at room temperature	175 mL
¾ cup	granulated sugar	175 mL
¼ cup	packed light brown sugar	60 mL
1	large egg	1
1 tbsp	vanilla extract	15 mL
¼ cup	heavy or whipping (35%) cream	60 mL

1. In a medium bowl, whisk together flour, salt and baking soda.

2. In bowl of stand mixer, beat peanut butter and butter on medium speed until light and fluffy, about 3 minutes. Add granulated sugar and brown sugar; beat for 2 minutes. Beat in egg and vanilla until well combined.

3. With the mixer on low speed, add flour mixture alternately with cream, making three additions of flour and two of cream and beating until combined.

4. Turn dough out onto a work surface and divide into three equal pieces. Shape each piece into a flat disk. Wrap each disk tightly in plastic wrap. Refrigerate for at least 1 hour, until cold, or for up to 3 days.

5. Preheat oven to 350°F (180°C), placing racks in the upper and lower thirds.

6. On a lightly floured work surface, roll out one disk of dough to a thickness of ¼ inch (0.5 cm). Using cookie cutter, cut out shapes and carefully transfer them to 2 prepared cookie sheets, spacing them about 1 inch (2.5 cm) apart. Reroll scraps as necessary. Repeat process with remaining disks of dough.

7. Bake for 11 to 15 minutes, switching positions of cookie sheets halfway through, until cookies are set and very lightly browned. Let cookies cool on cookie sheets for 10 minutes, then carefully transfer cookies to wire racks to cool completely before decorating.

8. Repeat steps 6 and 7 with the remaining dough.

Tips

If you don't have a stand mixer, you can use a handheld electric mixer for step 2, but in step 3, use a wooden spoon to stir in the flour mixture and cream.

This recipe was tested using regular peanut butter, as opposed to natural peanut butter. Regular peanut butter is creamy and thick at room temperature. Natural peanut butter has a thinner texture and tends to separate from the peanut oils at room temperature.

Vermont Maple Sugar Cookies

Makes 24 to 40 cookies

Tips

If you don't have a stand mixer, you can use a handheld electric mixer for step 2, but in step 3, use a wooden spoon to stir in the flour mixture.

It's easier to bake these cookies using 4 cookie sheets, rather than 2. While the first batch of cookies is baking, you can roll and cut shapes for the second batch so that they are ready to bake as soon as the first batch is done.

This recipe was tested using Grade B maple syrup, which tends to have a more concentrated maple flavor. It is more common to find Grade A (also known as fancy) maple syrup at the grocery store, and that will work fine as well.

If you like a less pronounced maple flavor, cut the maple extract to $\frac{1}{2}$ tsp (2 mL).

My husband grew up in Vermont, and his father makes his own maple syrup from the trees on their property. This means we are lucky enough to have a large shipment of maple syrup arrive on our doorstep every year, and I have fun experimenting with it in the kitchen! These lightly spiced cookies would be a perfect match for fall-themed cookies, such as Autumn Leaves (page 84) or Acorns (page 80).

- **Stand mixer (see tip, at left), fitted with paddle attachment**
- **Cookie cutter of choice**
- **2 to 4 cookie sheets, lined with parchment paper (see tip, at left)**

$3\frac{1}{2}$ cups	all-purpose flour	875 mL
$\frac{1}{2}$ tsp	ground cinnamon	2 mL
$\frac{1}{2}$ tsp	salt	2 mL
$\frac{1}{2}$ cup	granulated sugar	125 mL
$\frac{1}{2}$ cup	packed light brown sugar	125 mL
1 cup	unsalted butter, at room temperature	250 mL
1	large egg	1
$\frac{1}{2}$ cup	pure maple syrup	125 mL
1 tsp	vanilla extract	5 mL
1 tsp	maple extract	5 mL

1. In a medium bowl, whisk together flour, cinnamon and salt.

2. In bowl of stand mixer, beat granulated sugar, brown sugar and butter on medium speed until light and fluffy, about 3 minutes. Beat in egg, maple syrup, vanilla and maple extract until well combined.

3. With the mixer on low speed, gradually add flour mixture to the bowl, mixing until combined.

4. Turn dough out onto a work surface and divide into three equal pieces. Shape each piece into a flat disk. Wrap each disk tightly in plastic wrap. Refrigerate for at least 1 hour, until cold, or for up to 3 days.

5. Preheat oven to 350°F (180°C), placing racks in the upper and lower thirds.

6. On a lightly floured work surface, roll out one disk of dough to a thickness of $\frac{1}{4}$ inch (0.5 cm). Using cookie cutter, cut out shapes and carefully transfer them to 2 prepared cookie sheets, spacing them about 1 inch (2.5 cm) apart. Reroll scraps as necessary. Repeat process with remaining disks of dough.

7. Bake for 11 to 15 minutes, switching positions of cookie sheets halfway through, until cookies are set and very lightly browned. Let cookies cool on cookie sheets for 10 minutes, then carefully transfer cookies to wire racks to cool completely before decorating.

8. Repeat steps 6 and 7 with the remaining dough.

Pumpkin Spice Sugar Cookies

Over the past few years, pumpkin spice flavor has been popping up everywhere, from coffee to ice cream and even bagels! So why shouldn't this quintessential fall flavor be turned into sugar cookies too? Use this recipe to create Halloween cookies (pages 72–78) for all of your lucky trick-or-treaters.

- Stand mixer (see tip, page 42), fitted with paddle attachment
- Cookie cutter of choice
- 2 to 4 cookie sheets, lined with parchment paper (see tip, page 42)

4 cups + 2 tbsp	all-purpose flour	1 L + 30 mL
1/2 tsp	salt	2 mL
1/4 tsp	baking powder	1 mL
2 tsp	ground cinnamon	10 mL
1 tsp	ground ginger	5 mL
1/4 tsp	ground nutmeg	1 mL
1/4 tsp	ground allspice	1 mL
1 cup	packed light brown sugar	250 mL
1/2 cup	granulated sugar	125 mL
1 cup	unsalted butter, at room temperature	250 mL
1	large egg	1
1 cup	pumpkin purée (not pie filling)	250 mL
2 tsp	grated orange zest	10 mL
1 tsp	vanilla extract	5 mL

1. In a medium bowl, whisk together flour, salt, baking powder, cinnamon, ginger, nutmeg, and allspice.

2. In bowl of stand mixer, beat brown sugar, granulated sugar and butter on medium speed until light and fluffy, about 3 minutes. Beat in egg, pumpkin purée, orange zest and vanilla until well combined.

3. With the mixer on low speed, gradually add flour mixture to the bowl, mixing until combined.

4. Turn dough out onto a lightly floured work surface and divide into four equal pieces. Shape each piece into a flat disk. Wrap each disk tightly in plastic wrap. Refrigerate for at least 2 hours, until cold, or for up to 3 days.

5. Preheat oven to 350°F (180°C), placing racks in the upper and lower thirds.

6. On a generously floured work surface, roll out one disk of dough to a thickness of 1/4 inch (0.5 cm). Using cookie cutter, cut out shapes and carefully transfer them to 2 prepared cookie sheets, spacing them about 1 inch (2.5 cm) apart. Reroll scraps as necessary. Repeat process with remaining disks of dough.

7. Bake for 16 to 22 minutes, switching positions of cookie sheets halfway through, until cookies are set and very lightly browned. Let cookies cool on cookie sheets for 10 minutes, then carefully transfer cookies to wire racks to cool completely before decorating.

8. Repeat steps 6 and 7 with the remaining dough.

Tips

If you have pumpkin pie spice on hand, you can use 4 tsp (20 mL) in place of the cinnamon, ginger, allspice and nutmeg.

This dough tends to be a bit stickier than other cookie dough, so you will likely need extra flour when dividing it and rolling it out, to prevent it from sticking to the work surface.

If the dough starts to soften too much when you are rerolling scraps, wrap it and return it to the refrigerator for 20 minutes to firm up. Meanwhile, work with one of the other chilled disks.

Spicy Gingerbread Cut-Out Cookies

Tips

It's easier to bake these cookies using 4 cookie sheets, rather than 2. While the first batch of cookies is baking, you can roll and cut shapes for the second batch so that they are ready to bake as soon as the first batch is done.

Either light or dark brown sugar can be used in this recipe. Dark brown sugar will yield a richer molasses flavor.

This gingerbread dough baking in the oven immediately makes my home smell like Christmas! It conjures up memories of decorating gingerbread men with my brother during a snow day when school was cancelled. I wasn't a very skilled decorator back then, but I could always be counted on to polish off a few of my creations, along with a hot mug of spiced apple cider!

- **Stand mixer (see tip, page 42), fitted with paddle attachment**
- **Cookie cutter of choice**
- **2 to 4 cookie sheets, lined with parchment paper (see tip, at left)**

$3\frac{1}{2}$ cups	all-purpose flour	875 mL
1 tbsp	ground ginger	15 mL
2 tsp	ground cinnamon	10 mL
$\frac{1}{2}$ tsp	ground cloves	2 mL
$\frac{1}{2}$ tsp	salt	2 mL
$\frac{1}{2}$ tsp	baking soda	2 mL
1 cup	packed brown sugar (see tip, at left)	250 mL
$\frac{3}{4}$ cup + 2 tbsp	unsalted butter ($1\frac{3}{4}$ sticks), at room temperature	205 mL
$\frac{3}{4}$ cup	light (fancy) molasses	175 mL
2 tbsp	heavy or whipping (35%) cream	30 mL
1 tsp	vanilla extract	5 mL

1. In a medium bowl, whisk together flour, ginger, cinnamon, cloves, salt and baking soda.

2. In bowl of stand mixer, beat brown sugar and butter on medium speed until light and fluffy, about 3 minutes. Beat in molasses, cream and vanilla until well combined.

3. With the mixer on low speed, gradually add flour mixture to the bowl, mixing until combined.

4. Turn dough out onto a work surface and divide into three equal pieces. Shape each piece into a flat disk. Wrap each disk tightly in plastic wrap. Refrigerate for at least 2 hours, until cold, or for up to 3 days.

5. Preheat oven to 350°F (180°C), placing racks in the upper and lower thirds.

6. On a lightly floured work surface, roll out one disk of dough to a thickness of $\frac{1}{4}$ inch (0.5 cm). Using cookie cutter, cut out shapes and carefully transfer them to 2 prepared cookie sheets, spacing them about 1 inch (2.5 cm) apart. Reroll scraps as necessary. Repeat process with remaining disks of dough.

7. Bake for 11 to 15 minutes, switching positions of cookie sheets halfway through, until cookies are set and very lightly browned. Let cookies cool on cookie sheets for 10 minutes, then carefully transfer cookies to wire racks to cool completely before decorating.

8. Repeat steps 6 and 7 with the remaining dough.

Lemony Toasted Coconut Cookies

Makes 24 to 40 cookies

I love the smell and taste of toasted coconut, so I often incorporate it into my recipes. For these cookies, I paired the coconut with a generous amount of bright lemon zest, inspired by the two Meyer lemon trees in my backyard, which yield upward of 500 lemons a season! Use this dough for tropical-themed cookies, such as beachy Flip-flops (page 68) and Bikinis (page 65).

- **Food processor**
- **Stand mixer (see tip, at right), fitted with paddle attachment**
- **Cookie cutter of choice**
- **2 to 4 cookie sheets, lined with parchment paper (see tip, page 44)**

1½ cups	lightly toasted shredded sweetened coconut (see tip, at right)	375 mL
3¼ cups	all-purpose flour	800 mL
½ tsp	salt	2 mL
¾ cup	granulated sugar	175 mL
1¼ cups	unsalted butter, at room temperature	300 mL
2	large eggs	2
1½ tbsp	finely grated lemon zest	22 mL
1 tsp	pure vanilla extract	5 mL
1 tsp	coconut extract	5 mL

1. In food processor, process coconut until very finely ground.

2. In a large bowl, whisk together ground coconut, flour and salt.

3. In bowl of stand mixer, beat sugar and butter on medium speed until light and fluffy, about 3 minutes. Beat in eggs, lemon zest, vanilla and coconut extract until well combined.

4. With the mixer on low speed, gradually add flour mixture to the bowl, mixing until combined.

5. Turn dough out onto a work surface and divide into three equal pieces. Shape each piece into a flat disk. Wrap each disk tightly in plastic wrap. Refrigerate for at least 1 hour, until cold, or for up to 3 days.

6. Preheat oven to 350°F (180°C), placing racks in the upper and lower thirds.

7. On a lightly floured work surface, roll out one disk of dough to a thickness of ¼ inch (0.5 cm). Using cookie cutter, cut out shapes and carefully transfer them to 2 prepared cookie sheets, spacing them about 1 inch (2.5 cm) apart. Reroll scraps as necessary. Repeat process with remaining disks of dough.

8. Bake for 11 to 15 minutes, switching positions of cookie sheets halfway through, until cookies are set and very lightly browned. Let cookies cool on cookie sheets for 10 minutes, then carefully transfer cookies to wire racks to cool completely before decorating.

9. Repeat steps 7 and 8 with the remaining dough.

Tips

If you don't have a stand mixer, you can use a handheld electric mixer for step 3, but in step 4, use a wooden spoon to stir in the flour mixture.

To toast coconut, spread it in a single layer on a cookie sheet. Place cookie sheet in a preheated 300°F (150°C) oven for 10 to 15 minutes, stirring occasionally. Keep an eye on the coconut as it toasts — coconut can go from toasted to burned very quickly!

Variation

Use lime zest instead of lemon zest.

Nutty Pecan Cut-Out Cookies

Makes 30 to 48 cookies

Tips

If you don't have a stand mixer, you can use a handheld electric mixer for step 2, but in step 3, use a wooden spoon to stir in the flour mixture.

It's easier to bake these cookies using 4 cookie sheets, rather than 2. While the first batch of cookies is baking, you can roll and cut shapes for the second batch so that they are ready to bake as soon as the first batch is done.

While working with one disk of dough, keep the other disks in the refrigerator until ready to use. Chilled dough retains its shape better.

Variation

Substitute ground hazelnuts, almonds or walnuts for the pecans.

This recipe is a variation on my favorite linzer cookies, the nutty jam-filled sandwich cookies I make every Christmas. A hint of cinnamon and orange zest gives them a decidedly "holiday" feel, but I doubt anyone would mind if you chose to bake them during the summer!

- Stand mixer (see tip, at left), fitted with paddle attachment
- Cookie cutter of choice
- 2 to 4 cookie sheets, lined with parchment paper (see tip, at left)

3½ cups	all-purpose flour	875 mL
1½ tsp	ground cinnamon	7 mL
½ tsp	baking powder	2 mL
½ tsp	salt	2 mL
1¼ cups	granulated sugar	300 mL
1½ cups	unsalted butter, at room temperature	375 mL
1	large egg	1
1	large egg yolk	1
2 tsp	grated orange zest	10 mL
1 tsp	pure vanilla extract	5 mL
3 cups	finely ground pecans	750 mL

1. In a medium bowl, whisk together flour, cinnamon, baking powder and salt.

2. In bowl of stand mixer, beat sugar and butter on medium speed until light and fluffy, about 3 minutes. Beat in egg, egg yolk, orange zest and vanilla until well combined. Beat in ground pecans.

3. With the mixer on low speed, gradually add flour mixture to the bowl, mixing until combined.

4. Turn dough out onto a work surface and divide into three equal pieces. Shape each piece into a flat disk. Wrap each disk tightly in plastic wrap. Refrigerate for at least 2 hours, until cold, or for up to 3 days.

5. Preheat oven to 350°F (180°C), placing racks in the upper and lower thirds.

6. On a lightly floured work surface, roll out one disk of dough to a thickness of ¼ inch (0.5 cm). Using cookie cutter, cut out shapes and carefully transfer them to 2 prepared cookie sheets, spacing them about 1 inch (2.5 cm) apart. Reroll scraps as necessary. Repeat process with remaining disks of dough.

7. Bake for 11 to 15 minutes, switching positions of cookie sheets halfway through, until cookies are set and very lightly browned. Let cookies cool on cookie sheets for 10 minutes, then carefully transfer cookies to wire racks to cool completely before decorating.

8. Repeat steps 6 and 7 with the remaining dough.

Classic Royal Icing

If there is one common denominator for all of the cookies in this book, it is royal icing. Royal icing is a cookie decorator's best friend, allowing us to create colorful, multidimensional creations full of personality and individual style. Because it dries hard, royal icing is also perfect for packaging, shipping and delivering decorated cookie joy!

- **Stand mixer (see tip, at right), fitted with whisk attachment**

2 lbs	confectioners' (icing) sugar, sifted	1 kg
6 tbsp	meringue powder	90 mL
14 tbsp	warm water	210 mL
1 tbsp	freshly squeezed lemon juice	15 mL

1. In bowl of stand mixer, beat sugar and meringue powder on low speed until well combined.

2. In a measuring cup (preferably one with a spout), stir together water and lemon juice.

3. With the mixer on low speed, gradually add water mixture, mixing until combined. At this point, the icing will be fairly runny. (Don't worry!)

4. Increase mixer speed to medium and mix for 4 minutes, stopping to scrape down sides of bowl as necessary.

5. Increase mixer speed to high and beat for 3 to 5 minutes or until icing is stiff and glossy and the whisk attachment can stand up in the icing without sinking.

Makes about 6 cups (1.5 L)

Tips

If you don't have a stand mixer, a handheld electric mixer will work fine — it might just take a few extra minutes for the icing to reach the proper consistency.

I love a very lemony-tasting icing, as I think the tart flavor contrasts well with the sweet confectioners' sugar and cookies. I often replace some of the warm water in this recipe with lemon juice, depending on how tart/sweet I want the icing to taste!

If substituting another flavoring for the lemon juice, keep in mind that adding too much of an oil-based flavoring can cause royal icing to break down and affect how well it sets. My variations provide other flavoring options that work well.

Turn royal icing into two-step icing (page 24) to facilitate outlining and flooding cookies.

Variations

Peppermint Royal Icing: Replace the lemon juice with 1 to 2 tsp (5 to 10 mL) peppermint extract (depending on how minty you want it). This flavor pairs nicely with Dark Chocolate Sugar Cookies (page 40).

Vanilla Royal Icing: Replace the lemon juice with 1 tbsp (15 mL) vanilla extract. Try to find a clear variety, as dark extracts will tint the icing. Pair with Spicy Gingerbread Cut-Out Cookies (page 44) or Peanut Butter Sugar Cookies (page 41).

Coconut Royal Icing: Replace the lemon juice with 1 to 2 tsp (5 to 10 mL) coconut extract. Pair with Lemony Toasted Coconut Cookies (page 45).

Maple Royal Icing: Replace the lemon juice with 1 to 2 tsp (5 to 10 mL) maple extract. Since this extract tends to be dark, it may slightly darken the color of your icing. Use white gel paste to bring the color back to its original white. Pair this icing with Vermont Maple Sugar Cookies (page 42) or Nutty Pecan Cut-Out Cookies (page 46).

Orange, Lime or Lemon Royal Icing: Replace 1/4 cup (60 mL) of the water (or more if you want a more pronounced flavor) with orange, lime or lemon juice. Pair with Julie Anne's Classic Vanilla-Orange Sugar Cookies (page 36).

Almond Royal Icing: Replace the lemon juice with 1 to 2 tsp (5 to 10 mL) almond extract. This icing pairs well with Whole Wheat Sugar Cookies (page 39).

Vegan Royal Glaze

Tip

If you don't have a stand mixer, a handheld electric mixer will work fine — it might just take a few extra minutes for the icing to reach the proper consistency.

Variations

Substitute almond milk for the coconut milk

Substitute vanilla extract for the lemon juice. Try to find a clear variety, as dark extracts will tint the icing.

Because there's no egg-based meringue powder in this recipe, this vegan version of Classic Royal Icing (page 47) is more like a glaze, with a lovely shiny coat. Use this icing as you would the standard version, but give it a bit more time to set on your cookies, usually 1 to 2 days (the cookies can stand uncovered at room temperature during this time).

• **Stand mixer (see tip, at left), fitted with paddle attachment**

4 lbs	confectioners' (icing) sugar, sifted	2 kg
7 tbsp	unsweetened coconut milk	105 mL
1 tbsp	freshly squeezed lemon juice	15 mL
1/3 cup	light corn syrup	75 mL

1. Place confectioners' sugar in bowl of stand mixer.

2. In a measuring cup (preferably one with a spout), stir together coconut milk and lemon juice.

3. With the mixer on low speed, gradually add coconut milk mixture, mixing until combined. Add corn syrup and mix until combined.

4. Increase mixer speed to medium-high and mix for 2 to 3 minutes or until icing is smooth and glossy.

Part 2

Decorating Cookies

3

Seasonal Cookies

Easter Bunny

When the Easter Bunny hid Easter eggs and baskets at my house, my brother and I had our work cut out for us. This mischievous little guy never simply hid items in the more obvious locations, such as under the bed or behind a tree. We spent the better part of the day rummaging through everything from cereal boxes (to my mom's exasperation) to boxes in the back of the garage. It's a miracle we never left any undiscovered. Serve these funny bunny cookies after an exhausting morning of hunting eggs, which is sure to build up an appetite! **Makes about 30.**

What You Need

- 1 recipe cookie dough (pages 36–46)
- Bunny cookie cutter
- 1 recipe Classic Royal Icing (page 47)
- Black gel paste
- Burgundy or purple gel paste
- Pink gel paste
- 2 squeeze bottles
- Cornstarch
- Small rolling pin
- White fondant
- Pink fondant
- $1\frac{1}{4}$-inch (3 cm) round cutter (see tip)
- $\frac{3}{4}$-inch (2 cm) round cutter
- 2 disposable pastry bags
- 2 couplers
- 2 #2 round decorating tips

Techniques Used

- Tinting icing (page 22)
- Filling a squeeze bottle (page 24)
- Piping (page 27)
- Flooding (page 28)
- Working with fondant (page 30)
- Filling a pastry bag (page 24)

Getting Started

Bake cookies: Roll out dough and cut cookies with the bunny cookie cutter. Bake according to recipe directions. Let cool completely before decorating.

Tint and thin icing: Place $\frac{3}{4}$ cup (175 mL) icing in a bowl and tint it black. Place $\frac{1}{4}$ cup (60 mL) icing in a bowl and leave it white. Cover both bowls tightly and set aside. Place $1\frac{1}{2}$ cups (375 mL) icing in a bowl and tint it light burgundy or purple. Tint remaining icing pink. Thin burgundy and pink icing to two-step icing consistency (page 24) and transfer to squeeze bottles.

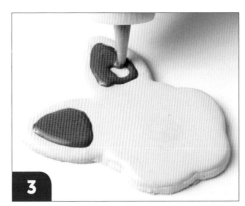

Using pink icing, outline bunnies. ■ Outline a triangular area inside each ear.

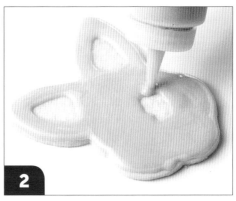

Flood bunnies with pink icing, leaving space for a different color inside the ears.

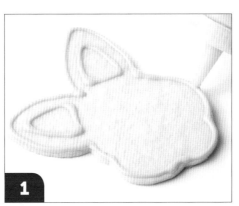

Using burgundy icing, flood the space inside the ears. ■ Let icing set for at least 6 hours or overnight.

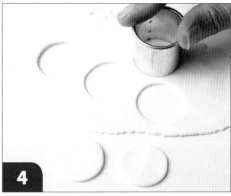

Meanwhile, on a work surface lightly dusted with cornstarch, roll out white fondant to $\frac{1}{16}$ inch (2 mm) thick. ■ Using the $1\frac{1}{4}$ inch (3 cm) round cutter, cut out 2 white circles per cookie.

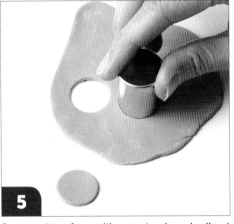

5

Dust work surface with cornstarch and roll out pink fondant to $1/16$ inch (2 mm) thick. ■ Using the $3/4$-inch (2 cm) cutter, cut out 1 pink circle per cookie. ■ Place all circles on a cookie sheet and let dry for at least 4 hours or overnight.

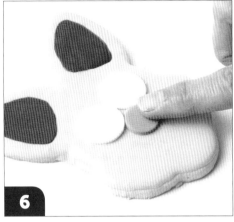

6

Dab the back of each fondant circle with icing and affix 2 white circles as eyes and 1 pink circle as a nose on each cookie. ■ The 3 circles should touch each other, without overlapping.

Tips

Because your bunny cutter might be slightly larger or smaller than mine, you may need larger or smaller cutters to cut out the fondant circles for the eyes and nose. Try to keep the same proportions as I have used.

Serve these hungry bunnies with Carrot cookies (page 54).

Variation

Use blue icing instead of pink to outline and flood your bunnies. Or make half pink and half blue.

7

Transfer black and white icing to pastry bags fitted with #2 tips. ■ Use white icing to pipe 2 square teeth at the bottom of each bunny's face.

8

Using black icing, pipe pupils looking to one side in each bunny's eyes. ■ Pipe whiskers extending from each bunny's nose. ■ Let cookies dry for at least 4 hours before serving.

Carrot

After the Easter Bunny is finished hiding all those eggs, he is most definitely ready to snack on some crunchy, juicy carrots! While this design is one of the easiest in the book, it also gives you some practice using the leaf piping tip, which comes in handy when decorating cakes too. Pair these cookies with the Easter Bunny cookies (page 52). **Makes about 36.**

What You Need

- 1 recipe cookie dough (pages 36–46)
- Carrot cookie cutter
- 1 recipe Classic Royal Icing (page 47)
- Green gel paste
- Orange gel paste
- Disposable pastry bag
- Coupler
- #66 or #67 leaf decorating tip (see tip)
- Squeeze bottle
- Small food-safe paintbrush
- Orange or gold luster dust

Techniques Used

- Tinting icing (page 22)
- Filling a pastry bag (page 24)
- Filling a squeeze bottle (page 24)
- Piping (page 27)
- Flooding (page 28)
- Adding sparkle (page 28)

Getting Started

Bake cookies: Roll out dough and cut cookies with the carrot cookie cutter. Bake according to recipe directions. Let cool completely before decorating.

Tint and thin icing: Place one-third of the icing in a bowl and tint it green. Transfer to a pastry bag fitted with a #66 or #67 leaf tip. Tint remaining icing orange, thin to two-step icing consistency (page 24) and transfer to a squeeze bottle.

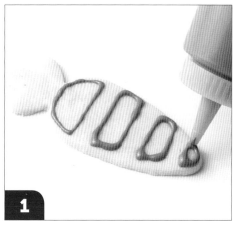

1 Using orange icing, outline every other section of carrots as shown.

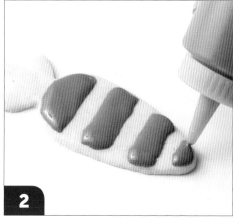

2 Flood the outlined sections with orange icing, so that each carrot is half covered in horizontal orange rows. ■ Let icing set for 15 minutes.

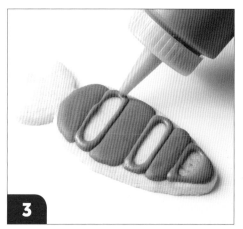

3 Outline the remaining carrot sections with orange icing.

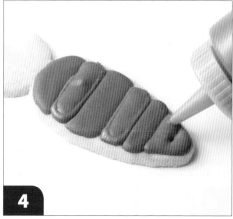

4 Flood the outlined sections with orange icing.

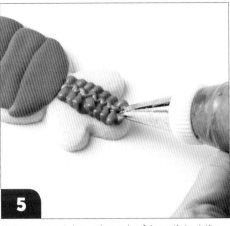

5 Using green icing, pipe a leaf (see tip) at the top center of each carrot, leaving room on either side.

6 Pipe another leaf to the right of each center leaf.

7 Pipe a third leaf to the left of each center leaf. ■ Let icing set for at least 6 hours or overnight.

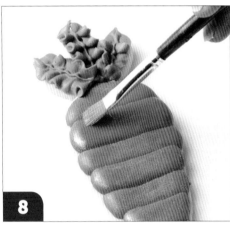

8 Using the small paintbrush, brush each carrot lightly with luster dust.

Tips

Tips #66 and #67 are leaf tips. These and other specialty tips can be found in the baking aisles of craft stores. While some tips are used only on occasion, leaf tips are more commonly required, so they are a good investment.

If all the orange icing does not fit in your squeeze bottle, cover the remaining icing tightly and refill the bottle as needed.

By outlining and flooding the carrot in sections, you create texture on the cookies.

To make leaf shapes, hold the bag at a 45-degree angle to the surface, touching it with the wider opening parallel to the surface. Apply pressure to the pastry bag to build up the base of the leaf, then relax pressure as you pull the tip toward you, bringing the leaf to a point. Stop squeezing and lift the bag away. You may want to practice on parchment paper before piping leaves on cookies.

Chick 'n' Egg

Which came first, the chicken or the egg? With this design, you get them both: a cute baby chick, complete with little orange feet and a tuft of feathers, *and* a brightly decorated egg, which completes the chick's outfit. Truly an egg-cellent idea! **Makes about 30.**

What You Need

- 1 recipe cookie dough (pages 36–46)
- Egg cookie cutter
- 1 recipe Classic Royal Icing (page 47)
- Blue gel paste
- Red gel paste
- Orange gel paste
- Yellow gel paste
- Squeeze bottle
- Orange fondant
- X-acto knife
- 4 disposable pastry bags
- 4 couplers
- 2 #2 round decorating tips
- 2 #1 round decorating tips
- Tweezers
- Royal icing eyes

Techniques Used

- Tinting icing (page 22)
- Filling a squeeze bottle (page 24)
- Piping (page 27)
- Flooding (page 28)
- Working with fondant (page 30)
- Using an X-acto knife (page 31)
- Filling a pastry bag (page 24)
- Adding embellishments (page 31)

Getting Started

Bake cookies: Roll out dough and cut cookies with the egg cookie cutter. Bake according to recipe directions. Let cool completely before decorating.

Tint and thin icing: Place $3/4$ cup (175 mL) icing in each of two bowls; tint one portion blue and leave one white. Place $1/2$ cup (125 mL) icing in a bowl and tint it red. Place $1/4$ cup (60 mL) icing in a bowl and tint it orange. Cover all bowls tightly and set aside. Tint remaining icing yellow, thin to two-step icing consistency (page 24) and transfer to a squeeze bottle.

1 Using yellow icing, outline and flood eggs. ■ Let icing set for at least 6 hours or overnight.

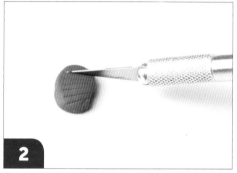

2 Meanwhile, to shape a tuft of feathers, mold a small amount of fondant into a small oval about $1/2$ inch (1 cm) wide and $3/4$ inch (2 cm) long. ■ Using the X-acto knife, gently cut marks in the oval, without cutting all the way through, creating a textured fan shape. ■ Make 1 piece per cookie.

3 Using small pieces of fondant, mold feet and legs for the chicks. ■ Make the feet flat and rounded, and the legs fairly skinny, with a flattened portion at the top that will lie flat against the back of the cookie when attached. ■ Make 2 legs per cookie. ■ Place all fondant pieces on a cookie sheet and let dry for at least 4 hours or overnight.

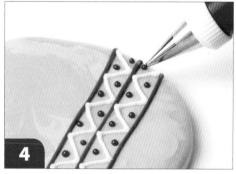

4 Transfer blue and white icing to pastry bags fitted with #2 tips. ■ Transfer red and orange icing to pastry bags fitted with #1 tips. ■ Use blue, white and red icing to pipe a zigzag and dot design onto the bottom third of each egg as shown.

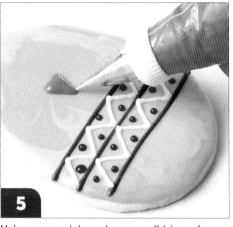

5

Using orange icing, pipe a small triangular beak on the upper portion of each egg.

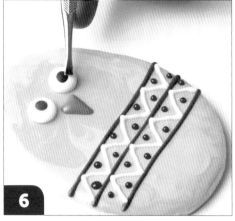

6

Using tweezers and a dab of icing on the back of each royal icing eye, place 2 eyes on each egg, just above the beak.

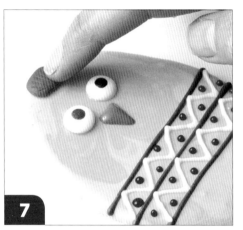

7

Dab the back of each tuft of feathers with icing and affix a tuft above the eyes at the top center of each egg.

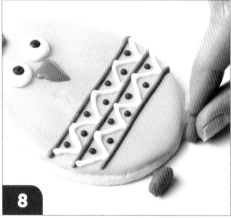

8

Using a dab of icing at the front of the flattened portion, affix 2 fondant legs to the back of each egg, at the bottom. ■ Let cookies dry for at least 6 hours before serving.

Tips

When you're piping the design in step 4, a ruler and an X-acto knife will help you create a template for piping straight, even lines.

Adding embellishments, such as the royal icing eyes, is easier if you use a pair of tweezers. Buy an extra pair and keep them handy with your decorating supplies.

If you don't have royal icing eyes on hand, pipe simple eyes using black icing and a pastry bag fitted with a #2 round decorating tip.

Pair these with Easter Bunny cookies (page 52) for special Easter basket treats.

Umbrella and Raindrops

What You Need

- 1 recipe cookie dough (pages 36–46)
- Umbrella cookie cutter
- Small raindrop cutter
- 1 recipe Classic Royal Icing (page 47)
- Black gel paste
- Pink gel paste
- Brown gel paste
- 3 squeeze bottles
- Fine blue sanding sugar
- Disposable pastry bag
- Coupler
- #2 round decorating tip

Techniques Used

- Tinting icing (page 22)
- Filling a squeeze bottle (page 24)
- Piping (page 27)
- Flooding (page 28)
- Adding sparkle (page 28)
- Wet-on-wet detailing (page 28)
- Filling a pastry bag (page 24)

April showers and plump raindrops require a large, and preferably fashionable, umbrella to keep you dry. This chic design is perfect for beginners, requiring only some basic piping and flooding skills, but the impressive results will yield a downpour of compliments. **Makes about 36.**

Getting Started

Bake cookies: Roll out dough and cut cookies with the umbrella cookie cutter. Cut 4 to 5 raindrop cookies per umbrella. Bake according to recipe directions. Let cool completely before decorating.

Tint and thin icing: Place 1 cup (250 mL) icing in each of two bowls; tint one portion black and leave one white. Cover black icing tightly and set aside. Divide remaining icing evenly between two bowls; tint one portion pink and one brown. Thin white, pink and brown icing to two-step icing consistency (page 24) and transfer to squeeze bottles.

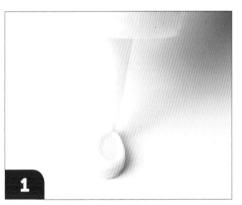

1 Working with one cookie at a time, use white icing to outline a raindrop cookie.

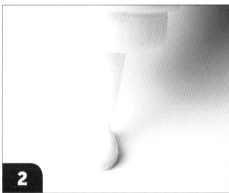

4 Meanwhile, using brown icing, outline umbrella tops.

2 Flood raindrop with white icing.

3 While the white icing is still wet, sprinkle the raindrop with sanding sugar, shaking off excess. ■ Repeat steps 1 to 3 for all raindrop cookies. ■ Let icing set for at least 6 hours or overnight.

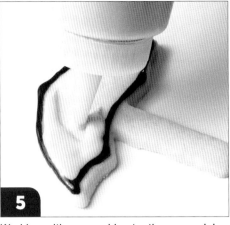

5

Working with one cookie at a time, use pink icing to flood an umbrella top.

6

While the pink icing is still wet, use brown icing to pipe a polka-dot pattern in the pink icing. ■ Repeat steps 5 and 6 for all umbrella cookies. ■ Let icing set for at least 6 hours or overnight.

Tips

Look for raindrop cutters in the baking aisle of craft stores.

When working with sanding sugar, shake excess off onto a sheet of parchment paper, which you can use to funnel it back into the jar. This helps to eliminate waste.

Don't be alarmed if excess sanding sugar sticks to the cookie even after you shake it. Wait until the icing dries completely, then gently brush off the unwanted sugar with a small food-safe paintbrush or a cotton swab.

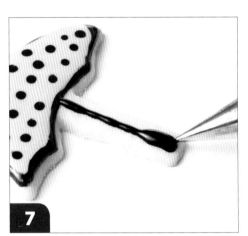

7

Transfer black icing to a pastry bag fitted with a #2 tip. ■ Pipe a handle, including a thicker end, on each umbrella cookie.

8

Using brown icing, pipe 3 lines on each umbrella top: one down the center, one curving to the left and one curving to the right, dividing each umbrella top into 4 sections. ■ Let cookies dry for at least 4 hours before serving.

Polka-Dot Bonnet

What You Need

- 1 recipe cookie dough (pages 36–46)
- Bonnet cookie cutter
- 1 recipe Classic Royal Icing (page 47)
- Blue gel paste
- 2 squeeze bottles
- Cornstarch
- Small rolling pin
- Pink fondant
- Small flower cutter
- Light pink sanding sugar

Techniques Used

- Tinting icing (page 22)
- Filling a squeeze bottle (page 24)
- Piping (page 27)
- Flooding (page 28)
- Wet-on-wet detailing (page 28)
- Working with fondant (page 30)
- Adding sparkle (page 28)

I love a stylish hat. Well, let me rephrase: I love the *idea* of a stylish hat, yet I never seem to wear them. (I blame my large head.) Fortunately, these beautiful bonnets fit perfectly in the palm of your hand. Make them for a special Mother's Day gift or a Kentucky Derby party treat. **Makes about 36.**

Getting Started

Bake cookies: Roll out dough and cut cookies with the bonnet cookie cutter. Bake according to recipe directions. Let cool completely before decorating.

Tint and thin icing: Divide icing evenly between two bowls; tint one portion light blue and leave one white. Thin blue and white icing to two-step icing consistency (page 24) and transfer to squeeze bottles.

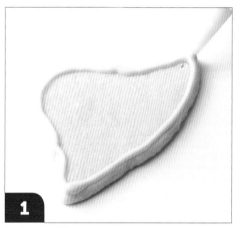

1

Working with one cookie at a time, use blue icing to outline a bonnet.

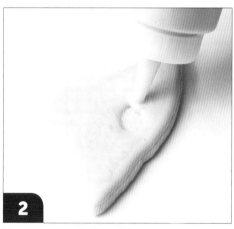

2

Flood bonnet with blue icing.

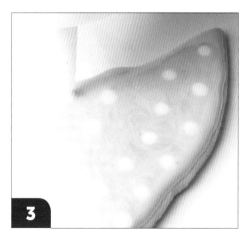

3

While the blue icing is still wet, use white icing to pipe a polka-dot pattern on the bonnet. ■ Repeat steps 1 to 3 for all cookies. ■ Let icing set for at least 6 hours or overnight.

4

Meanwhile, on a work surface lightly dusted with cornstarch, roll out fondant to $1/16$ inch (2 mm) thick. ■ Using the flower cutter, cut out 3 flowers per cookie. ■ Place flowers on a cookie sheet and let dry for at least 4 hours or overnight.

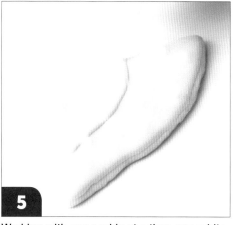

5

Working with one cookie at a time, use white icing to pipe a thick horizontal band across the center of a bonnet.

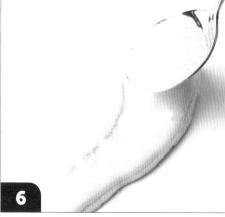

6

While the white icing is still wet, sprinkle the band with sanding sugar, shaking off excess.
■ Repeat steps 5 and 6 for all cookies.

7

Dab the back of each flower with icing and affix 3 flowers in a row across each band.

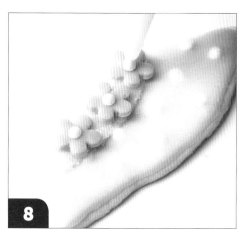

8

Using blue icing, pipe a small dot in the center of each flower. ■ Let cookies dry for at least 6 hours before serving.

Tips

If all the light blue and white icings do not fit in your squeeze bottles, cover the remaining icings tightly and refill the bottles as needed.

Keep any fondant you are not presently working with tightly wrapped in plastic wrap, as it can quickly dry out, rendering it unusable.

Adding embellishments, such as the flowers, is easier if you use a pair of tweezers. Buy an extra pair and keep them handy with your decorating supplies.

Variations

Mix and match the colors of the bonnet and polka-dots to make a variety of bonnets. Try combining brown and light pink, or black, white and red.

Instead of placing fondant flowers on the band, cut out a fondant bow to affix.

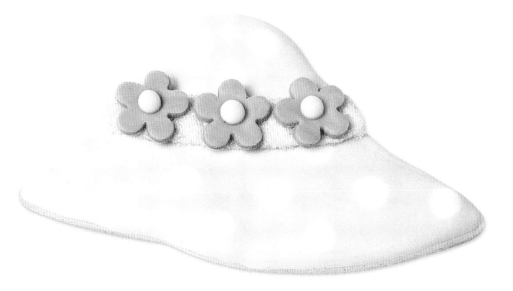

Butterfly

I vividly remember running through the grass in my bare feet, chasing bright butterflies but rarely catching them. These show-stopping cookies use the monarch butterfly as inspiration. They are much easier than they look, but you don't need to tell anyone! **Makes about 30.**

What You Need

- 1 recipe cookie dough (pages 36–46)
- Butterfly cookie cutter
- 1 recipe Classic Royal Icing (page 47)
- Black gel paste
- Orange gel paste
- Yellow gel paste
- 4 squeeze bottles
- Toothpick

Techniques Used

- Tinting icing (page 22)
- Filling a squeeze bottle (page 24)
- Piping (page 27)
- Flooding (page 28)

Getting Started

Bake cookies: Roll out dough and cut cookies with the butterfly cookie cutter. Bake according to recipe directions. Let cool completely before decorating.

Thin and tint icing: Thin icing to two-step icing consistency (page 24). Divide icing equally among four bowls; tint one portion black, one orange and one yellow, and leave one white. Transfer all icings to squeeze bottles.

1

Working with one cookie at a time, use black icing to outline the upper and lower sections on the left wing of a butterfly.

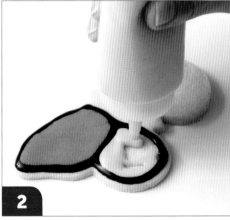

2

Flood the upper section of the left wing with orange icing and the lower section with yellow icing.

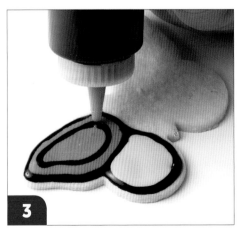

3

Using black icing, pipe a line around the inside of the orange section, following the contour of the outline.

4

Place the end of the toothpick on the outer black outline and drag it through the orange icing and inner black line toward the center of the orange icing. ■ Repeat several more times, working around the orange section in a counterclockwise direction.

5

Using black icing, pipe a line around the inside of the yellow section, following the contour of the outline. ■ Repeat step 4 in the yellow section.

6

Using white icing, pipe dots on the black outline of the wing, spacing the dots evenly around the top, left side and bottom, as well as on the line that divides the orange and yellow sections, but leaving the area closest to the center of the butterfly solid black.

7

Repeat steps 1 to 6 on the right side of the butterfly.

8

Using black icing, pipe the butterfly's head and long, thin body, attaching it to the wings. ■ Repeat steps 1 to 8 for all cookies. ■ Let cookies dry for at least 6 hours before serving.

Tips

Cookie dough retains its shape best when cold. If the rolled-out dough gets too warm while you're cutting shapes, carefully transfer it to a cookie sheet and place it in the refrigerator for 15 minutes before continuing.

Sometimes air bubbles are created when you flood a cookie with icing. If this happens, use the tip of a toothpick to pop the bubbles.

Variation

Experiment with different color combinations on the wings, such as hot pink and bright blue.

Sunglasses

You simply cannot go to the pool or the beach during the summer without a pair of cool shades to complete your look. This sparkly pair is sure to catch the eye of many other sunbathers. Make them any color you like, matching the disco dust color to the icing. **Makes about 36.**

What You Need

- 1 recipe cookie dough (pages 36–46)
- Sunglasses cookie cutter
- 1 recipe Classic Royal Icing (page 47)
- Disposable pastry bag
- Coupler
- #1 round decorating tip
- Black gel paste
- Blue gel paste
- 2 squeeze bottles
- Blue disco dust

Techniques Used

- Tinting icing (page 22)
- Filling a pastry bag (page 24)
- Filling a squeeze bottle (page 24)
- Piping (page 27)
- Flooding (page 28)
- Adding sparkle (page 28)

Getting Started

Bake cookies: Roll out dough and cut cookies with the sunglasses cookie cutter. Bake according to recipe directions. Let cool completely before decorating.

Tint and thin icing: Transfer 1/4 cup (60 mL) white icing to a pastry bag fitted with a #1 tip. Divide remaining icing evenly between two bowls; tint one portion black and one blue. Thin black and blue icing to two-step icing consistency (page 24) and transfer to squeeze bottles.

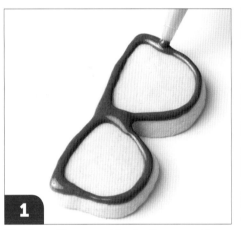

1 Working with one cookie at a time, use blue icing to outline and flood the rim of a pair of sunglasses, leaving space for the lenses.

2 While the blue icing is still wet, sprinkle the rim with disco dust, shaking off excess. ■ Repeat steps 1 and 2 for all cookies. ■ Let icing set for 10 minutes.

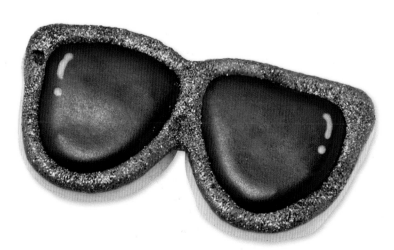

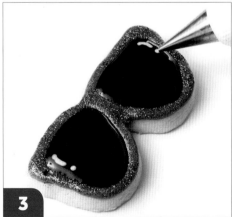

3 Working with one cookie at a time, use black icing to flood the lenses. ■ Immediately pipe 2 white accent marks on the outer edge of each lens. ■ Repeat for all cookies. ■ Let cookies dry for at least 6 hours before serving.

Bikini

These adorable itsy-bitsy-teeny-weeny bikini cookies would be perfect for a beach picnic or pool party. Have fun with the design, mixing and matching colors and patterns. Try making these with Lemony Toasted Coconut cookie dough (page 45) and Lemon Royal Icing (variation, page 47). **Makes about 36.**

Getting Started

Bake cookies: Roll out dough and cut cookies with the bikini cookie cutter. Bake according to recipe directions. Let cool completely before decorating.

Tint and thin icing: Place 1/2 cup (125 mL) icing in each of two bowls; tint one portion yellow and leave one white. Cover tightly and set aside. Tint remaining icing teal, thin to two-step icing consistency (page 24) and transfer to a squeeze bottle (cover any remaining teal icing tightly and refill the bottle as needed).

What You Need

- 1 recipe cookie dough (pages 36–46)
- Bikini cookie cutter
- 1 recipe Classic Royal Icing (page 47)
- Yellow gel paste
- Teal gel paste
- Squeeze bottle
- 2 disposable pastry bags
- 2 couplers
- #1 round decorating tip
- #2 round decorating tip

Techniques Used

- Tinting icing (page 22)
- Filling a squeeze bottle (page 24)
- Piping (page 27)
- Flooding (page 28)
- Filling a pastry bag (page 24)

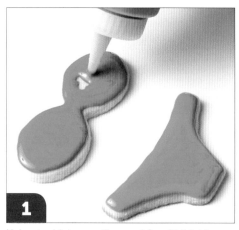

1

Using teal icing, outline and flood bikini tops and bottoms. ■ Let icing set for at least 6 hours or overnight.

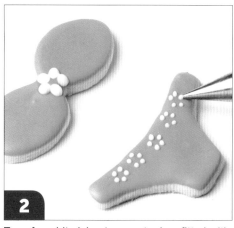

2

Transfer white icing to a pastry bag fitted with a #1 tip. ■ Pipe a large daisy in the center of each bikini top. ■ Pipe 5 small daisies along the waistline of each bikini bottom, leaving room at the corners.

3

Transfer yellow icing to a pastry bag fitted with a #2 tip. ■ Pipe dots in the center of all daisies and a small bow on each corner of bikini bottoms. ■ Let cookies dry for at least 3 hours before serving.

Swimming Trunks

What You Need

- 1 recipe cookie dough (pages 36–46)
- Shorts cookie cutter
- 1 recipe Classic Royal Icing (page 47)
- Green gel paste
- Peach or orange gel paste
- 2 squeeze bottles
- White fondant
- Disposable pastry bag
- Coupler
- #2 round decorating tip
- Tweezers

Techniques Used

- Tinting icing (page 22)
- Filling a squeeze bottle (page 24)
- Piping (page 27)
- Flooding (page 28)
- Working with fondant (page 30)
- Filling a pastry bag (page 24)

Just like the Bikini cookies (page 65), these colorful swimming trunks would be a fun portable treat for a day at the beach or a pool party. If you really want to create a splash, make an entire themed cookie tray, including Sunglasses (page 64), Flip-flops (page 68), and Starfish (page 148)! **Makes about 36.**

Getting Started

Bake cookies: Roll out dough and cut cookies with the shorts cookie cutter. Bake according to recipe directions. Let cool completely before decorating.

Tint and thin icing: Divide icing even between two bowls; tint one portion light green and one peach or orange. Transfer half the peach icing to another bowl, cover tightly and set aside. Thin green and remaining peach icing to two-step icing consistency (page 24) and transfer to squeeze bottles.

1. Working with one cookie at a time, use green icing to outline a pair of shorts.

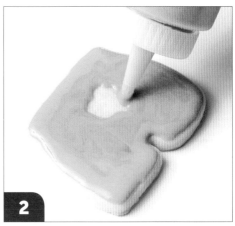

2. Flood shorts with green icing.

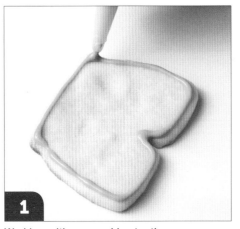

3. While the green icing is still wet, use the squeeze bottle of peach icing to pipe a flower or star pattern on the shorts. ■ Repeat steps 1 to 3 for all cookies. ■ Let icing set for at least 6 hours or overnight.

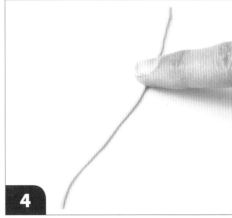

4. Meanwhile, roll fondant into thin ropes about 1/8 inch (3 mm) in diameter.

5

Shape each rope into a simple bow. ■ Make 1 bow per cookie. ■ Place bows on a cookie sheet and let dry for at least 2 hours or overnight.

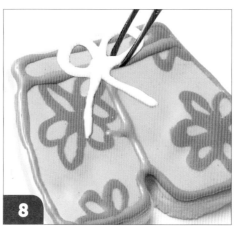

6

Transfer reserved peach icing to a pastry bag fitted with a #2 tip. ■ Working with one cookie at a time, pipe a border around outside of shorts.

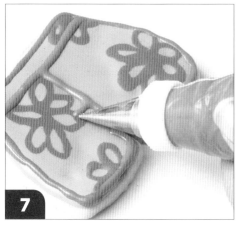

7

Pipe a peach waistband and center line on shorts as shown.

8

While the peach icing is still wet, use tweezers to place a fondant bow at the top center of the shorts. ■ Repeat steps 6 to 8 for all cookies. ■ Let cookies dry for at least 3 hours before serving.

Tips

Keep any fondant you are not presently working with tightly wrapped in plastic wrap, as it can quickly dry out, rendering it unusable.

Adding embellishments, such as the bows, is easier if you use a pair of tweezers. Buy an extra pair and keep them handy with your decorating supplies.

Variation

Instead of making fondant bows, you can pipe bows onto the shorts using white icing in a pastry bag fitted with a #1 tip.

Flip-flops

What You Need

- 1 recipe cookie dough (pages 36–46)
- Flip-flop cookie cutter (see tip)
- 1 recipe Classic Royal Icing (page 47)
- Peach gel paste
- Bright blue gel paste
- Hot pink gel paste
- 3 squeeze bottles
- Cornstarch
- Small rolling pin
- Blue fondant
- Peach fondant
- Small star cutter
- Ruler
- X-acto knife

Techniques Used

- Tinting icing (page 22)
- Filling a squeeze bottle (page 24)
- Piping (page 27)
- Flooding (page 28)
- Wet-on-wet detailing (page 28)
- Working with fondant (page 30)
- Using an X-acto knife (page 31)

During the summer, the daytime temperatures where I live rarely dip below 100°F, so comfort is key when it comes to attire. For me, this means lots of sundresses and brightly colored flip-flops. I used my growing collection as inspiration for these cookies, which would be a fun indoor project on those days when it's just too hot to stay outside. **Makes about 30.**

Getting Started

Bake cookies: Roll out dough and cut cookies with the flip-flop cookie cutter. Bake according to recipe directions. Let cool completely before decorating.

Thin and tint icing: Thin icing to two-step icing consistency (page 24). Place ¾ cup (175 mL) icing in each of two bowls; tint one portion peach and one bright blue. Tint remaining icing hot pink. Transfer all icings to squeeze bottles.

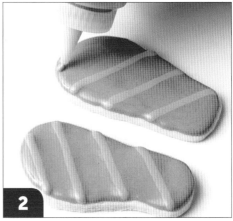

1

Working with one cookie at a time, use hot pink icing to outline and flood a flip-flop.

2

While the pink icing is still wet, use peach icing to pipe 4 diagonal lines across the flip-flop (see tip), spacing them evenly.

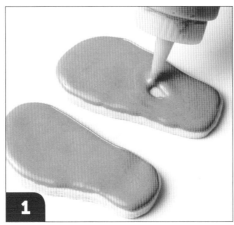

3

Use blue icing to pipe a diagonal line immediately below each peach line. ■ Repeat steps 1 to 3 for all cookies. ■ Let icing set for at least 6 hours or overnight.

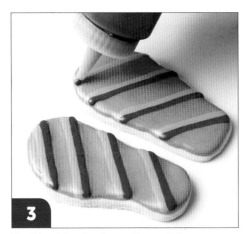

4

Meanwhile, on a work surface lightly dusted with cornstarch, roll out blue fondant to ¹⁄₁₆ inch (2 mm) thick. ■ Using the star cutter, cut out 1 star per flip-flop. ■ Place stars on a cookie sheet and let dry for at least 4 hours or overnight.

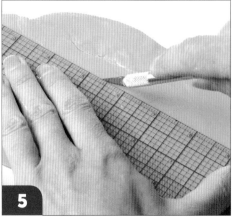

5 Dust work surface with cornstarch and roll out peach fondant to $\frac{1}{16}$ inch (2 mm) thick. ■ With the ruler as a guide, use the X-acto knife to cut strips about $\frac{1}{2}$ inch (1 cm) wide and long enough to span half the length of each flip-flop. ■ Make 2 strips per cookie.

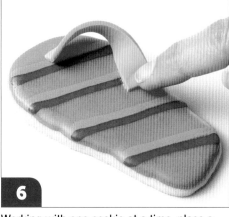

6 Working with one cookie at a time, place a dab of icing at the top center of a flip-flop and another halfway down the flip-flop on the right side. ■ Affix one end of a fondant strip to the top dot and the other end to the bottom dot, curving the strip in a C shape to look like the strap of a flip-flop.

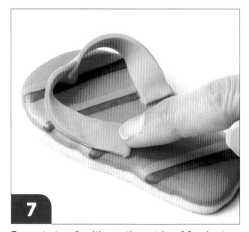

7 Repeat step 6 with another strip of fondant on the left side of the flip-flop. ■ Repeat steps 6 and 7 for all cookies.

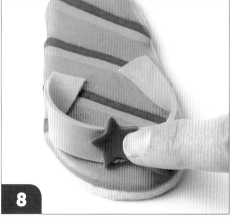

8 Dab the back of each fondant star with icing and affix a star to the point where the fondant strips meet at the top of each flip-flop. ■ Let cookies dry for at least 6 hours before serving.

Tips

When cutting out flip-flop shapes, be sure to cut half the cookies for a right flip-flop and half for a left flip-flop. To do this, flip the cutter over for half the cookies.

If all the hot pink icing does not fit in your squeeze bottle, cover the remaining icing tightly and refill the bottle as needed.

In step 2, pipe your diagonal lines in opposite directions for left and right feet.

An X-acto knife is a good investment if you plan to work with fondant often. Its blade is sharper than a paring knife, allowing for a more "x-act" cut.

Ice Cream Cone

I'm not a huge dessert person, but I seldom turn down a bowl of ice cream or, even better, an ice cream cone. On a hot summer day, a scoop of ice cream is almost mandatory, and this generous cone features one of my favorite flavors: mint chocolate chip, with a cherry on top! **Makes about 24.**

What You Need

- 1 recipe cookie dough (pages 36–46)
- Ice cream cone cookie cutter
- 1 recipe Classic Royal Icing (page 47)
- Brown gel paste
- Mint or avocado green gel paste
- Disposable pastry bag
- Coupler
- #1 round decorating tip
- 3 squeeze bottles
- Red fondant
- Tweezers

Techniques Used

- Tinting icing (page 22)
- Filling a pastry bag (page 24)
- Filling a squeeze bottle (page 24)
- Piping (page 27)
- Flooding (page 28)
- Wet-on-wet detailing (page 28)
- Working with fondant (page 30)

Getting Started

Bake cookies: Roll out dough and cut cookies with the ice cream cone cookie cutter. Bake according to recipe directions. Let cool completely before decorating.

Tint and thin icing: Divide icing evenly among four bowls; tint one portion dark brown, one light brown and one mint or avocado green, and leave one white. Transfer dark brown icing to a pastry bag fitted with a #1 tip. Thin light brown, green and white icing to two-step icing consistency (page 24) and transfer to squeeze bottles.

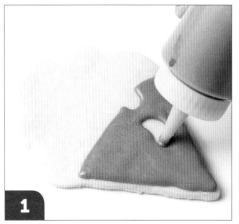

1

Using light brown icing, outline and flood cones as shown, leaving a curved space at the top for an ice cream "drip."

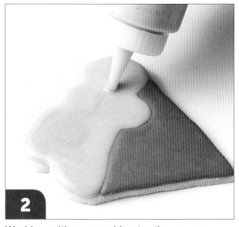

2

Working with one cookie at a time, use green icing to outline and flood the ice cream section of a cookie, leaving space at the top for whipped cream.

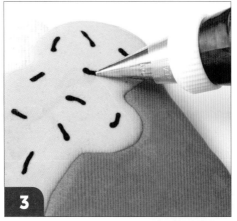

3

While the green icing is still wet, pipe several dark brown chocolate chips in the ice cream. ■ Repeat steps 2 and 3 for all cookies.

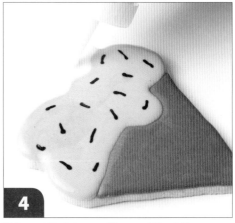

4

Using white icing, outline and flood the remaining whipped cream section of each cookie. ■ Let icing set for at least 6 hours or overnight.

5

Meanwhile, mold 2 tsp (10 mL) fondant into a cherry shape. ■ Flatten the back so the cherry will lie flat.

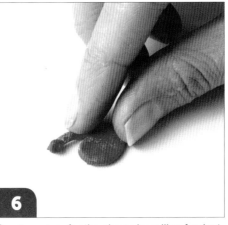

6

Create a stem for the cherry by rolling fondant into a thin, slightly curved rope. ■ Dab the end of the stem with water and press it lightly against the top of the cherry to affix. ■ Make 1 cherry per cookie. ■ Place cherries on a cookie sheet and let dry for at least 4 hours or overnight.

Tips

Adding embellishments, such as the cherries, is easier if you use a pair of tweezers. Buy an extra pair and keep them handy with your decorating supplies.

Make these cookies with Dark Chocolate cookie dough (page 40) paired with Peppermint Royal Icing (variation, page 47).

Variations

Change the color of the ice cream to look like your favorite flavor.

Make the cone a double scoop by turning the whipped cream section into a second scoop of ice cream.

Instead of putting a cherry on top, scatter the top with a layer of colored sprinkles while the icing is still wet.

7

Using dark brown icing, pipe a crisscross pattern on each cone, spacing the lines evenly in both directions.

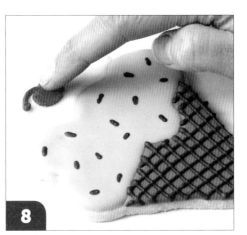

8

Dab the back of each fondant cherry with icing and affix a cherry to the whipped cream section of each cookie. ■ Let cookies dry for at least 4 hours before serving.

Witch's Hat

What You Need

- 1 recipe cookie dough (pages 36–46)
- Witch hat cookie cutter
- 1 recipe Classic Royal Icing (page 47)
- Blue gel paste
- Black gel paste
- Purple gel paste
- Squeeze bottle
- Purple or blue disco dust
- Cornstarch
- Small rolling pin
- Orange fondant
- Ruler
- X-acto knife
- 2 disposable pastry bags
- 2 couplers
- 2 #1 round decorating tips

Techniques Used

- Tinting icing (page 22)
- Filling a squeeze bottle (page 24)
- Piping (page 27)
- Flooding (page 28)
- Adding sparkle (page 28)
- Working with fondant (page 30)
- Using an X-acto knife (page 31)
- Filling a pastry bag (page 24)

I think I was a witch for Halloween at least three times when I was growing up. Needless to say, I never won the most original costume award! These cookies turn plain black witches' caps into something special with a touch of sparkly purple magic — no potion required! **Makes about 30.**

Getting Started

Bake cookies: Roll out dough and cut cookies with the witch's hat cookie cutter. Bake according to recipe directions. Let cool completely before decorating.

Tint and thin icing: Place 1 cup (250 mL) icing in a bowl and tint it blue. Place ½ cup (125 mL) icing in a bowl and tint it black. Cover both bowls tightly and set aside. Tint remaining icing purple, thin to two-step icing consistency (page 24) and transfer to a squeeze bottle.

1 Working with one cookie at a time, use purple icing to outline a hat.

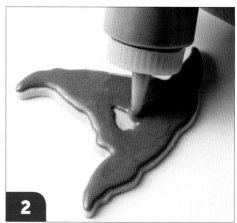

2 Flood hat with purple icing.

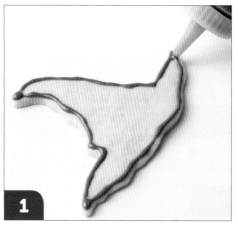

3 While purple icing is still wet, sprinkle the hat with disco dust, shaking off excess. ■ Repeat steps 1 to 3 for all cookies. ■ Let icing set for at least 6 hours or overnight.

4 Meanwhile, on a work surface lightly dusted with cornstarch, roll out fondant to ⅛ inch (3 mm) thick.

5

With the ruler as a guide, use the X-acto knife to cut strips about $\frac{1}{2}$ inch (1 cm) wide and long enough to span the bottom of the triangular portion of a witch's hat. ■ Make 1 strip per cookie. ■ Place strips on a cookie sheet and let dry for at least 4 hours or overnight.

6

Transfer blue and black icing to pastry bags fitted with #1 tips. ■ Use blue icing to pipe small dots in a polka-dot pattern on each hat.

7

Dab the back of each fondant strip with icing and affix a strip across the bottom of the triangular portion of each hat.

8

Using black icing, pipe a buckle in the center of each strip, extending onto the hat. ■ Let cookies dry for at least 6 hours before serving.

Tips

If all the purple icing does not fit in your squeeze bottle, cover the remaining icing tightly and refill the bottle as needed.

After rolling out fondant, let it rest for about 15 minutes (but not much longer!) before cutting out shapes. This allows it to harden a bit, making for cleaner cuts.

Keep any fondant you are not presently working with tightly wrapped in plastic wrap, as it can quickly dry out, rendering it unusable.

Variation

Instead of sprinkling hats with purple or blue disco dust, paint them with purple or blue luster dust for a more matte sparkle. After purple icing has dried completely, mix luster dust with vodka or lemon juice (see page 30) and carefully brush onto the surface. Let dry completely, several hours or overnight.

Witch's Broom

What You Need

- 1 recipe cookie dough (pages 36–46)
- Broom cookie cutter
- 1 recipe Classic Royal Icing (page 47)
- Red gel paste
- Yellow gel paste
- Brown gel paste
- Squeeze bottle
- Small food-safe paintbrush
- Gold or yellow luster dust
- Brown or mahogany luster dust
- 2 disposable pastry bags
- 2 couplers
- 2 #2 round decorating tips

Techniques Used

- Tinting icing (page 22)
- Filling a squeeze bottle (page 24)
- Piping (page 27)
- Flooding (page 28)
- Adding sparkle (page 28)
- Filling a pastry bag (page 24)

Housework would be much more enjoyable if I had a few of these cookies to nibble on between chores! Make these simple sweepers as part of your Halloween party dessert platter. Pair them with the purple Witch's Hat cookies (page 72) for a colorful display. **Makes about 40.**

Getting Started

Bake cookies: Roll out dough and cut cookies with the broom cookie cutter. Bake according to recipe directions. Let cool completely before decorating.

Tint and thin icing: Place ¾ cup (175 mL) icing in a bowl and tint it red. Cover tightly and set aside. Divide remaining icing evenly between two bowls; tint one portion yellow and one brown. Transfer yellow icing to a pastry bag fitted with a #2 tip. Thin brown icing to two-step icing consistency (page 24) and transfer to a squeeze bottle.

1 Using brown icing, outline and flood broomsticks.

2 Use yellow icing to make individual broom bristles. ■ For each broom, pipe a layer of 10 to 15 lines, starting at the base of the broomstick and extending straight to the halfway point of the broom, then tapering out in various directions to the end of the broom. ■ Let icing set for 10 minutes.

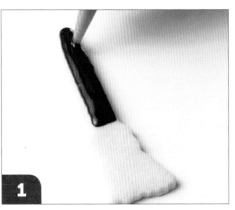

3 Pipe a second layer of 10 to 15 lines on each broom. ■ Let icing set for 10 minutes.

4 Pipe a third layer of lines on each broom, creating texture for the bristles. ■ Let icing set for at least 6 hours or overnight.

5

Using the small paintbrush, brush the bristles lightly with gold luster dust.

6

Brush the broomsticks lightly with brown luster dust.

7

Using brown icing, pipe a border around each broomstick.

8

Transfer red icing to a pastry bag fitted with a #2 tip. ■ Pipe a band at the halfway point of each broom. ■ Pipe another band halfway between the first band and the broomstick. ■ Let cookies dry for at least 4 hours before serving.

Tips

Cookie dough retains its shape best when cold. If the rolled-out dough gets too warm while you're cutting shapes, carefully transfer it to a cookie sheet and place it in the refrigerator for 15 minutes before continuing.

Keep royal icing tightly covered when you're not using it, as it tends to dry out quickly.

When applying luster dust, make sure the paintbrush you use is dry; otherwise, the dust will clump rather than covering the surface in a light, even layer.

Mummy Trick-or-Treater

What You Need

- 1 recipe cookie dough (pages 36–46)
- Gingerbread man cookie cutter
- 1 recipe Classic Royal Icing (page 47)
- Black gel paste
- Squeeze bottle
- Cornstarch
- Small rolling pin
- Orange fondant
- Black fondant
- White fondant
- Ruler
- X-acto knife
- Edible marker
- Disposable pastry bag
- Coupler
- #1 round decorating tip
- Tweezers
- Royal icing eyes

Techniques Used

- Tinting icing (page 22)
- Filling a squeeze bottle (page 24)
- Piping (page 27)
- Flooding (page 28)
- Working with fondant (page 30)
- Using an X-acto knife (page 31)
- Filling a pastry bag (page 24)
- Adding embellishments (page 31)

Be the hit of your Halloween party by passing out these adorable mummy cookies. You might even turn the decorating process into a fun party activity. All you need is a lot of white fondant… and a *little* patience! **Makes about 30.**

Getting Started

Bake cookies: Roll out dough and cut cookies with the gingerbread man cookie cutter. Bake according to recipe directions. Let cool completely before decorating.

Tint and thin icing: Place $1/2$ cup (125 mL) icing in a bowl and tint it black. Cover tightly and set aside. Thin remaining white icing to two-step icing consistency (page 24) and transfer to a squeeze bottle.

Using white icing, outline and flood cookies. ■ Let icing set for at least 6 hours or overnight.

Meanwhile, create goodie bags. ■ On a work surface lightly dusted with cornstarch, roll out orange fondant to $1/16$ inch (2 mm) thick. ■ Using the ruler and X-acto knife, cut out a $1^1/2$- by 1-inch (4 by 2.5 cm) rectangle. ■ Make 1 rectangle per cookie.

Roll black fondant into very thin ropes. ■ Cut ropes into 1-inch (2.5 cm) sections and bend each into a handle shape. ■ Dab the ends of each handle with water and press them lightly against an orange rectangle to affix. ■ Place goodie bags on a cookie sheet and let dry for at least 6 hours or overnight.

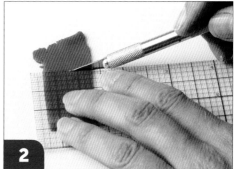

Dust work surface with cornstarch and roll out white fondant to $1/16$ inch (2 mm) thick. ■ With the ruler as a guide, use the X-acto knife to cut long strips about $1/2$ inch (1 cm) wide. ■ Make several strips for each cookie.

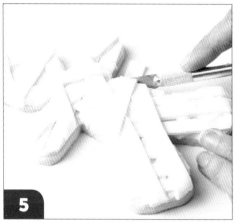

5

To make each cookie look wrapped like a mummy, use dabs of icing to affix white strips in various directions, trimming the strips at the edges of the cookie and pressing the ends down. ■ Leave small spaces for eyes and a mouth.

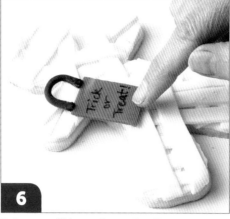

6

Using an edible marker, write "Trick or Treat!" on each goodie bag. ■ Dab the back of each bag with icing and affix a bag to each mummy's hand.

7

Using tweezers and a dab of icing on the back of each royal icing eye, place two eyes on each mummy's face.

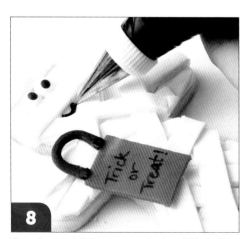

8

Transfer black icing to a pastry bag fitted with a #1 tip. ■ Pipe a mouth on each mummy. ■ Let cookies dry for at least 6 hours before serving.

Pumpkin

What You Need

- 1 recipe cookie dough (pages 36–46)
- Pumpkin cookie cutter
- 1 recipe Classic Royal Icing (page 47)
- Brown gel paste
- Orange gel paste
- 2 squeeze bottles
- Cornstarch
- Small rolling pin
- Avocado green fondant
- Small leaf cutter
- Pointed fondant modeling tool (see tip)
- Small food-safe paintbrush
- Gold or orange luster dust
- Disposable pastry bag
- Coupler
- #2 round decorating tips

Techniques Used

- Tinting icing (page 22)
- Filling a squeeze bottle (page 24)
- Piping (page 27)
- Flooding (page 28)
- Working with fondant (page 30)
- Adding sparkle (page 28)
- Filling a pastry bag (page 24)

One of my favorite fall memories is taking our annual trip to the local pumpkin patch with my dad, where my brother and I would select the perfect pumpkin to carve into a jack-o'-lantern. I always chose one that was round and plump, just like these cookies. Bake them with (what else?) my Pumpkin Spice cookie dough (page 43) and use Vanilla Royal Icing (variation, page 47.) **Makes about 36.**

Getting Started

Bake cookies: Roll out dough and cut cookies with the pumpkin cookie cutter. Bake according to recipe directions. Let cool completely before decorating.

Tint and thin icing: Place $1/2$ cup (125 mL) icing in a bowl and tint it brown. Tint remaining icing orange. Place half the orange icing in another bowl, cover tightly and set aside. Thin brown and remaining orange icing to two-step icing consistency (page 24) and transfer to squeeze bottles.

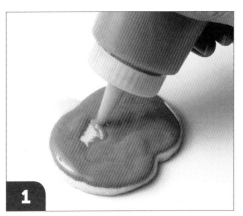

1 Using the squeeze bottle of orange icing, outline and flood pumpkins.

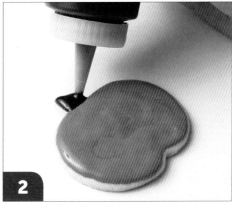

2 Using brown icing, outline and flood pumpkin stems. ■ Let icing set for at least 6 hours or overnight.

3 Meanwhile, on a work surface lightly dusted with cornstarch, roll out fondant to $1/8$ inch (3 mm) thick. ■ Using the leaf cutter, cut out 1 leaf per cookie. ■ Use the modeling tool to create a shallow crease in each leaf.

4 Roll fondant ropes about $1/4$ inch (5 mm) in diameter and 3 inches (7.5 cm) long. ■ Coil each rope around itself a few times, pinching the ends to a point. ■ Make 1 coil per cookie. ■ Place leaves and coils on a cookie sheet and let dry for at least 6 hours or overnight.

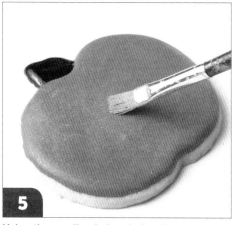

5 Using the small paintbrush, brush each pumpkin lightly with luster dust.

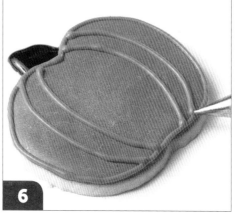

6 Transfer reserved orange icing to a pastry bag fitted with a #2 tip. ■ Pipe a border around each pumpkin. ■ Pipe 2 curved lines on each side of center on each pumpkin, as shown.

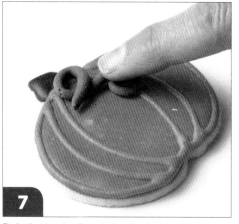

7 Dab the back of each fondant coil with icing and affix a coil to each pumpkin so that it is trailing down from the stem.

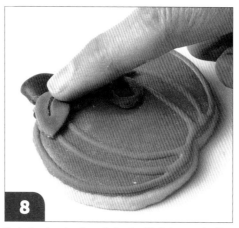

8 Dab the back of each leaf with icing and affix a leaf to each pumpkin so that the wider end of the leaf covers the top end of the coil. ■ Let cookies dry for at least 4 hours before serving.

Tips

The number of cookies this recipe will yield depends on the size of your cutter. I used a 3-inch (7.5 cm) pumpkin cutter.

If you don't have a leaf-shaped cutter, simply cut a leaf freehand from rolled-out fondant.

If you don't have a modeling tool, use the tip of a dull butter knife to make the crease in each leaf.

Variation

Turn these pumpkins into jack-o'-lanterns! Pipe and flood eyes, a nose and a wide toothy grin using black icing in a squeeze bottle. Draw the design first with an edible marker if you want a guide for piping.

Acorn

I grew up in New Jersey, where we had plenty of large oak trees in our front and backyards. I loved to search for acorns, especially those with intact caps, which could be used for decorations or art class projects. Pair these with the hungry Squirrel cookies (page 82) and make them with Nutty Pecan cookie dough (page 46)! **Makes about 30.**

What You Need

- 1 recipe cookie dough (pages 36–46)
- Acorn cookie cutter
- 1 recipe Classic Royal Icing (page 47)
- Brown gel paste
- 2 squeeze bottles
- Small food-safe paintbrush
- Brown or mahogany luster dust
- Disposable pastry bag
- Coupler
- #2 round decorating tip
- Brown sanding sugar

Techniques Used

- Tinting icing (page 22)
- Filling a squeeze bottle (page 24)
- Piping (page 27)
- Flooding (page 28)
- Adding sparkle (page 28)
- Filling a pastry bag (page 24)

Getting Started

Bake cookies: Roll out dough and cut cookies with the acorn cookie cutter. Bake according to recipe directions. Let cool completely before decorating.

Tint and thin icing: Divide icing evenly between two bowls; tint one portion light brown and one dark brown. Transfer half the dark brown icing to another bowl, cover tightly and set aside. Thin light brown and remaining dark brown icing to two-step icing consistency (page 24) and transfer to squeeze bottles.

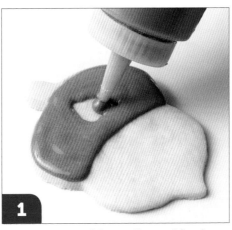

1 Using light brown icing, outline and flood acorn caps, excluding the stem.

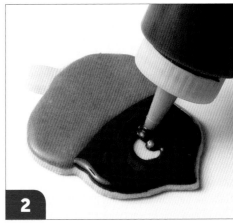

2 Working with one cookie at a time, use the squeeze bottle of dark brown icing to outline and flood bottom section of acorns.

3 While the dark brown icing is still wet, use light brown icing to pipe 2 accent marks on each acorn. ■ Repeat steps 2 and 3 for all cookies. ■ Let icing set for at least 6 hours or overnight.

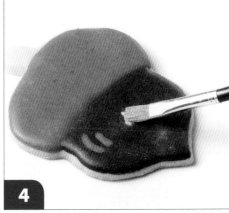

4 Using the small paintbrush, brush the bottom section of each acorn lightly with luster dust.

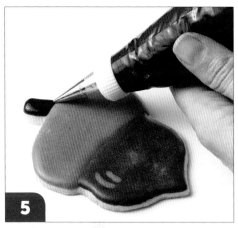

5 Transfer reserved dark brown icing to a pastry bag fitted with a #2 tip. ■ Pipe a stem for each acorn.

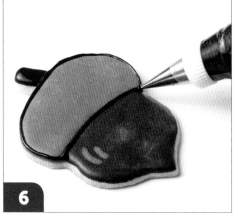

6 Working with one cookie at a time, pipe a dark brown border around each acorn cap.

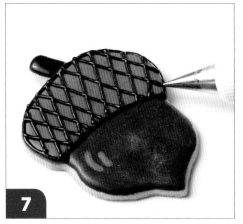

7 Pipe a dark brown crisscross pattern within each acorn cap, spacing the lines evenly in both directions.

8 While the icing is still wet, sprinkle the acorn cap with sanding sugar, shaking off excess. ■ Repeat steps 6 to 8 for all cookies. ■ Let cookies dry for at least 6 hours before serving.

Tips

The number of cookies this recipe will yield depends on the size of your cutter. I used a 3-inch (7.5 cm) acorn cutter.

When applying luster dust, make sure the paintbrush you use is dry; otherwise, the dust will clump rather than covering the surface in a light, even layer.

Don't be alarmed if excess sanding sugar sticks to the cookie even after you shake it. Wait until the icing dries completely, then gently brush off the unwanted sugar with a small food-safe paintbrush or a cotton swab.

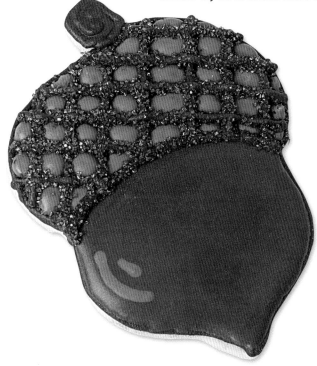

Squirrel

This hungry squirrel is running through the forest in search of acorns to gather for a snack. (They're on page 80.) Make these cookies as part of a fall-themed arrangement, or add them to other animal cookies as part of a farm theme (pages 119–130). **Makes about 24.**

What You Need

- 1 recipe cookie dough (pages 36–46)
- Squirrel cookie cutter
- 1 recipe Classic Royal Icing (page 47)
- Brown gel paste
- Black gel paste
- 2 squeeze bottles
- Fine dark brown sanding sugar
- Fine black sanding sugar
- 2 disposable pastry bags
- 2 couplers
- 2 #1 round decorating tips
- Tweezers
- Royal icing eyes

Techniques Used

- Tinting icing (page 22)
- Filling a squeeze bottle (page 24)
- Piping (page 27)
- Flooding (page 28)
- Adding sparkle (page 28)
- Filling a pastry bag (page 24)
- Adding embellishments (page 31)

Getting Started

Bake cookies: Roll out dough and cut cookies with the squirrel cookie cutter. Bake according to recipe directions. Let cool completely before decorating.

Tint and thin icing: Place ¼ cup (60 mL) icing in each of two bowls; tint one portion dark brown and one black. Cover tightly and set aside. Place 1½ cups (375 mL) icing in a bowl and leave it white. Tint remaining icing light brown. Thin white and light brown icing to two-step icing consistency (page 24) and transfer to squeeze bottles.

1 Using light brown icing, outline and flood each squirrel's body, excluding the tail. ■ Let icing set for at least 6 hours or overnight.

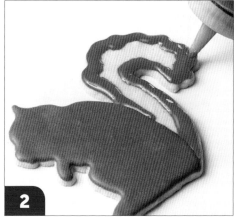

2 Working with one cookie at a time, use light brown icing to outline and flood the outside of the tail.

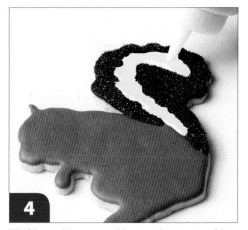

3 While the light brown icing is still wet, sprinkle it with dark brown sanding sugar, shaking off excess. ■ Repeat steps 2 and 3 for all cookies.

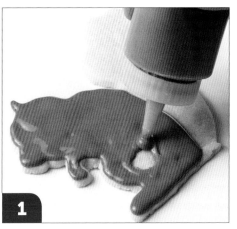

4 Working with one cookie at a time, use white icing to flood the interior of the tail.

5

While the white icing is still wet, sprinkle it with black sanding sugar, shaking off excess. ■ Repeat steps 4 and 5 for all cookies.

6

Transfer dark brown and black icing to pastry bags fitted with #1 tips. ■ Use dark brown icing to pipe a nose, front claws and back claws on each squirrel. ■ Use black icing to pipe whiskers and a mouth.

7

Using tweezers and a dab of icing, affix a royal icing eye on each squirrel.

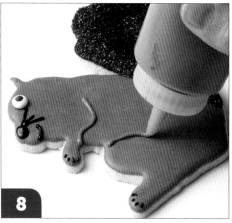

8

Using light brown icing, outline each squirrel's arm and haunch as shown. ■ Dab a bit of white icing inside each squirrel's ear. ■ Let cookies dry for at least 6 hours before serving.

Tips

Adding embellishments, such as the royal icing eyes, is easier if you use a pair of tweezers. Buy an extra pair and keep them handy with your decorating supplies.

If you don't have royal icing eyes on hand, pipe simple eyes using black icing and a pastry bag fitted with a #2 round decorating tip.

Don't be alarmed if excess sanding sugar sticks to the cookie even after you shake it. Wait until the icing dries completely, then gently brush off the unwanted sugar with a small food-safe paintbrush or a cotton swab.

Autumn Leaves

Raking colorful leaves is one of the best parts of fall. Well, let me rephrase: the raking part isn't necessarily fun, but jumping into the freshly raked pile of leaves is a blast! Create your own pile of swirly, jewel-toned leaf cookies for a platter. Everyone will be sure to dive in! **Makes about 30.**

What You Need

- 1 recipe cookie dough (pages 36–46)
- Leaf cookie cutter
- 1 recipe Classic Royal Icing (page 47)
- Yellow gel paste
- Red gel paste
- Brown gel paste
- Orange gel paste
- 4 squeeze bottles
- Toothpick
- Small food-safe paintbrush
- Orange or gold luster dust

Techniques Used

- Tinting icing (page 22)
- Filling a squeeze bottle (page 24)
- Piping (page 27)
- Flooding (page 28)
- Adding sparkle (page 28)

Variation

Add a little extra sparkle by piping an orange border around each leaf after it has dried, using a pastry bag fitted with a #2 round decorating tip. Immediately sprinkle the border with fine orange sanding sugar, shaking off excess. Let dry for several hours before serving.

Getting Started

Bake cookies: Roll out dough and cut cookies with the leaf cookie cutter. Bake according to recipe directions. Let cool completely before decorating.

Thin and tint icing: Thin icing to two-step icing consistency (page 24). Place 1 cup (250 mL) icing in each of two bowls; tint one portion yellow and one red. Place ½ cup (125 mL) icing in a bowl and tint it brown. Tint remaining icing orange. Transfer all icings to squeeze bottles.

1 Working with one cookie at a time, use brown icing to outline and flood the stem. ■ Use orange icing to outline and flood the leaf.

2 While the orange icing is still wet, pipe several yellow and red dots on the leaf, spacing them evenly. ■ Draw the end of the toothpick through the leaf, connecting the dots in sweeping motions. ■ Repeat steps 1 and 2 for all cookies. ■ Let icing set for at least 6 hours or overnight.

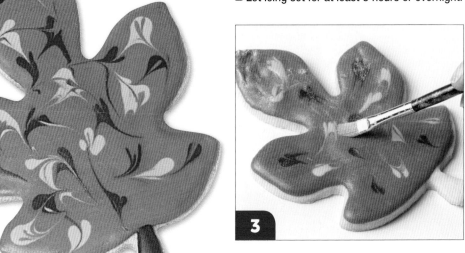

3 Using the small paintbrush, brush each leaf lightly with luster dust.

Snowman

Growing up, my friends and I would eagerly await the first big snowfall. We were almost guaranteed a day off from school, and we could spend the day playing in the winter wonderland: sledding, creating snow forts and, of course, building a snowman (and the occasional snow lady). This stylish snowman is very well dressed, with a dapper black hat, a colorful sweater and the requisite carrot nose. **Makes about 30.**

What You Need

- 1 recipe cookie dough (pages 36–46)
- Snowman cookie cutter
- 1 recipe Classic Royal Icing (page 47)
- Black gel paste
- Red gel paste
- Blue gel paste
- 3 squeeze bottles
- Orange fondant
- Toothpick
- Disposable pastry bag
- Coupler
- #1 round decorating tip
- Tweezers
- Royal icing flowers

Techniques Used

- Tinting icing (page 22)
- Filling a squeeze bottle (page 24)
- Piping (page 27)
- Flooding (page 28)
- Working with fondant (page 30)
- Filling a pastry bag (page 24)

Getting Started

Bake cookies: Roll out dough and cut cookies with the snowman cookie cutter. Bake according to recipe directions. Let cool completely before decorating.

Tint and thin icing: Place ¼ cup (60 mL) icing in a bowl and tint it black. Cover tightly and set aside. Place 1 cup (250 mL) icing in each of three bowls; tint one portion black, one red and one blue, and leave one white. Thin all four icings to two-step icing consistency (page 24) and transfer to squeeze bottles.

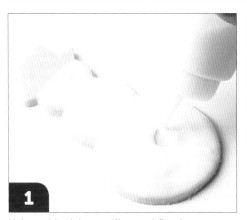

1

Using white icing, outline and flood snowmen, leaving space at the top for the hat.

2

Using black icing, outline and flood hats. ■ Let icing set for at least 6 hours or overnight.

3

Meanwhile, mold fondant into small carrots for snowmen noses. ■ The noses can be a variety of lengths, but the ends should be flat so that they attach easily to cookies. ■ Make 1 carrot per cookie. ■ Place carrots on a cookie sheet and let dry for at least 4 hours or overnight.

4

Working with one cookie at a time, use red icing to outline and flood a scarf as shown.

continued...

Tips

Keep royal icing tightly covered when you're not using it, as it tends to dry out quickly.

Be sure to wear disposable latex gloves when coloring fondant so the gel paste does not stain your hands.

Keep any fondant you are not presently working with tightly wrapped in plastic wrap, as it can quickly dry out, rendering it unusable.

5

While the red icing is still wet, pipe alternating blue and white lines vertically across the neckline of the scarf, spacing evenly.

6

Immediately drag the end of the toothpick through the center of the blue and white lines, working inward from the left end of the neckline to the center of the scarf, and from the right end to the center.

7

Pipe alternating blue and white lines horizontally across each long tail of the scarf, spacing evenly.

8

Immediately drag the end of the toothpick through the center of the blue and white lines, working downward from the neckline to the end of each tail. ■ Repeat steps 4 to 8 for all cookies.

9

Pipe individual white, blue and red strands at the end of each scarf tail, creating a fringe.

10

Working with one cookie at a time, use blue icing to pipe a band across the center of each snowman's hat.

11

While the blue icing is still wet, use tweezers to place a royal icing flower on one side of the band. ■ Repeat steps 10 and 11 for all cookies.

12

Transfer reserved black icing to a pastry bag fitted with a #1 tip. ■ Pipe eyes and a dotted "coal" mouth on each snowman.

13

Pipe a few black buttons on each snowman's body.

14

Dab the end of each fondant carrot with icing and affix a carrot nose on each snowman. ■ Let cookies dry for at least 6 hours before serving.

Tips

Adding embellishments, such as the flowers and carrot noses, is easier if you use a pair of tweezers. Buy an extra pair and keep them handy with your decorating supplies.

Royal icing flowers can be found in the baking aisle of many craft stores or check the Source Guide (page 253) for other vendors.

Instead of using royal icing flowers, you could pipe a flower onto each hat freehand, using red icing in a pastry bag fitted with a #1 round decorating tip.

Snowflake

What You Need

- 1 recipe cookie dough (pages 36–46)
- Snowflake cookie cutter
- 1 recipe Classic Royal Icing (page 47)
- Light blue gel paste
- Squeeze bottle
- Disposable pastry bag
- Coupler
- #2 round decorating tip
- Fine white or blue sanding sugar
- Tweezers
- Silver dragées or white edible pearls

Techniques Used

- Tinting icing (page 22)
- Filling a squeeze bottle (page 24)
- Piping (page 27)
- Flooding (page 28)
- Filling a pastry bag (page 24)
- Adding sparkle (page 28)
- Adding embellishments (page 31)

Like La Tour Eiffel (page 226) and the "Batter Up" Baseball cookies (page 157), snowflake cookies are a great way to practice your piping skills. You can follow my design exactly or feel free to switch it up a bit. No two snowflakes are alike, after all! **Makes about 24.**

Getting Started

Bake cookies: Roll out dough and cut cookies with the snowflake cookie cutter. Bake according to recipe directions. Let cool completely before decorating.

Tint and thin icing: Divide icing evenly between two bowls; tint one portion light blue and leave one white. Cover white icing tightly and set aside. Thin light blue icing to two-step icing consistency (page 24) and transfer to a squeeze bottle.

1 Using blue icing, outline and flood snowflakes. ■ Let icing set for at least 6 hours or overnight.

2 Transfer white icing to a pastry bag fitted with a #2 tip. ■ Working with one cookie at a time, pipe a border around a snowflake.

3 While the white icing is still wet, sprinkle the border with sanding sugar, shaking off excess. ■ Repeat steps 2 and 3 for all cookies.

4 Working with one cookie at a time, use white icing to pipe a design inside a snowflake as shown (or create your own design).

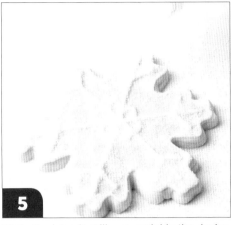

5

While the icing is still wet, sprinkle the design with sanding sugar, shaking off excess. ■ Repeat steps 4 and 5 for all cookies.

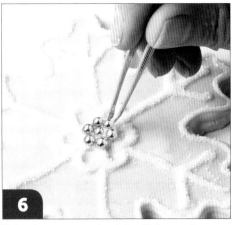

6

Using tweezers and a dab of icing on the back of each dragée, affix 7 dragées in a cluster in the center of each snowflake.

7

Affix 1 dragée between each point of each snowflake.

8

Affix 1 dragée at each outermost tip of each snowflake. ■ Let cookies dry for at least 6 hours before serving.

Tips

Don't be alarmed if excess sanding sugar sticks to the cookie even after you shake it. Wait until the icing dries completely, then gently brush off the unwanted sugar with a small food-safe paintbrush or a cotton swab.

Adding embellishments, such as the dragées, is easier if you use a pair of tweezers. Buy an extra pair and keep them handy with your decorating supplies.

Variation

When making a set of snowflakes, swap the colors so that some have a blue base with white detail and some have a white base with blue detail. This variety will make for a prettier presentation.

Mittens

These cookies would be a fun project for a cold and dreary winter day when the last thing you want to do is go outside. Match them with Winter Hat cookies (page 91) to make a set, or decorate them to look like your own favorite pair of mittens. **Makes about 30.**

What You Need

- 1 recipe cookie dough (pages 36–46)
- Mitten cookie cutter
- 1 recipe Classic Royal Icing (page 47)
- Blue gel paste
- Pink gel paste
- 3 squeeze bottles
- Toothpick
- Fine white sanding sugar

Techniques Used

- Tinting icing (page 22)
- Filling a squeeze bottle (page 24)
- Piping (page 27)
- Flooding (page 28)
- Feathering (page 29)
- Adding sparkle (page 28)

Tips

If you are planning to make pairs of mittens, remember to cut half the cookies for a left hand and half for a right hand. To do this, flip the cutter over for half the cookies.

Before baking these cookies, cut a small hole in the bottom of each mitten. After the cookies have been decorated, loop a ribbon through each hole and use the cookies as edible ornaments.

Getting Started

Bake cookies: Roll out dough and cut cookies with the mitten cookie cutter. Bake according to recipe directions. Let cool completely before decorating.

Thin and tint icing: Thin icing to two-step icing consistency (page 24). Divide icing evenly among three bowls; tint one portion light blue and one light pink, and leave one white. Transfer all icings to squeeze bottles.

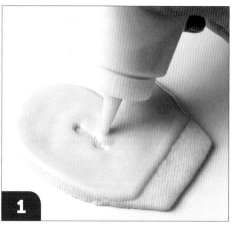

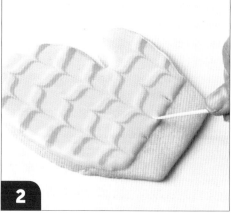

Working with one cookie at a time, use blue icing to outline and flood a mitten, leaving a band at the wrist un-iced.

Immediately pipe 5 horizontal pink lines across the blue icing, spacing evenly. ■ Pipe a white line just above each pink line. ■ Feather vertically through the pink and white lines. ■ Repeat steps 1 and 2 for all cookies. ■ Let icing set for at least 6 hours or overnight.

Working with one cookie at a time, use white icing to outline and flood the wristband of a mitten. ■ Immediately sprinkle wet icing with sanding sugar, shaking off excess. ■ Repeat for all cookies. ■ Let cookies dry for at least 6 hours before serving.

Winter Hat

These hats are meant to be paired with the Mittens (page 90), but they are certainly cute enough to stand on their own. I had a hat just like this when I was growing up, which I loved to pair with my powder pink ski jacket. I was very easy to pick out as I sped (or on occasion tumbled) down the slopes. **Makes about 30.**

What You Need

- 1 recipe cookie dough (pages 36–46)
- Winter hat cookie cutter
- 1 recipe Classic Royal Icing (page 47)
- Pink gel paste
- Blue gel paste
- Disposable pastry bag
- Coupler
- #2 round decorating tip
- 3 squeeze bottles
- Fine pink sanding sugar

Techniques Used

- Tinting icing (page 22)
- Filling a pastry bag (page 24)
- Filling a squeeze bottle (page 24)
- Piping (page 27)
- Flooding (page 28)
- Wet-on-wet detailing (page 28)
- Adding sparkle (page 28)

Getting Started

Bake cookies: Roll out dough and cut cookies with the winter hat cookie cutter. Bake according to recipe directions. Let cool completely before decorating.

Tint and thin icing: Divide icing evenly among three bowls; tint one portion light pink and one light blue, and leave on white. Transfer half the white icing to a pastry bag fitted with a #2 tip. Thin pink, blue and remaining white icing to two-step icing consistency (page 24) and transfer to squeeze bottles.

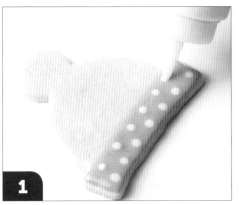

1

Working with one cookie at a time, use pink icing to outline and flood the band at the base of a hat. ■ Using the squeeze bottle of white icing, immediately pipe a polka-dot pattern in the pink icing.

2

Use pink icing to outline and flood the ball at the top of a hat. ■ Immediately sprinkle the ball with sanding sugar, shaking off excess.

3

Use blue icing to outline and flood the center of a hat. ■ Using the pastry bag of white icing, immediately pipe a snowflake design in the center of the hat as shown (or create your own design). ■ Repeat steps 1 to 3 for all cookies. ■ Let cookies dry for at least 6 hours before serving.

Tip

As with the Mittens (page 90), you can turn these cookies into edible ornaments. Before baking, cut a small hole in the ball at the top of each hat. After decorating, loop a ribbon through each hole.

Festive Christmas Sweater

What You Need

- 1 recipe cookie dough (pages 36–46)
- Sweater cookie cutter
- 1 recipe Classic Royal Icing (page 47)
- Yellow gel paste
- Blue gel paste
- Red gel paste
- Squeeze bottle
- Cornstarch
- Small rolling pin
- Green fondant
- Mini Christmas tree cutter (see tip)
- Fine red sanding sugar
- 3 disposable pastry bags
- 3 couplers
- 3 #2 round decorating tips

Techniques Used

- Tinting icing (page 22)
- Filling a squeeze bottle (page 24)
- Piping (page 27)
- Flooding (page 28)
- Working with fondant (page 30)
- Adding sparkle (page 28)
- Filling a pastry bag (page 24)

The "ugly Christmas sweater" was once a dreaded holiday gift that you were forced to wear for the family photo. Now it is celebrated at annual parties where the ugliest sweater wins a prize. The great thing about these cookies is that they can never be too over-the-top. The more decorations, colors and glitter you add, the better they look! **Makes about 30.**

Getting Started

Bake cookies: Roll out dough and cut cookies with the sweater cookie cutter. Bake according to recipe directions. Let cool completely before decorating.

Tint and thin icing: Place ¼ cup (60 mL) icing in each of three bowls; tint one portion yellow and one blue, and leave one white. Cover tightly and set aside. Tint remaining icing red, thin to two-step icing consistency (page 24) and transfer to a squeeze bottle.

Using red icing, outline sweaters.

Flood sweaters with red icing. ■ Let icing set for at least 6 hours or overnight.

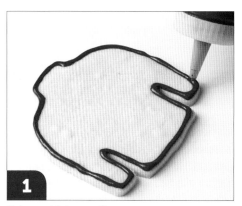

Meanwhile, on a work surface lightly dusted with cornstarch, roll out fondant to ¹⁄₁₆ inch (2 mm) thick. ■ Using the tree cutter, cut out 1 Christmas tree per cookie. ■ Place trees on a cookie sheet and let dry for at least 4 hours or overnight.

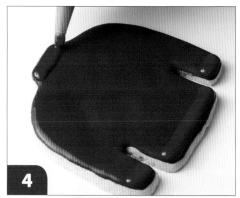

Working with one cookie at a time, use red icing to pipe thick lines across the cuffs, bottom edge and collar of each sweater.

5 While the red icing is still wet, sprinkle it with sanding sugar, shaking off excess. ■ Repeat steps 5 and 6 for all cookies.

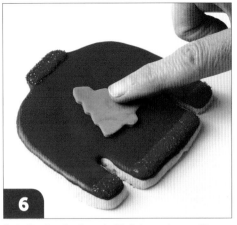

6 Dab the back of each Christmas tree with icing and affix a tree to the center of each sweater.

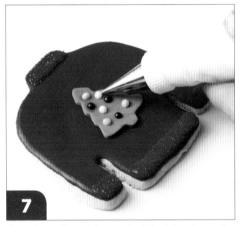

7 Transfer yellow, blue and white icing to pastry bags fitted with #2 tips. ■ Pipe small balls in alternating colors on trees. ■ Using yellow icing, pipe a star on top of each tree.

8 Using red icing, pipe evenly spaced red dots on the sleeves and around the tree on the body of the sweater. ■ Pipe red lines to define the sleeves. ■ Let cookies dry for at least 2 hours before serving.

Tips

If you don't have a small Christmas tree cutter, you can draw your own small tree template on parchment paper and trace around it with an X-acto knife or a small paring knife.

Don't be alarmed if excess sanding sugar sticks to the cookie even after you shake it. Wait until the icing dries completely, then gently brush off the unwanted sugar with a small food-safe paintbrush or a cotton swab.

Variation

Instead of a tree, cut other shapes for the center of each sweater, such as a candy cane, an ornament or a wreath.

Christmas Tree

What You Need

- 1 recipe cookie dough (pages 36–46)
- Christmas tree cookie cutter
- 1 recipe Classic Royal Icing (page 47)
- Yellow gel paste
- Blue gel paste
- Red gel paste
- Brown gel paste
- Green gel paste
- 3 squeeze bottles
- Cornstarch
- Small rolling pin
- Yellow fondant
- Small star cutter (see tip)
- Mini white dragées
- 3 disposable pastry bags
- 3 couplers
- 3 #1 round decorating tips
- Tweezers
- Silver nonpareils
- Small food-safe paintbrush
- Gold luster dust

Techniques Used

- Tinting icing (page 22)
- Filling a squeeze bottle (page 24)
- Piping (page 27)
- Flooding (page 28)
- Working with fondant (page 30)
- Adding embellishments (page 31)
- Filling a pastry bag (page 24)
- Adding sparkle (page 28)

"O Christmas Tree, O Christmas Tree / How lovely are thy royal icing branches!" Okay, I changed the lyrics a bit, but it's hard to not think of this song while you're decorating these cookies. I love how the "snow" adds an outdoor wintery look. Serve these at a tree-trimming party. **Makes about 24.**

Getting Started

Bake cookies: Roll out dough and cut cookies with the Christmas tree cookie cutter. Bake according to recipe directions. Let cool completely before decorating.

Tint and thin icing: Place $\frac{1}{4}$ cup (60 mL) icing in each of three bowls; tint one portion yellow, one blue and one red. Cover tightly and set aside. Place $1\frac{1}{2}$ cups (375 mL) icing in a bowl and leave it white. Place 1 cup (250 mL) icing in a bowl and tint it brown. Tint remaining icing green. Thin white, brown and green icing to two-step icing consistency (page 24) and transfer to squeeze bottles.

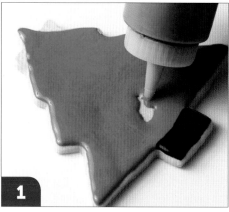

1

Using brown icing, outline and flood tree trunks. ■ Using green icing, outline and flood the remainder of each tree. ■ Let icing set for at least 6 hours or overnight.

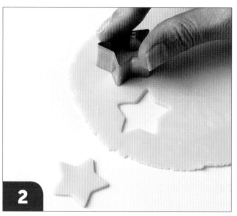

2

Meanwhile, on a work surface lightly dusted with cornstarch, roll out fondant to $\frac{1}{8}$ inch (3 mm) thick. ■ Using the star cutter, cut out 1 star per cookie. ■ Place stars on a cookie sheet and let dry for at least 4 hours or overnight.

3

Working with one cookie at a time, use white icing to pipe thick snow-like borders along the bottom of each tier of the tree.

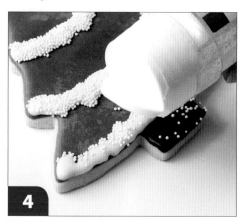

4

While the white icing is still wet, sprinkle the borders with dragées, shaking off excess. ■ Repeat steps 3 and 4 for all cookies.

5

Transfer yellow, blue and red icing to pastry bags fitted with #1 tips. ■ Working with one cookie at a time, pipe small balls in alternating colors on the green sections of the tree.

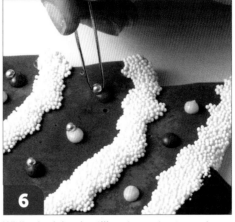

6

While the icing is still wet, use tweezers to place a silver nonpareil at the top of each ball. ■ Repeat steps 5 and 6 for all cookies.

7

Using the small paintbrush, brush each fondant star with gold luster dust.

8

Dab the back of each star with icing and affix a star to the top of each tree. ■ Let cookies dry for at least 6 hours before serving.

Tips

Instead of creating a star out of fondant, you can pipe one freehand using yellow icing in a pastry bag fitted with a #2 round decorating tip. After filling in the star, sprinkle it with gold disco dust for extra sparkle.

Adding embellishments, such as the silver nonpareils, is easier if you use a pair of tweezers. Buy an extra pair and keep them handy with your decorating supplies.

When applying luster dust, make sure the paintbrush you use is dry; otherwise, the dust will clump rather than covering the surface in a light, even layer.

Christmas Bulb

What You Need

- 1 recipe cookie dough (pages 36–46)
- Christmas bulb cookie cutter
- 1 recipe Classic Royal Icing (page 47)
- Red gel paste
- Green gel paste
- Blue gel paste
- Yellow gel paste
- 4 squeeze bottles
- Disposable pastry bag
- Coupler
- #2 round decorating tip
- Fine silver sanding sugar

Techniques Used

- Tinting icing (page 22)
- Filling a squeeze bottle (page 24)
- Piping (page 27)
- Flooding (page 28)
- Filling a pastry bag (page 24)
- Adding sparkle (page 28)

When I was growing up, decorating the Christmas tree was always a big event, with everyone in my family participating. My dad was in charge of putting the lights on the tree, but first my brother and I had the chore of untangling long strings of brightly colored bulbs. Make these festive cookies to set out when you decorate your own tree, as a reward for untangling all those knots! **Makes about 40.**

Getting Started

Bake cookies: Roll out dough and cut cookies with the Christmas bulb cookie cutter. Bake according to recipe directions. Let cool completely before decorating.

Tint and thin icing: Divide icing evenly among five bowls; tint one portion red, one green, one blue and one yellow, and leave one white. Transfer white icing to a pastry bag fitted with a #2 tip. Thin red, green, blue and yellow icing to two-step icing consistency (page 24) and transfer to squeeze bottles.

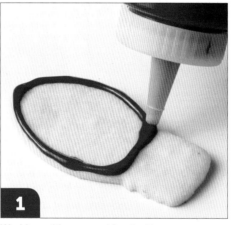

1 Working with one cookie at a time, use red icing to outline the top section of a Christmas bulb.

2 Flood the bulb with red icing.

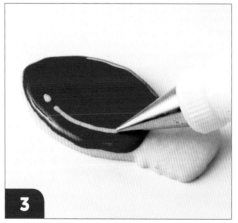

3 While the red icing is still wet, use white icing to pipe highlight marks on the left side of the bulb as shown. ■ Repeat steps 1 to 3 to make 10 red bulbs.

4 Using green icing, outline and flood the top section of a bulb. ■ Immediately pipe white highlight marks on the left side. ■ Repeat to make 10 green bulbs.

5 Using blue icing, outline and flood the top section of a bulb. ■ Immediately pipe white highlight marks on the left side. ■ Repeat to make 10 blue bulbs.

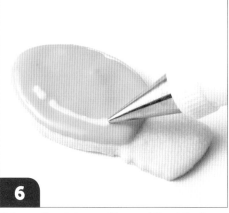

6 Using yellow icing, outline and flood the top section of a bulb. ■ Immediately pipe white highlight marks on the left side. ■ Repeat to make 10 yellow bulbs. ■ Let icing set for at least 6 hours or overnight.

7 Working with one cookie at a time, use white icing to pipe a screw design on the stem of a bulb.

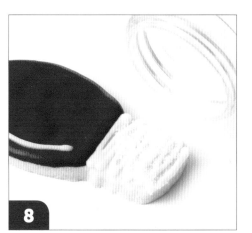

8 While the white icing is still wet, sprinkle it with sanding sugar, shaking off excess. ■ Repeat steps 7 and 8 for all cookies. ■ Let cookies dry for at least 2 hours before serving.

Tips

Before baking these cookies, cut a small hole in the stem of each bulb. After the cookies have been decorated, loop a ribbon through each hole and hang the bulbs on your tree as edible ornaments.

If you have filled a pastry bag with icing but are not using it for a while, set it upright in a tall drinking glass until you're ready for it.

To display these cookies, arrange them on a large plate or tray along a piece of thin rope candy, to simulate a string of lights.

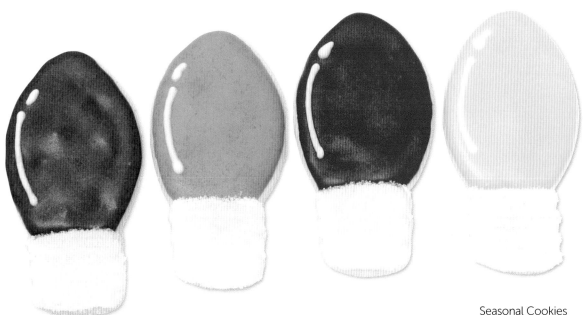

Peppermint Candy

What You Need

- 1 recipe cookie dough (pages 36–46)
- Wrapped candy cookie cutter
- 1 recipe Classic Royal Icing (page 47)
- Green gel paste
- Red gel paste
- 3 squeeze bottles
- Toothpick
- Disposable pastry bag
- Coupler
- #2 round decorating tip
- Fine white sanding sugar (optional)

Techniques Used

- Tinting icing (page 22)
- Filling a squeeze bottle (page 24)
- Piping (page 27)
- Flooding (page 28)
- Filling a pastry bag (page 24)
- Adding sparkle (page 28)

The design of these cookies might look advanced, but you will be surprised to discover how easy they are — and so impressed with yourself after you make them! Bring them to a holiday potluck or ship them off as homemade gifts. I like to make them using Dark Chocolate cookie dough (page 40) paired with Peppermint Royal Icing (variation, page 47). **Makes about 40.**

Getting Started

Bake cookies: Roll out dough and cut cookies with the wrapped candy cookie cutter. Bake according to recipe directions. Let cool completely before decorating.

Tint and thin icing: Place ¾ cup (175 mL) icing in each of three bowls; tint one portion green and one red, and leave one white. Cover white icing tightly and set aside. Thin green, red and remaining white icing to two-step icing consistency (page 24) and transfer to squeeze bottles.

1 Working with one cookie at a time, use the squeeze bottle of white icing to outline a cookie.

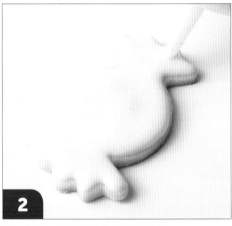

2 Flood the cookie with white icing.

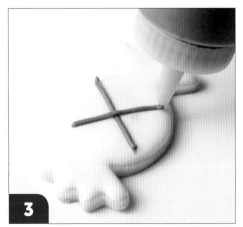

3 While the white icing is still wet, use green icing to pipe an X across the round section of the cookie.

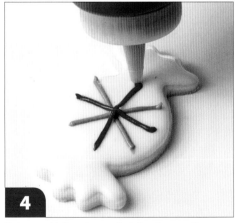

4 Using red icing, immediately pipe another X across the round section of the cookie, 45 degrees away from the green X.

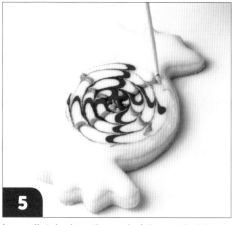

5

Immediately drag the end of the toothpick through the red and green lines, starting at the center of the cookie and spiraling toward the outer edge. ■ Repeat steps 1 to 5 for all cookies. ■ Let icing set for at least 6 hours or overnight.

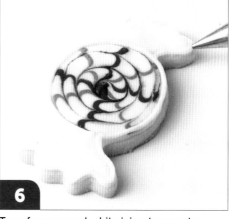

6

Transfer reserved white icing to a pastry bag fitted with a #2 tip. ■ Working with one cookie at a time, pipe a border around the round section of a cookie and around the "wrapper" sections on either side.

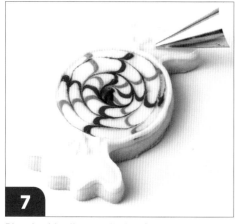

7

Pipe 3 white lines radiating from the round section into the wrapper on each side.

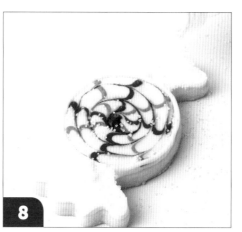

8

If desired, while the white icing is still wet, sprinkle it with sanding sugar, shaking off excess. ■ Repeat steps 6 to 8 for all cookies. ■ Let cookies dry for at least 2 hours before serving.

Tips

If all the white icing does not fit in your squeeze bottle, cover the remaining icing tightly and refill the bottle as needed.

Sometimes air bubbles are created when you flood a cookie with icing. If this happens, use the tip of a toothpick to pop the bubbles.

Variation

Make the spiral design using all red or all green for an easier design.

Christmas Stocking

Peeking out of these adorable stockings are an oversized candy cane and a snuggly teddy bear! **Makes about 30.**

What You Need

- 1 recipe cookie dough (pages 36–46)
- Stocking cookie cutter
- 1 recipe Classic Royal Icing (page 47)
- Green gel paste
- Blue gel paste
- Black gel paste
- Red gel paste
- 2 squeeze bottles
- White disco dust
- Cornstarch
- Small rolling pin
- White fondant
- Brown fondant
- Mini candy cane cutter
- Mini bear cutter
- 3 disposable pastry bags
- 3 couplers
- #2 round decorating tip
- 2 #1 round decorating tips

Techniques Used

- Tinting icing (page 22)
- Filling a squeeze bottle (page 24)
- Piping (page 27)
- Flooding (page 28)
- Adding sparkle (page 28)
- Working with fondant (page 30)
- Filling a pastry bag (page 24)

Getting Started

Bake cookies: Roll out dough and cut cookies with the stocking cookie cutter. Bake according to recipe directions. Let cool completely before decorating.

Tint and thin icing: Place 1 cup (250 mL) icing in a bowl and tint it green. Place ³⁄₄ cup (175 mL) icing in a bowl and tint it blue. Place ¹⁄₄ cup (60 mL) icing in a bowl and tint it black. Cover all bowls tightly and set aside. Place 1¹⁄₂ cups (375 mL) icing in a bowl and leave it white. Tint remaining icing red. Thin white and red icing to two-step icing consistency (page 24) and transfer to squeeze bottles.

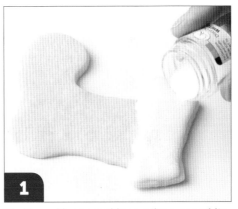

1 Working with one cookie at a time, use white icing to outline and flood the top of a stocking. ■ Immediately sprinkle the wet icing with disco dust, shaking off excess. ■ Repeat for all cookies.

2 Using red icing, outline and flood the bottom of each stocking. ■ Let icing set for at least 6 hours or overnight.

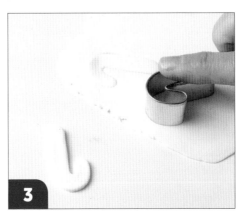

3 Meanwhile, on a work surface lightly dusted with cornstarch, roll out white fondant to ¹⁄₁₆ inch (2 mm) thick. ■ Using the candy cane cutter, cut out 1 candy cane per cookie.

4 Dust work surface with cornstarch and roll out brown fondant to ¹⁄₁₆ inch (2 mm) thick. ■ Using the bear cutter, cut out 1 bear per cookie. ■ Place candy canes and bears on a cookie sheet and let dry for at least 4 hours or overnight.

5 Transfer green icing to a pastry bag fitted with a #2 tip. ■ Pipe a crisscross pattern on the red part of each stocking, spacing the lines evenly in both directions.

6 Transfer blue and black icing to pastry bags fitted with #1 tips. ■ Use blue icing to personalize the top of each stocking with a name. ■ Use white icing to pipe a border around the top of each stocking.

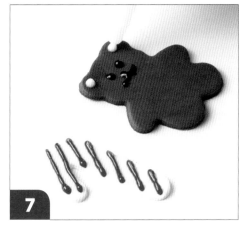

7 Use red icing to pipe stripes across each fondant candy cane. ■ Use black icing to pipe a face on each bear, and dab white icing in the interior of each bear's ears.

8 Using dabs of icing, affix a candy cane and a bear to the back of each cookie so that they appear to be emerging from the top. ■ Let cookies dry for at least 6 hours before serving.

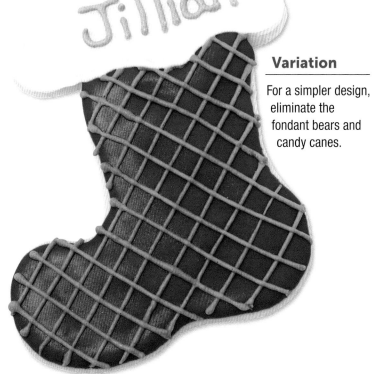

Tips

Make these cookies for a school or office Christmas party, personalizing each stocking with a student or co-worker's name.

Be sure to wear disposable latex gloves when coloring fondant so the gel paste does not stain your hands.

Keep any fondant you are not presently working with tightly wrapped in plastic wrap, as it can quickly dry out, rendering it unusable.

Variation

For a simpler design, eliminate the fondant bears and candy canes.

Rudolph the Red-Nosed Reindeer

What You Need

- 1 recipe cookie dough (pages 36–46)
- Reindeer cookie cutter
- 1 recipe Classic Royal Icing (page 47)
- Red gel paste
- Green gel paste
- Black gel paste
- Brown gel paste
- 5 disposable pastry bags
- 5 couplers
- #3 round decorating tip
- Squeeze bottle
- 2 #1 round decorating tips
- 2 #2 round decorating tips
- Tweezers
- Royal icing eyes

Techniques Used

- Tinting icing (page 22)
- Filling a squeeze bottle (page 24)
- Piping (page 27)
- Flooding (page 28)
- Filling a pastry bag (page 24)
- Adding embellishments (page 31)

Make a tray of these cookies for a holiday party or pass them out to lucky neighborhood carolers (providing, of course, that they sing "Rudolph the Red-Nosed Reindeer" first!) The relatively simple design makes this a great cookie to work on with kids who are home on holiday break. **Makes about 30.**

Getting Started

Bake cookies: Roll out dough and cut cookies with the reindeer cookie cutter. Bake according to recipe directions. Let cool completely before decorating.

Tint and thin icing: Place $\frac{1}{4}$ cup (60 mL) icing in each of four bowls; tint one portion red, one green and one black, and leave one white. Cover tightly and set aside. Divide remaining icing evenly between two bowls; tint one portion dark brown and one medium brown. Transfer dark brown icing to a pastry bag fitted with a #3 tip. Thin medium brown icing to two-step icing consistency (page 24) and transfer to a squeeze bottle.

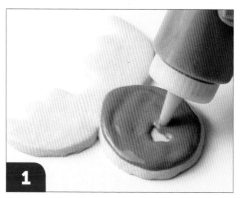

1 Using medium brown icing, outline and flood Rudolph's head in an egg shape on each cookie.

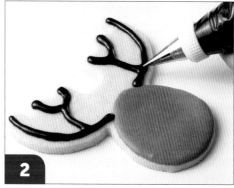

2 Using dark brown icing, pipe antlers on each head as shown. ■ Let icing set for at least 6 hours or overnight.

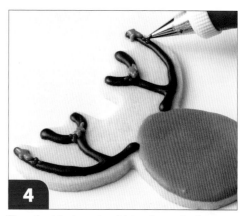

3 Transfer green and white icing to pastry bags fitted with #1 tips. ■ Use green icing to pipe a holly leaf on each branch of the antlers on each cookie.

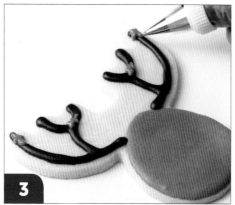

4 Transfer black and red icing to pastry bags fitted with #2 tips. ■ Use red icing to pipe a cluster of holly berries underneath each holly leaf.

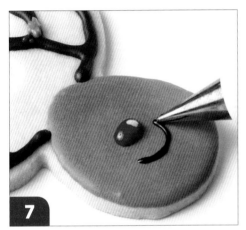

5

Working with one cookie at a time, use red icing to pipe a big red nose in the center of a reindeer's head.

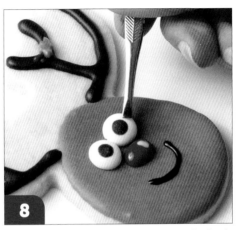

6

While the red icing is still wet, use white icing to pipe a small curved line on the nose to make it look shiny. ■ Repeat steps 5 and 6 for all cookies.

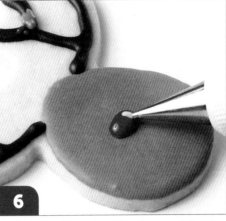

7

Using black icing, pipe a smile on each reindeer.

8

Using tweezers and a dab of icing on the back of each royal icing eye, place two eyes close together on each reindeer. ■ Let cookies dry for at least 4 hours before serving.

Tips

Adding embellishments, such as the royal icing eyes, is easier if you use a pair of tweezers. Buy an extra pair and keep them handy with your decorating supplies.

If you don't have royal icing eyes on hand, pipe simple eyes using black icing and a pastry bag fitted with a #2 round decorating tip.

If you like, you can use a red hot candy as Rudolph's nose instead of piping it.

Holly Leaf Place Card

This is a great "starter" design if you are fairly new to cookie decorating, but your guests won't find it any less impressive when they realize their place cards are as delicious as they are beautiful! **Makes about 40.**

What You Need

- 1 recipe cookie dough (pages 36–46)
- Holly leaf cookie cutter
- 1 recipe Classic Royal Icing (page 47)
- Red gel paste
- Green gel paste
- Squeeze bottle
- Cornstarch
- Small rolling pin
- Red fondant
- Small round cutter
- Disposable pastry bag
- Coupler
- #1 round decorating tip
- Small food-safe paintbrush (optional)
- Red luster dust (optional)

Techniques Used

- Tinting icing (page 22)
- Filling a squeeze bottle (page 24)
- Piping (page 27)
- Flooding (page 28)
- Working with fondant (page 30)
- Filling a pastry bag (page 24)
- Adding sparkle (page 28)

Variation

Instead of using fondant for the holly berries, pipe them using red icing in a pastry bag fitted with a #2 tip. Or use round red candies.

Getting Started

Bake cookies: Roll out dough and cut cookies with the holly leaf cookie cutter. Bake according to recipe directions. Let cool completely before decorating.

Tint and thin icing: Place 1 cup (250 mL) icing in a bowl and tint it red. Cover tightly and set aside. Tint remaining icing green, thin to two-step icing consistency (page 24) and transfer to a squeeze bottle (cover any remaining green icing tightly and refill the bottle as needed).

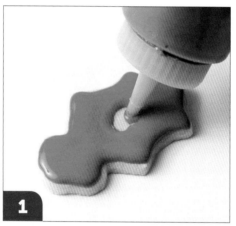

1

Using green icing, outline and flood holly leaves. ■ Let icing set for at least 6 hours or overnight.

2

On a work surface lightly dusted with cornstarch, roll out fondant to $\frac{1}{16}$ inch (2 mm) thick. ■ Using the round cutter, cut out 3 berries per cookie. ■ Dab the back of each berry with icing and affix a cluster of 3 berries to each leaf. ■ If desired, use the small paintbrush to brush berries with luster dust.

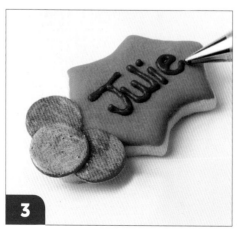

3

Transfer red icing to a pastry bag fitted with a #1 tip. ■ Personalize each leaf by piping a name across it. ■ Let cookies dry for at least 2 hours before serving.

4

Cookies for Kids

Party Hat

Although party hats are a staple of most children's birthday parties, the tight strap under your chin makes them quite uncomfortable to wear. Here's a better solution that's guaranteed to be more popular: traditional colorful hats in the form of fun and festive cookies. **Makes about 30.**

What You Need

- 1 recipe cookie dough (pages 36–46)
- Party hat cookie cutter
- 1 recipe Classic Royal Icing (page 47)
- Yellow gel paste
- Squeeze bottle
- Cornstarch
- Small rolling pin
- Red fondant
- Blue fondant
- #10 round decorating tip (see tips)
- Ruler
- X-acto knife

Techniques Used

- Tinting icing (page 22)
- Filling a squeeze bottle (page 24)
- Piping (page 27)
- Flooding (page 28)
- Working with fondant (page 30)

Getting Started

Bake cookies: Roll out dough and cut cookies with the party hat cookie cutter. Bake according to recipe directions. Let cool completely before decorating.

Thin and tint icing: Thin icing to two-step icing consistency (page 24), tint it yellow and transfer to a squeeze bottle.

1 Using yellow icing, outline and flood party hats. ■ Let icing set for at least 6 hours or overnight.

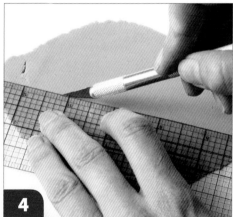

2 Meanwhile, on a work surface lightly dusted with cornstarch, roll out red fondant to ⅛ inch (3 mm) thick. ■ Using the round back side of the #10 tip, cut out 6 circles per cookie.

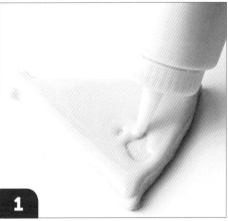

3 Using the front side of the #10 tip, cut out 7 circles per cookie. ■ Place all circles on a cookie sheet and let dry for at least 4 hours or overnight.

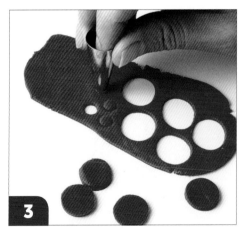

4 Dust work surface with cornstarch and roll out blue fondant to ⅛ inch (3 mm) thick. ■ With the ruler as a guide, use the X-acto knife to cut 4 long strips about ¼ inch (5 mm) wide.

5

Lay the 4 strips diagonally across a hat, spacing evenly. ■ Trim each strip to align with the edges of the cookie. ■ Use these 4 strips as templates and cut 4 matching strips per cookie.

6

Dab the back of each strip with icing and affix 4 strips to each hat, pressing the ends of the strips into the sides of the cookies for an even look.

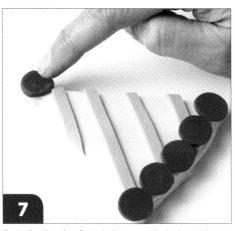

7

Dab the back of each large red circle with icing and affix 5 circles along the bottom edge of each hat. ■ Affix 1 circle at the top point of each hat.

8

Dab the back of each small red circle with icing and affix circles in between blue strips as shown. ■ Let cookies dry for at least 6 hours before serving.

Tips

If all the icing does not fit in your squeeze bottle, cover the remaining icing tightly and refill the bottle as needed.

If you don't have a #10 decorating tip, use the back side of another decorating tip to cut the circles in step 2, and use the end of a drinking straw to cut the circles in step 3. Alternatively, you could pipe the smaller circles using red icing in a pastry bag fitted with a #2 tip.

When cutting out fondant circles with the decorating tip, prevent sticking by dipping the tip in cornstarch between cuts or spraying the inside lightly with nonstick spray.

Piece of Cake

These cookies are a piece of cake to make! I chose to make them look like red velvet cake, as I love the dramatic color contrast with the icing, but feel free to mix up the colors to match own favorite flavors. **Makes about 30.**

What You Need

- 1 recipe cookie dough (pages 36–46)
- Piece of cake cookie cutter
- 1 recipe Classic Royal Icing (page 47)
- Burgundy gel paste
- Brown gel paste
- 2 squeeze bottles
- Ruler
- X-acto knife
- Blue fondant
- Yellow fondant
- Disposable pastry bag
- Coupler
- #13 star decorating tip

Techniques Used

- Tinting icing (page 22)
- Filling a squeeze bottle (page 24)
- Using an X-acto knife (page 31)
- Piping (page 27)
- Flooding (page 28)
- Working with fondant (page 30)
- Filling a pastry bag (page 24)

Getting Started

Bake cookies: Roll out dough and cut cookies with the piece of cake cookie cutter. Bake according to recipe directions. Let cool completely before decorating.

Tint and thin icing: Divide icing evenly between two bowls; tint one portion a red velvet color, using burgundy and brown gel paste, and leave one white. Transfer 1 cup (250 mL) red velvet icing to another bowl, cover tightly and set aside. Thin white and remaining red velvet icing to two-step icing consistency (page 24) and transfer to squeeze bottles.

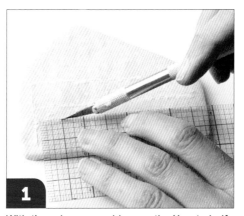

1 With the ruler as a guide, use the X-acto knife to lightly trace the outline of a layer of icing on top of each cake slice, a thick layer along the back side of the slice, and a thick layer through the middle of the slice.

2 Using white icing, outline and flood the icing layers on each cookie. ■ Using the squeeze bottle of red velvet icing, outline and flood the remaining sections of each cookie. ■ Let icing set for at least 6 hours or overnight.

3 Meanwhile, roll blue and yellow fondant into long ropes about $\frac{1}{4}$ inch (1 cm) in diameter. ■ Place ropes side by side and press them gently together. ■ Holding the ropes at the top and bottom, twist them until you have what resembles a spiral straw.

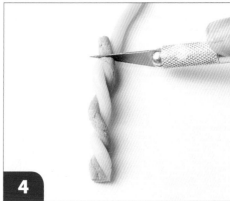

4 Cut spiraled ropes into 2-inch (5 cm) long pieces. ■ Flatten the back of each piece so it will lie flat.

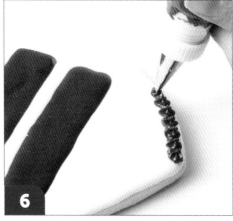

5

Mold a small piece of yellow fondant into a flame shape. ■ Use a dab of water to attach the flame to the top of a spiraled piece, pressing them lightly together. ■ Make 1 candle per cookie. ■ Place candles on a cookie sheet and let dry for at least 4 hours or overnight.

6

Transfer remaining red velvet icing to a pastry bag fitted with a #13 star tip. ■ Pipe stars along the top back edge of each slice.

7

Using white icing, pipe a border along the other two sides at the top of each slice.

8

Dab the back of each fondant candle with icing and affix a candle to the middle of the icing on top of each slice. ■ Let cookies dry for at least 6 hours before serving.

Tips

Use birthday cake flavoring to enhance your cookie dough and give the cookies an authentic cake taste. Birthday cake flavoring is not as common as vanilla or almond flavorings, but you may find it in the baking aisle of craft stores or some well-stocked grocery stores. See the Source Guide (page 253) for other options. Use 1 tsp (5 mL) flavoring in addition to the vanilla extract in Julie Anne's Classic Vanilla-Orange Sugar Cookies (page 36), and omit the orange zest.

If you don't have an X-acto knife, you can use an edible marker to trace the outlines in step 1.

Keep any fondant you are not presently working with tightly wrapped in plastic wrap, as it can quickly dry out, rendering it unusable.

Rocket Ship

Children (and many adults!) are fascinated with all things outer space. Create these sparkly rocket ship cookies for an astronaut-themed birthday party. You can even pipe the child's age onto the cookies as part of the decoration (see variation). Everyone will think the results are out of this world! **Makes about 36.**

What You Need

- 1 recipe cookie dough (pages 36–46)
- 1 recipe Classic Royal Icing (page 47)
- Rocket cookie cutter
- Red gel paste
- Orange gel paste
- Yellow gel paste
- Blue gel paste
- 2 squeeze bottles
- Blue disco dust
- 3 disposable pastry bags
- 3 couplers
- #2 round decorating tip
- 2 #1 round decorating tips
- Red disco dust

Techniques Used

- Tinting icing (page 22)
- Filling a squeeze bottle (page 24)
- Piping (page 27)
- Flooding (page 28)
- Adding sparkle (page 28)
- Filling a pastry bag (page 24)

Getting Started

Bake cookies: Roll out dough and cut cookies with the rocket cookie cutter. Bake according to recipe directions. Let cool completely before decorating.

Tint and thin icing: Place 1 cup (250 mL) icing in a bowl and tint it red. Place ¼ cup (60 mL) icing in each of two bowls; tint one portion orange and one yellow. Cover all bowls tightly and set aside. Divide remaining icing evenly between two bowls; tint one portion blue and leave one white. Thin blue and white icing to two-step icing consistency (page 24) and transfer to squeeze bottles.

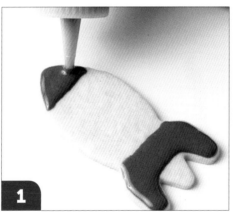

1 Working with one cookie at a time, use blue icing to outline and flood the bottom and top sections of a rocket as shown, leaving the center un-iced.

2 While the blue icing is still wet, sprinkle it with blue disco dust, shaking off excess. ■ Repeat steps 1 and 2 for all cookies.

3 Working with one cookie at a time, use white icing to outline and flood the center section a rocket.

4 While the white icing is still wet, use blue icing to pipe a curved accent line at the top of the white icing and another one at the bottom. ■ Repeat steps 3 and 4 for all cookies. ■ Let icing set for at least 6 hours or overnight.

5

Transfer red icing to a pastry bag fitted with a #2 tip. ■ Working with one cookie at a time, pipe a square in the center of the white icing. ■ Pipe a star inside the square.

6

While the red icing is still wet, sprinkle it with red disco dust, shaking off excess. ■ Repeat steps 5 and 6 for all cookies.

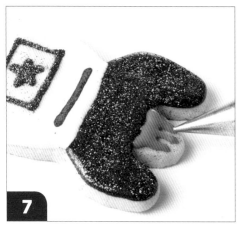

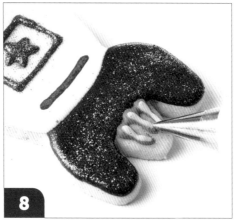

7

Transfer orange and yellow icing to pastry bags fitted with #1 tips. ■ Using orange icing, pipe 3 flames emerging from the bottom of each rocket.

8

On top of each orange flame, pipe a thinner yellow flame. ■ Let cookies dry for at least 6 hours before serving.

Tips

Sometimes air bubbles are created when you flood a cookie with icing. If this happens, use the tip of a toothpick to pop the bubbles.

Don't be alarmed if excess disco dust sticks to the cookie even after you shake it. Wait until the icing dries completely, then gently brush off the unwanted dust with a small food-safe paintbrush or a cotton swab.

Variation

Replace the star in the center of the rocket with a number representing the birthday boy or girl's age, or an initial representing his or her name. Sprinkle with disco dust as directed.

Choo-Choo Train

Like many little boys, my brother was obsessed with trains as a child. Although I'm *fairly* certain his train phase has passed, I'm positive his cookie phase has not. He would love these engine cookies just as much now. **Makes about 24.**

What You Need

- 1 recipe cookie dough (pages 36–46)
- Train cookie cutter
- 1 recipe Classic Royal Icing (page 47)
- Blue gel paste
- Yellow gel paste
- Black gel paste
- Red gel paste
- 4 squeeze bottles
- Cornstarch
- Small rolling pin
- Black fondant
- 2 small round cutters, one slightly larger than the other (see tip)
- 2 disposable pastry bags
- 2 couplers
- 2 #2 round decorating tips
- Gold disco dust
- Tweezers
- Silver dragées

Techniques Used

- Tinting icing (page 22)
- Filling a squeeze bottle (page 24)
- Working with fondant (page 30)
- Piping (page 27)
- Flooding (page 28)
- Filling a pastry bag (page 24)
- Adding sparkle (page 28)
- Adding embellishments (page 31)

Getting Started

Bake cookies: Roll out dough and cut cookies with the train cookie cutter. Bake according to recipe directions. Let cool completely before decorating.

Tint and thin icing: Place ¾ cup (175 mL) icing in each of four bowls; tint two portions blue and one yellow, and leave one white. Cover white and one blue portion tightly and set aside. Place ½ cup (125 mL) icing in a bowl and tint it black. Tint remaining icing red. Thin yellow, black, red and remaining blue icing to two-step icing consistency (page 24) and transfer to squeeze bottles.

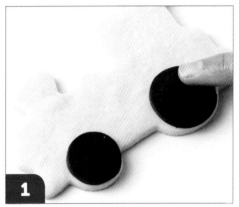

1 On a work surface lightly sprinkled with cornstarch, roll out fondant to ⅛ inch (3 mm) thick. ■ Using the round cutters, cut out 1 small circle and 1 large circle per cookie. ■ Dab the back of each circle with icing and affix a small circle to the smaller wheel and a large circle to the larger wheel on each cookie.

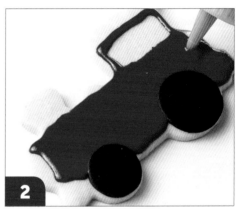

2 Using red icing, outline and flood each train engine, leaving sections un-iced as shown.

3 Using the squeeze bottle of blue icing, outline and flood the steam dome, window and cab roof of each train.

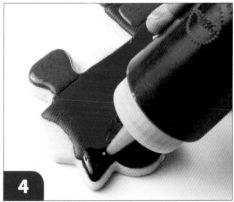

4 Using black icing, flood the bumper at the bottom front of each train. ■ Let icing set for at least 6 hours or overnight.

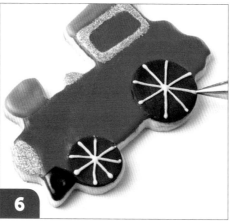

5 Working with one cookie at a time, use yellow icing to outline the window. ■ Outline and flood the circle at the front of the train and the small dome on top. ■ Immediately sprinkle the wet icing with disco dust, shaking off excess. ■ Repeat for all cookies.

6 Transfer white and reserved blue icing to pastry bags fitted with #2 tips. ■ Using white icing, pipe 8 spokes in each wheel, spacing evenly.

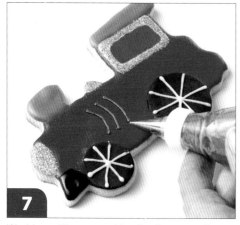

7 Working with one cookie at a time, use the pastry bag of blue icing to pipe 3 curved accent lines on the side of the train, a border around the cab roof and a connector line from wheel to wheel.

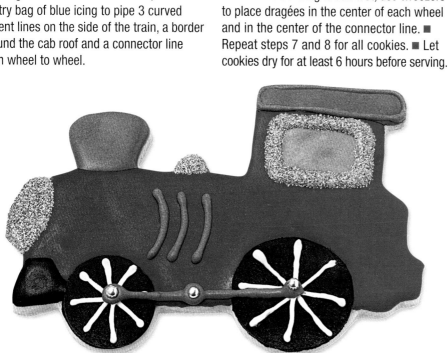

8 While the blue icing is still wet, use tweezers to place dragées in the center of each wheel and in the center of the connector line. ■ Repeat steps 7 and 8 for all cookies. ■ Let cookies dry for at least 6 hours before serving.

Tips

Choose round cutters that match the size of the train cutter's wheels, which may vary from mine. I used 1-inch (2.5 cm) and 1½ inch (4 cm) round cutters for my wheels.

Don't be alarmed if excess disco dust sticks to the cookie even after you shake it. Wait until the icing dries completely, then gently brush off the unwanted dust with a small food-safe paintbrush or a cotton swab.

Adding embellishments, such as the dragées, is easier if you use a pair of tweezers. Buy an extra pair and keep them handy with your decorating supplies.

Sailboat

The first time I tried sailing a small boat by myself, I ended up capsizing and screaming at the top of my lungs for help. That was also the last time I sailed by myself. Clearly I needed a few more lessons! I think, for now at least, I will stick to making sailboat cookies instead. **Makes about 36.**

What You Need

- 1 recipe cookie dough (pages 36–46)
- Sailboat cookie cutter
- 1 recipe Classic Royal Icing (page 47)
- Black gel paste
- Red gel paste
- Yellow gel paste
- Blue gel paste
- Disposable pastry bag
- Coupler
- #2 round decorating tip
- 3 squeeze bottles
- Toothpick

Techniques Used

- Tinting icing (page 22)
- Filling a pastry bag (page 24)
- Filling a squeeze bottle (page 24)
- Piping (page 27)
- Flooding (page 28)
- Feathering (page 29)

Getting Started

Bake cookies: Roll out dough and cut cookies with the sailboat cookie cutter. Bake according to recipe directions. Let cool completely before decorating.

Tint and thin icing: Place $1/2$ cup (125 mL) icing in a bowl and tint it black. Transfer to a pastry bag fitted with a #2 tip. Divide remaining icing evenly among three bowls; tint one portion red, one blue and one yellow. Thin red, blue and yellow icing to two-step icing consistency (page 24) and transfer to squeeze bottles.

1 Using blue icing, outline and flood the hull of each boat.

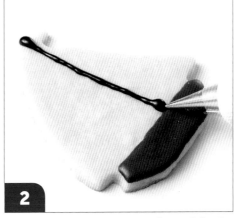

2 Using black icing, pipe a mast for each boat, starting at the tip of the sails with a round dot for a finial and piping straight down to the base.

3 Using red icing, outline and flood the smaller sail on each boat.

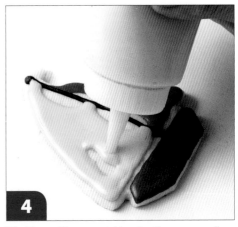

4 Working with one cookie at a time, use yellow icing to outline and flood the larger sail.

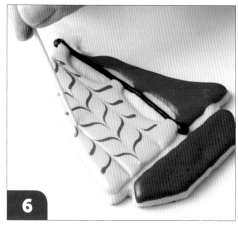

5

While the yellow icing is still wet, use blue icing to pipe 5 to 6 horizontal lines across the yellow sail, spacing evenly.

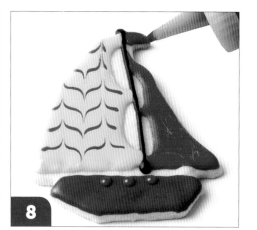

6

Using the end of the toothpick, feather vertically through the blue lines. ■ Repeat steps 4 to 6 for all cookies.

7

Using red icing, pipe 3 dots in the top center of each hull.

8

Pipe a small red flag at the top of each mast. ■ Let cookies dry for at least 6 hours before serving.

Tips

Sometimes air bubbles are created when you flood a cookie with icing. If this happens, use the tip of a toothpick to pop the bubbles.

These cookies would also go well with other sports-themed cookies (pages 154–170).

When you're piping the mast in step 2, a ruler and an X-acto knife will help you create a template for a straight, even line.

Sparkly Tutu

I only took ballet lessons for a few years as a child (I was better at figure skating), but I kept my tutus for playing dress-up with my friends. I loved the sparkly sequins and the satiny floral embellishments. These cookies are sure to make any budding ballerina *jeté* for joy, whether you serve them at her birthday party or as a special post-recital treat. **Makes about 30.**

What You Need

- 1 recipe cookie dough (pages 36–46)
- Tutu cookie cutter
- 1 recipe Classic Royal Icing (page 47)
- Purple gel paste
- 2 squeeze bottles
- White disco dust
- Cornstarch
- Small rolling pin
- White fondant
- Small flower cutter
- Ruler
- X-acto knife
- Tweezers
- White edible pearls

Techniques Used

- Tinting icing (page 22)
- Filling a squeeze bottle (page 24)
- Piping (page 27)
- Flooding (page 28)
- Adding sparkle (page 28)
- Working with fondant (page 30)
- Adding embellishments (page 31)

Getting Started

Bake cookies: Roll out dough and cut cookies with the tutu cookie cutter. Bake according to recipe directions. Let cool completely before decorating.

Thin and tint icing: Thin icing to two-step icing consistency (page 24). Divide icing evenly between two bowls; tint one portion purple and leave one white. Transfer purple and white icing to squeeze bottles.

Working with one cookie at a time, use white icing to outline the skirt section of a tutu.

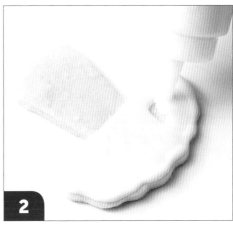

Flood the skirt with white icing.

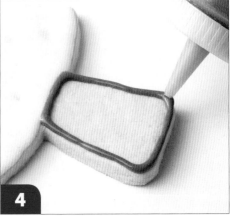

While the white icing is still wet, sprinkle it with disco dust, shaking off excess. ■ Repeat steps 1 to 3 for all cookies.

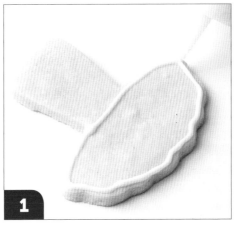

Using purple icing, outline the bodice section of each tutu.

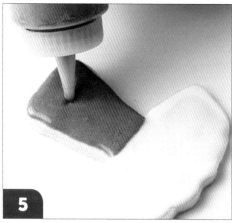

5 Flood each bodice with purple icing. ■ Let icing set for at least 6 hours or overnight.

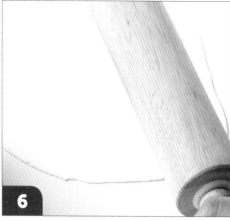

6 On a work surface lightly dusted with cornstarch, roll out fondant to 1/8 inch (3 mm) thick.

7 Using the flower cutter, cut out 1 flower per cookie.

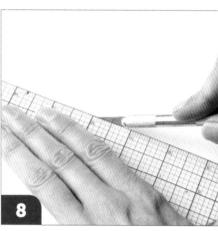

8 With the ruler as a guide, use the X-acto knife to cut fondant strips about 1/4 inch (5 mm) wide and slightly longer than the waistline of a tutu.

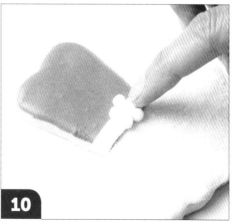

9 Dab the back of each fondant strip with icing and affix a strip to the waistline of each tutu, pressing the ends of the strips into the sides of the cookies for an even look.

10 Dab the back of each fondant flower with icing and affix a flower to the center of each strip.

continued...

Tips

Keep any fondant you are not presently working with tightly wrapped in plastic wrap, as it can quickly dry out, rendering it unusable.

After rolling out fondant, let it rest for about 15 minutes (but not much longer!) before cutting out shapes. This allows it to harden a bit, making for cleaner cuts.

An X-acto knife is a good investment if you plan to work with fondant often. Its blade is sharper than a paring knife, allowing for a more "x-act" cut.

Tip

Adding embellishments, such as the edible pearls, is easier if you use a pair of tweezers. Buy an extra pair and keep them handy with your decorating supplies.

Variations

Use the birthday girl's favorite color in place of the purple gel paste.

Pipe your own white flowers by hand if you don't have a small flower cutter. Use a pastry bag fitted with a #2 tip to create simple five-petal designs.

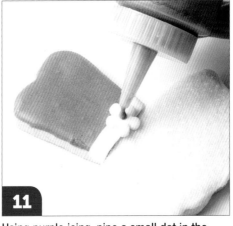

11 Using purple icing, pipe a small dot in the center of each flower.

12 Pipe a wide purple border along the bottom edge of each skirt.

13 Working with one cookie at a time, pipe a narrow purple border along the top edge of the bodice.

14 While the purple icing is still wet, use tweezers to place a line of edible pearls along the top of the bodice. ■ Repeat steps 13 and 14 for all cookies. ■ Let cookies dry for at least 6 hours before serving.

Cow

Can't you just hear these cow cookies saying "Moo"? This is a simple design that is fun for decorators of all levels and ages. These cookies go perfectly with (what else?) a glass of ice-cold milk! **Makes about 36.**

Getting Started

Bake cookies: Roll out dough and cut cookies with the cow head cookie cutter. Bake according to recipe directions. Let cool completely before decorating.

Thin and tint icing: Thin icing to two-step icing consistency (page 24). Place 1 cup (250 mL) icing in a bowl and tint it pink. Divide remaining icing evenly between two bowls; tint one portion black and leave one white. Transfer pink, black and white icing to squeeze bottles.

1

Working with one cookie at a time, use black icing to outline and flood the sides of the cow's head as shown, leaving space for the inner ears, nose and center stripe. ■ Using tweezers, immediately place 2 royal icing eyes on the cow, one on each black section. ■ Repeat for all cookies.

2

Working with one cookie at a time, use pink icing to outline and flood the inner ears and nose. ■ Immediately pipe 2 black nostrils in the nose. ■ Repeat for all cookies.

3

Using white icing, outline and flood the center stripe down each cow's head. ■ Let cookies dry for at least 6 hours before serving.

What You Need

- 1 recipe cookie dough (pages 36–46)
- Cow head cookie cutter
- 1 recipe Classic Royal Icing (page 47)
- Pink gel paste
- Black gel paste
- 3 squeeze bottles
- Tweezers
- Royal icing eyes

Techniques Used

- Tinting icing (page 22)
- Filling a squeeze bottle (page 24)
- Piping (page 27)
- Flooding (page 28)
- Adding embellishments (page 31)

Tips

Before piping designs onto cookies, I like to lightly trace them onto the cookie with an X-acto knife or edible marker, then use the trace marks as a guide for piping. That way, I know in advance how the finished design will look, which I find easier than piping it freehand.

If you don't have royal icing eyes on hand, pipe simple eyes using black icing in a pastry bag fitted with a #2 round decorating tip.

Little Lamb

My mother-in-law raises lambs in Vermont, so these sweet cookies would be perfect for her (although hers don't wear big pink bows). These would also be fun to make for a class that is learning nursery rhymes, such as "Mary Had a Little Lamb." I love how well the individually piped dots mimic the fluffy wool of a lamb's coat. **Makes about 36.**

What You Need

- 1 recipe cookie dough (pages 36–46)
- Lamb cookie cutter
- 1 recipe Classic Royal Icing (page 47)
- Black gel paste
- Pink gel paste
- Squeeze bottle
- Cornstarch
- Small rolling pin
- Pink fondant
- Small bow cutter
- 3 disposable pastry bags
- 3 couplers
- #2 round decorating tip
- 2 #1 round decorating tips

Techniques Used

- Tinting icing (page 22)
- Filling a squeeze bottle (page 24)
- Piping (page 27)
- Flooding (page 28)
- Working with fondant (page 30)
- Filling a pastry bag (page 24)

Getting Started

Bake cookies: Roll out dough and cut cookies with the lamb cookie cutter. Bake according to recipe directions. Let cool completely before decorating.

Tint and thin icing: Place $1/2$ cup (125 mL) icing in each of two bowls; tint one portion black and one pink. Cover tightly and set aside. Divide remaining icing evenly between two bowls. Cover one bowl tightly and set aside. Thin remaining white icing to two-step icing consistency (page 24) and transfer to a squeeze bottle.

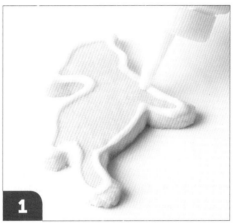

1

Using the squeeze bottle of white icing, outline lambs, leaving a bit of space for hooves.

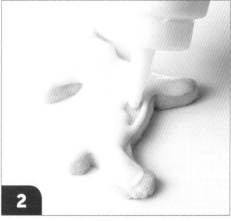

2

Flood lambs with white icing. ■ Let icing set for at least 6 hours or overnight.

3

Meanwhile, on a work surface lightly dusted with cornstarch, roll out fondant to $1/8$ inch (3 mm) thick.

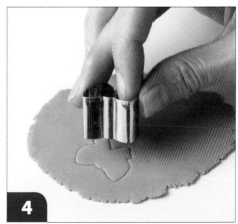

4

Using bow cutter, cut out 1 bow per cookie. ■ Place bows on a cookie sheet and let dry for at least 4 hours or overnight.

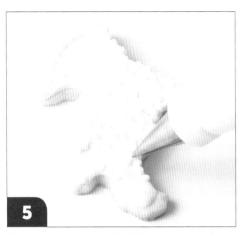

5 Transfer reserved white icing to a pastry bag fitted with a #2 tip. ■ Pipe dots, one next to the other, all over each lamb, leaving space for the inner ears and face.

6 Transfer black and pink icing to pastry bags fitted with a #1 tip. ■ Use black icing to pipe each lamb's eyes, nose and hooves.

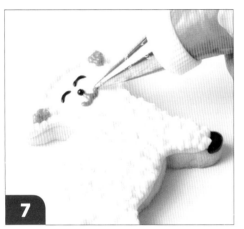

7 Using pink icing, fill the inner ears and pipe a mouth on each lamb.

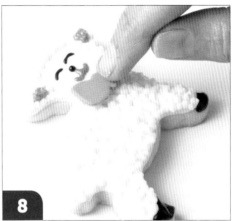

8 Dab the back of each fondant bow with icing and affix a bow to each lamb's neck. ■ Let cookies dry for at least 6 hours before serving.

Tips

Keep royal icing tightly covered when you're not using it, as it tends to dry out quickly.

Be sure to wear disposable latex gloves when coloring fondant so the gel paste does not stain your hands.

If you don't have a small bow cutter, mold a small piece of fondant into a bow shape with your fingers. Alternatively, pipe a bow onto each lamb's neck using pink icing in a pastry bag fitted with a #2 round decorating tip.

Smiling Pig

What You Need

- 1 recipe cookie dough (pages 36–46)
- Pig cookie cutter
- 1 recipe Classic Royal Icing (page 47)
- Black gel paste
- Yellow gel paste
- Pink gel paste
- Squeeze bottle
- 3 disposable pastry bags
- 3 couplers
- 3 #1 round decorating tips
- Cotton swab
- Pink luster dust

Techniques Used

- Tinting icing (page 22)
- Filling a pastry bag (page 24)
- Filling a squeeze bottle (page 24)
- Piping (page 27)
- Flooding (page 28)
- Working with fondant (page 30)

We've all heard the saying "As happy as a pig in mud," but this little guy, with rosy cheeks and a chain of fresh daisies around his neck, is happy because he is cleaner (and cuter) than the average pig! Like the other farm animals, this cookie is great for beginning pipers. **Makes about 36.**

Getting Started

Bake cookies: Roll out dough and cut cookies with the pig cookie cutter. Bake according to recipe directions. Let cool completely before decorating.

Tint and thin icing: Place 1/2 cup (125 mL) icing in each of three bowls; tint one portion black and one yellow, and leave one white. Cover all bowls tightly and set aside. Tint remaining icing pink, thin to two-step icing consistency (page 24) and transfer to a squeeze bottle.

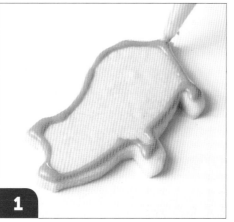

1 Using pink icing, outline pigs, leaving a bit of space for hooves.

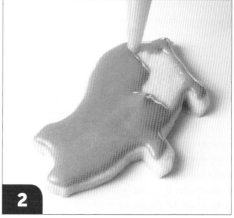

2 Flood pigs with pink icing. ■ Let icing set for at least 6 hours or overnight.

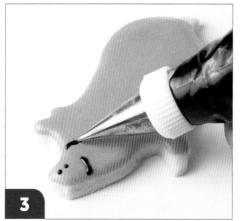

3 Transfer black, yellow and white icing to pastry bags fitted with #1 tips. ■ Use black icing to pipe an eye, nostrils and a smile on each pig's face.

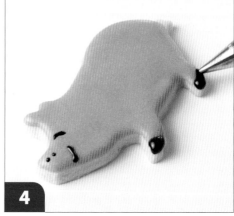

4 Pipe black hooves on each pig.

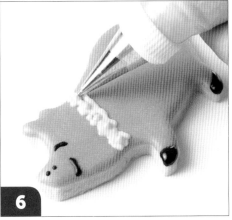

5

Using white icing, pipe a chain of daisies around each pig's neck.

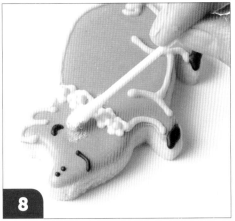

6

Using yellow icing, pipe a dot in the center of each daisy.

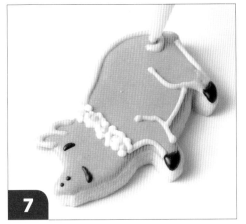

7

Using pink icing, pipe a border around each pig's legs, stomach, rump and back. ■ Outline each pig's ears and pipe a squiggly tail.

8

Using the cotton swab, dab a bit of luster dust onto each pig's cheek, rubbing it in a small circle. ■ Let cookies dry for at least 4 hours before serving.

Tips

Keep royal icing tightly covered when you're not using it, as it tends to dry out quickly.

Sometimes air bubbles are created when you flood a cookie with icing. If this happens, use the tip of a toothpick to pop the bubbles.

Variation

Pipe a black slit on the top of pig and turn the design into piggy bank cookies.

Mouse and Cheese

This little mouse scurried to the corner of the barn so he could enjoy his piece of cheese without being bothered by the Curious Owl (page 126). From "Three Blind Mice" to Stuart Little, friendly mice are a common childhood theme. That said, you don't need to be a kid to love these cookies. **Makes about 30.**

What You Need

- 1 recipe cookie dough (pages 36–46)
- Mouse cookie cutter
- 1 recipe Classic Royal Icing (page 47)
- Brown gel paste
- Pink gel paste
- Black gel paste
- 2 squeeze bottles
- Cornstarch
- Small rolling pin
- Ivory fondant
- Ruler
- X-acto knife
- Round decorating tips in various sizes (see tip)
- Toothpick
- Disposable pastry bag
- Coupler
- #1 round decorating tip
- Tweezers
- Royal icing eyes

Techniques Used

- Tinting icing (page 22)
- Filling a squeeze bottle (page 24)
- Piping (page 27)
- Flooding (page 28)
- Working with fondant (page 30)
- Filling a pastry bag (page 24)
- Adding embellishments (page 31)

Getting Started

Bake cookies: Roll out dough and cut cookies with the mouse cookie cutter. Bake according to recipe directions. Let cool completely before decorating.

Tint and thin icing: Place ¼ cup (60 mL) icing in a bowl and tint it brown. Cover tightly and set aside. Place 1 cup (250 mL) icing in a bowl and tint it pink. Tint remaining icing gray (see tip). Thin pink and gray icing to two-step icing consistency (page 24) and transfer to squeeze bottles.

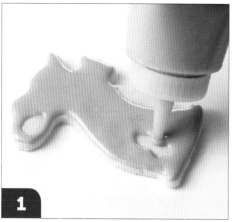

1

Using gray icing, outline and flood each mouse, leaving space for the inner ear and belly.

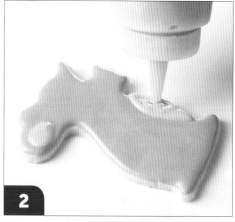

2

Using pink icing, outline and flood each mouse's inner ear and belly. ■ Let icing set for at least 6 hours or overnight.

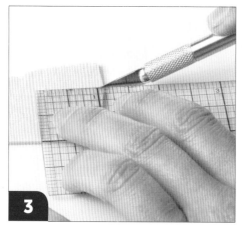

3

Meanwhile, on a work surface lightly dusted with cornstarch, roll out fondant to ¹⁄₁₆ inch (2 mm) thick. ■ With the ruler as a guide, use the X-acto knife to cut out 1-inch (2.5 cm) squares. ■ Make 1 square per cookie.

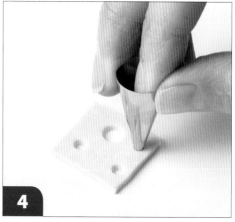

4

Using decorating tips in various sizes, cut holes in each square to make it resemble a piece of Swiss cheese. ■ Place squares on a cookie sheet and let dry for at least 4 hours or overnight.

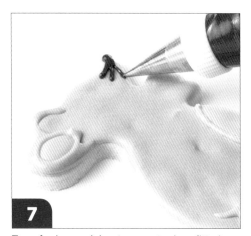

5

Using pink icing, pipe a squiggly tail on each mouse. ■ Create a point for the tail by quickly dragging the end of the toothpick out from the end of the tail.

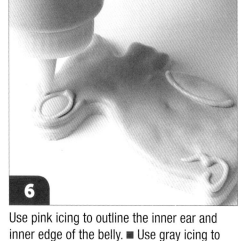

6

Use pink icing to outline the inner ear and inner edge of the belly. ■ Use gray icing to pipe a border around the outside of each mouse's ears.

Tips

I used #3 and #5 round decorating tips for Swiss cheese piece.

To tint icing gray, mix in black gel paste a tiny dab at a time until you reach the desired shade.

Adding embellishments, such as the royal icing eyes, is easier if you use a pair of tweezers. Buy an extra pair and keep them handy with your decorating supplies.

If you don't have royal icing eyes on hand, pipe simple eyes using black icing and a pastry bag fitted with a #2 round decorating tip.

7

Transfer brown icing to a pastry bag fitted with a #1 tip. ■ Pipe a nose and whiskers on each mouse.

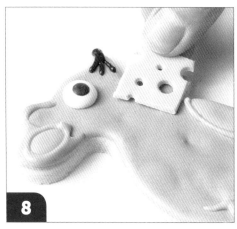

8

Using tweezers and a dab of icing on the back of each royal icing eye, place an eye on each mouse. ■ Dab the back of each fondant square with icing and affix a square to each mouse's front paws. ■ Let cookies dry for at least 6 hours before serving.

Curious Owl

These curious owls are one of the designs I had the most fun creating. For a fun display, pipe the eyes to look in all different directions. **Makes about 24.**

What You Need

- 1 recipe cookie dough (pages 36–46)
- Owl cookie cutter
- 1 recipe Classic Royal Icing (page 47)
- Black gel paste
- Green gel paste
- Squeeze bottle
- Cornstarch
- Small rolling pin
- Light blue fondant
- White fondant
- Brown fondant
- Orange fondant
- 1-inch (2.5 cm) round cutter
- ¾-inch (2 cm) round cutter
- X-acto knife
- Owl wing template (page 252)
- 2 disposable pastry bags
- 2 couplers
- 2 #2 round decorating tips

Techniques Used

- Tinting icing (page 22)
- Filling a squeeze bottle (page 24)
- Piping (page 27)
- Flooding (page 28)
- Working with fondant (page 30)
- Using an X-acto knife (page 31)
- Working with templates (page 32)
- Filling a pastry bag (page 24)

Getting Started

Bake cookies: Roll out dough and cut cookies with the owl cookie cutter. Bake according to recipe directions. Let cool completely before decorating.

Tint and thin icing: Place 1 cup (250 mL) icing in a bowl and leave it white. Place ½ cup (125 mL) icing in a bowl and tint it black. Cover both bowls tightly and set aside. Tint remaining icing green, thin to two-step icing consistency (page 24) and transfer to a squeeze bottle.

1 Using green icing, outline and flood owls. ■ Let icing set for at least 6 hours or overnight.

2 Meanwhile, on a work surface lightly dusted with cornstarch, roll out blue and white fondant to 1⁄16 inch (2 mm) thick. ■ Using the 1-inch (2.5 cm) round cutter, cut out 2 blue circles per cookie. ■ Using the ¾-inch (2 cm) round cutter, cut out 2 white circles per cookie.

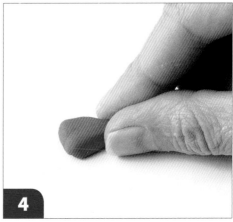

3 Dust the work surface with cornstarch and roll out brown fondant to 1⁄16 inch (2 mm) thick. ■ Using the X-acto knife and owl wing template, cut out 2 wings per cookie.

4 Mold a small piece of orange fondant into a rounded triangular shape, for the owl's nose. ■ Make 1 nose per cookie. ■ Place all fondant pieces on a cookie sheet and let dry for at least 4 hours or overnight.

5

Dab the back of each fondant wing with icing and affix a wing on each side of each owl.

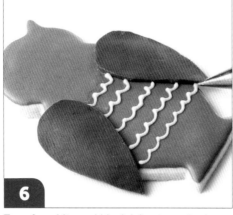

6

Transfer white and black icing to pastry bags fitted with #2 tips. ■ Use white icing to pipe wavy lines across each owl's body, to simulate chest feathers.

Tips

If all the green icing does not fit in your squeeze bottle, cover the remaining icing tightly and refill the bottle as needed.

After rolling out fondant, let it rest for about 15 minutes (but not much longer!) before cutting out shapes. This allows it to harden a bit, making for cleaner cuts.

An X-acto knife is a good investment if you plan to work with fondant often. Its blade is sharper than a paring knife, allowing for a more "x-act" cut.

7

Dab the back of each blue circle with icing and affix 2 circles to each owl's head. ■ Affix a white circle on top of each blue circle, placing it near an edge of the blue circle, depending on where you want the owl to be looking. ■ Using black icing, pipe a pupil inside each white circle, again positioning it depending on where the owl is looking.

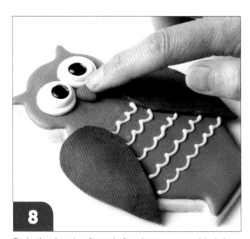

8

Dab the back of each fondant nose with icing and affix a nose on each owl. ■ Let cookies dry for at least 6 hours before serving.

Clucking Chicken

What You Need

- 1 recipe cookie dough (pages 36–46)
- Chicken cookie cutter
- 1 recipe Classic Royal Icing (page 47)
- Red gel paste
- Orange gel paste
- Yellow gel paste
- Squeeze bottle
- 2 disposable pastry bags
- 2 couplers
- 2 #2 round decorating tips
- Tweezers
- Royal icing eyes

Techniques Used

- Tinting icing (page 22)
- Filling a squeeze bottle (page 24)
- Piping (page 27)
- Flooding (page 28)
- Filling a pastry bag (page 24)
- Adding embellishments (page 31)

You can practically picture these bright yellow cookies springing to life and clucking their way around the barnyard, picking up grains with their little red beaks. This is another very simple design, ideal for beginning decorators. **Makes about 24.**

Getting Started

Bake cookies: Roll out dough and cut cookies with the chicken cookie cutter. Bake according to recipe directions. Let cool completely before decorating.

Tint and thin icing: Place 1½ cups (375 mL) icing in a bowl and tint it red. Place ¼ cup (60 mL) icing in a bowl and tint it orange. Cover both bowls tightly and set aside. Tint remaining icing yellow, thin to two-step icing consistency (page 24) and transfer to a squeeze bottle.

1 Using yellow icing, outline chickens, leaving space for feet.

2 Flood chickens with yellow icing. ■ Let icing set for at least 6 hours or overnight.

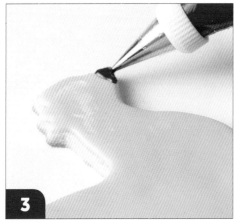

3 Transfer red and orange icing to pastry bags fitted with #2 tips. ■ Use red icing to pipe a beak on each chicken.

4 Pipe a red crest on each chicken's head and tail feathers on its rump.

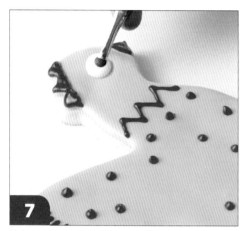

5

Pipe a wavy red line at each chicken's neckline and a red polka-dot pattern on its body, leaving space for a wing on the chicken's side.

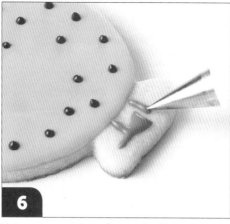

6

Using orange icing, pipe each chicken's feet. ■ Let icing set for 15 minutes.

7

Using tweezers and a dab of icing on the back of each royal icing eye, place an eye on each chicken.

8

Using yellow icing, outline and fill a wing on each chicken's side. ■ Let cookies dry for at least 6 hours before serving.

Tips

Adding embellishments, such as the royal icing eyes, is easier if you use a pair of tweezers. Buy an extra pair and keep them handy with your decorating supplies.

If you don't have royal icing eyes on hand, pipe simple eyes using black icing and a pastry bag fitted with a #2 round decorating tip.

You could also pair these cookies with the Chick 'n' Egg Cookies (page 56).

Goose

When I finished this design, I couldn't help but think of Gussy and Golly, the two chatty geese from the book (and movie) *Charlotte's Web*. In fact, this entire set of farm animals would be perfect for a party theme based on the popular children's book (one of my favorites) or one based on nursery rhymes (such as Mother Goose). **Makes about 24.**

What You Need

- 1 recipe cookie dough (pages 36–46)
- Goose cookie cutter
- 1 recipe Classic Royal Icing (page 47)
- Orange gel paste
- 2 squeeze bottles
- Cornstarch
- Small rolling pin
- Blue fondant
- Small bow cutter
- Tweezers
- Royal icing eyes

Techniques Used

- Tinting icing (page 22)
- Filling a squeeze bottle (page 24)
- Piping (page 27)
- Flooding (page 28)
- Working with fondant (page 30)
- Adding embellishments (page 31)

Getting Started

Bake cookies: Roll out dough and cut cookies with the goose cookie cutter. Bake according to recipe directions. Let cool completely before decorating.

Thin and tint icing: Thin icing to two-step icing consistency (page 24). Place 1½ cups (375 mL) icing in a bowl and tint it orange. Leave remaining icing white. Transfer orange and white icing to squeeze bottles.

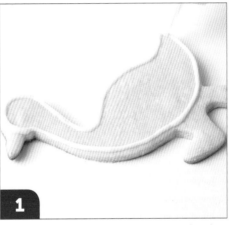

1 Using white icing, outline each goose, leaving space for the beak and feet.

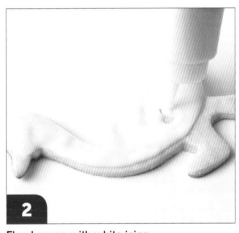

2 Flood geese with white icing.

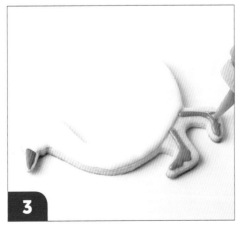

3 Using orange icing, pipe and flood each goose's beak and feet. ■ Let icing set for at least 6 hours or overnight.

4 Meanwhile, on a work surface lightly dusted with cornstarch, roll out fondant to ⅛ inch (3 mm) thick.

5 Using the bow cutter, cut out 1 bow per cookie. ■ Place bows on a cookie sheet and let dry for at least 4 hours or overnight.

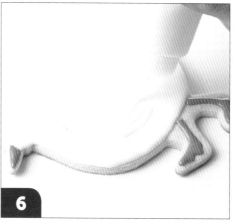

6 Using white icing, pipe 3 curved accent lines on the side of each goose, where its wing would be.

7 Using tweezers and a dab of icing on the back of each royal icing eye, place an eye on each goose.

8 Dab the back of each fondant bow with icing and affix a bow to each goose's neck. ■ Let cookies dry for at least 4 hours before serving.

Tips

If all the white icing does not fit in your squeeze bottle, cover the remaining icing tightly and refill the bottle as needed.

If you don't have a small bow cutter, mold a small piece of fondant into a bow shape with your fingers. Alternatively, pipe a bow onto each goose's neck using blue icing in a pastry bag fitted with a #2 round decorating tip.

If you don't have royal icing eyes on hand, pipe simple eyes using black icing and a pastry bag fitted with a #2 round decorating tip.

Zebra

If you're looking to take your piping skills to the next level, this is the perfect cookie design for you! I love that the design *looks* really difficult, but is actually relatively straightforward. You'll earn your piping "stripes" in no time! **Makes about 30.**

What You Need

- 1 recipe cookie dough (pages 36–46)
- Horse or zebra cookie cutter
- 1 recipe Classic Royal Icing (page 47)
- Black gel paste
- Squeeze bottle
- Disposable pastry bag
- Coupler
- #1 round decorating tip
- Tweezers
- Royal icing eyes

Techniques Used

- Tinting icing (page 22)
- Filling a squeeze bottle (page 24)
- Piping (page 27)
- Flooding (page 28)
- Filling a pastry bag (page 24)
- Adding embellishments (page 31)

Getting Started

Bake cookies: Roll out dough and cut cookies with the horse cookie cutter. Bake according to recipe directions. Let cool completely before decorating.

Tint and thin icing: Divide icing evenly between two bowls; tint one portion black and leave one white. Cover black icing tightly and set aside. Thin white icing to two-step icing consistency (page 24) and transfer to a squeeze bottle.

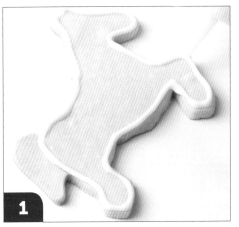

Using white icing, outline zebras, leaving the tail un-iced.

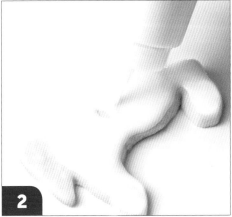

Flood zebras with white icing. ■ Let icing set for at least 6 hours or overnight.

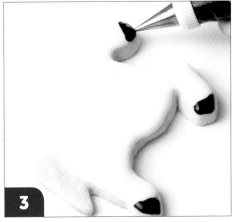

Transfer black icing to a pastry bag fitted with a #1 tip. ■ Pipe hooves and a snout onto each zebra.

Pipe 2 small triangles for ears and a small hairline under the ears.

5

Pipe a zebra stripe pattern onto each zebra's body as shown. ■ Leave the head unstriped.

6

Starting at the zebra's rump (inside the tail section) pipe 10 to 12 lines down to the end of the tail, overlapping some of the lines, to form a thick black tail.

7

Using tweezers and a dab of icing on the back of each royal icing eye, place an eye on each zebra.

8

Using white icing, pipe a small nostril on each zebra's snout. ■ Let cookies dry for at least 6 hours before serving.

Tips

If you can't find a horse or zebra cookie cutter, look around for a suitable substitute. For example, you could use a carousel horse cookie cutter and cut the carousel pole off before baking.

Adding embellishments, such as the royal icing eyes, is easier if you use a pair of tweezers. Buy an extra pair and keep them handy with your decorating supplies.

If you don't have royal icing eyes on hand, pipe simple eyes using black icing and a pastry bag fitted with a #2 round decorating tip.

Giraffe

Giraffes manage to look sweet and gentle despite their massive size. My favorite parts of this cookie are the cute little fondant horns (or rather, ossicones) and swishy tail — but the spots are cool too! **Makes about 24.**

What You Need

- 1 recipe cookie dough (pages 36–46)
- Giraffe cookie cutter
- 1 recipe Classic Royal Icing (page 47)
- Black gel paste
- Copper gel paste
- Brown gel paste
- Yellow gel paste
- 3 squeeze bottles
- Brown fondant
- Rounded fondant modeling tool (see tip)
- X-acto knife
- Tweezers
- Royal icing eyes
- Disposable pastry bag
- Coupler
- #1 round decorating tip

Techniques Used

- Tinting icing (page 22)
- Filling a squeeze bottle (page 24)
- Piping (page 27)
- Flooding (page 28)
- Working with fondant (page 30)
- Using an X-acto knife (page 31)
- Adding embellishments (page 31)
- Filling a pastry bag (page 24)

Getting Started

Bake cookies: Roll out dough and cut cookies with the giraffe cookie cutter. Bake according to recipe directions. Let cool completely before decorating.

Tint and thin icing: Place 1/4 cup (60 mL) icing in a bowl and tint it black. Cover tightly and set aside. Place 1 1/2 cups (375 mL) icing in a bowl and tint it copper. Place 1 cup (250 mL) icing in a bowl and tint it dark brown. Tint remaining icing yellow. Thin copper, brown and yellow icing to two-step icing consistency (page 24) and transfer to squeeze bottles.

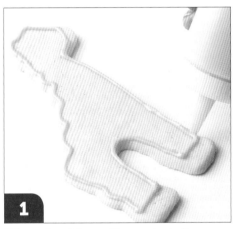

1 Using yellow icing, outline each giraffe, leaving space for the hooves and snout.

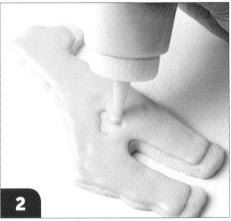

2 Flood giraffes with yellow icing. ■ Let icing set for at least 6 hours or overnight.

3 Meanwhile, roll fondant into a thin rope about 1/8 inch (3 mm) in diameter. ■ Cut a piece about 1/2 inch (1 cm) long. ■ Mold a small piece of fondant into a ball slightly larger than 1/8 inch (3 mm) in diameter. ■ Dab the ball with water and press it lightly against one end of the rope piece to affix. ■ Make 2 horns per cookie.

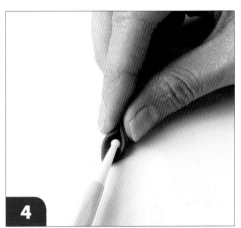

4 Mold a small piece of fondant into a triangle. ■ Press the top of the modeling tool into the triangle to form a curved ear shape. ■ Make 1 ear per cookie.

5

Roll fondant into a thin rope about $\frac{1}{8}$ inch (3 mm) in diameter. ■ Cut a piece about 2 inches (5 cm) long, to serve as a tail. ■ At the bottom of the tail, use the X-acto knife to gently draw lines that simulate individual hairs. ■ Make 1 tail per cookie. ■ Place all fondant pieces on a cookie sheet and let dry for at least 4 hours or overnight.

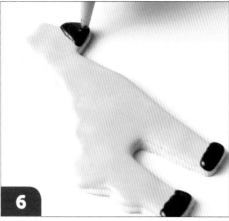

6

Using brown icing, pipe hooves and a snout on each giraffe.

7

Pipe a brown border down each giraffe's back, from head to rump.

8

Using copper icing, pipe and flood a giraffe pattern on each giraffe from the legs up to the neck, as shown.

9

Dab the bottom of each fondant horn with icing and affix 2 horns to the top of each giraffe's head.

10

Using brown icing, pipe hair over the ends of the horns to hide them.

Tips

Keep royal icing tightly covered when you're not using it, as it tends to dry out quickly.

Sometimes air bubbles are created when you flood a cookie with icing. If this happens, use the tip of a toothpick to pop the bubbles.

Be sure to wear disposable latex gloves when coloring fondant so the gel paste does not stain your hands.

Keep any fondant you are not presently working with tightly wrapped in plastic wrap, as it can quickly dry out, rendering it unusable.

If you don't have fondant modeling tools, use a wooden skewer or a kitchen tool with a similar shape to form the ears.

If you don't have an X-acto knife, any small, sharp knife will work fine.

continued…

Tips

Adding embellishments, such as the fondant pieces and the royal icing eyes, is easier if you use a pair of tweezers. Buy an extra pair and keep them handy with your decorating supplies.

If you don't have royal icing eyes on hand, pipe simple eyes using black icing and a pastry bag fitted with a #2 round decorating tip.

11

Dab the back of each fondant ear with icing and affix an ear behind the horns on each giraffe's head.

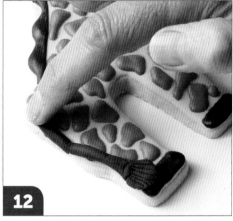

12

Dab the back of each fondant tail with icing and affix a tail to each giraffe's rump.

13

Using tweezers and a dab of icing on the back of each royal icing eye, place an eye on each giraffe.

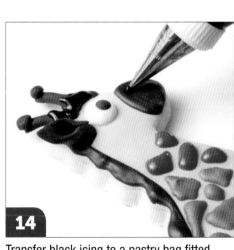

14

Transfer black icing to a pastry bag fitted with a #1 tip. ■ Pipe a small nostril on each giraffe's snout. ■ Let cookies dry for at least 6 hours before serving.

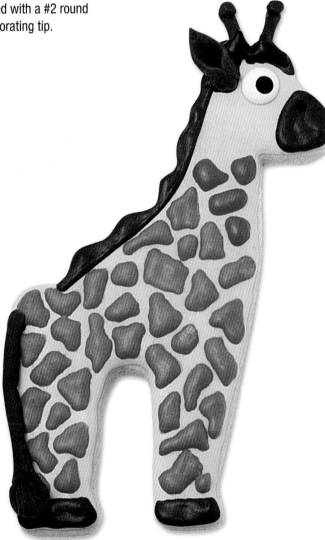

Blue Elephant

Sweet blue elephant cookies would be just as perfect for a themed baby shower (pages 208–212) as they are alongside the rest of their zoo animal friends. Since elephants are known to love peanuts, make these with Peanut Butter cookie dough (page 41.) **Makes about 30.**

Getting Started

Bake cookies: Roll out dough and cut cookies with the elephant cookie cutter. Bake according to recipe directions. Let cool completely before decorating.

Tint and thin icing: Place 1 cup (250 mL) icing in a bowl and tint it light blue. Place ¼ cup (60 mL) icing in each of two bowls; tint one portion black and leave one white. Cover all bowls tightly and set aside. Tint remaining icing light blue, thin to two-step icing consistency (page 24) and transfer to a squeeze bottle.

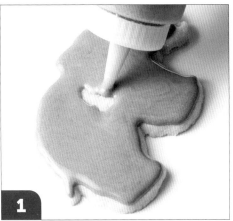

1 Using the squeeze bottle of blue icing, outline and flood each elephant, leaving the tusk un-iced. ■ Let icing set for at least 6 hours or overnight.

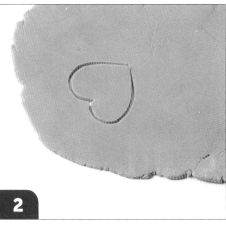

2 Meanwhile, on a work surface lightly dusted with cornstarch, roll out pink fondant to ¹⁄₁₆ inch (2 mm) thick. ■ Using the heart cutter, cut out 1 heart for every 2 cookies.

3 Using the X-acto knife, cut each heart in half vertically.

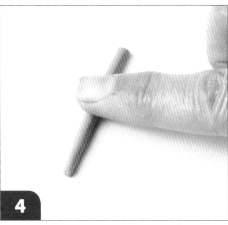

4 Roll pink fondant into a rope about ⅛ inch (3 mm) in diameter. ■ Cut a piece about 1½ inches (4 cm) long, to serve as a tail.

What You Need

- 1 recipe cookie dough (pages 36–46)
- Elephant cookie cutter
- 1 recipe Classic Royal Icing (page 47)
- Blue gel paste
- Black gel paste
- Squeeze bottle
- Cornstarch
- Small rolling pin
- Pink fondant
- Black fondant
- 1-inch (2.5 cm) heart cutter
- X-acto knife
- #10 round decorating tip (see tips)
- Small food-safe paintbrush (optional)
- Blue or silver luster dust (optional)
- 3 disposable pastry bags
- 3 couplers
- #2 round decorating tip
- 2 #1 round decorating tips
- Tweezers

Techniques Used

- Tinting icing (page 22)
- Filling a squeeze bottle (page 24)
- Piping (page 27)
- Flooding (page 28)
- Working with fondant (page 30)
- Using an X-acto knife (page 31)
- Adding sparkle (page 28)
- Filling a pastry bag (page 24)

continued… Cookies for Kids **137**

Tips

Be sure to wear disposable latex gloves when coloring fondant so the gel paste does not stain your hands.

Keep any fondant you are not presently working with tightly wrapped in plastic wrap, as it can quickly dry out, rendering it unusable.

If you don't have a heart-shaped cutter, cut your hearts freehand using an X-acto knife or a small, sharp knife.

If you don't have a #10 decorating tip, use the end of a drinking straw as a cutter.

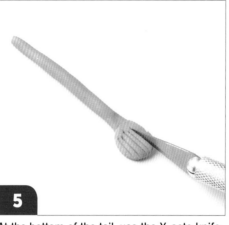

5

At the bottom of the tail, use the X-acto knife to gently draw lines that simulate individual hairs. ■ Make 1 tail per cookie.

6

Dust work surface lightly with cornstarch and roll out black fondant to $\frac{1}{16}$ inch (2 mm) thick. ■ Using the #10 tip as a cutter, cut out 9 circles per cookie. ■ Place all fondant pieces on a cookie sheet and let dry for at least 4 hours or overnight.

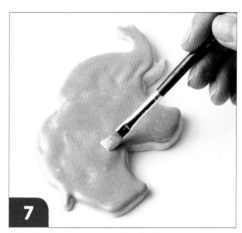

7

If desired, use the small paintbrush to brush each elephant lightly with luster dust.

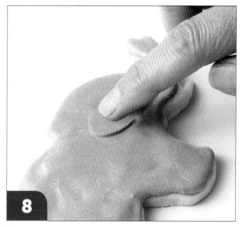

8

Turn each halved heart so that the point is facing down and the straight edge is facing the same direction as your elephant's face. ■ Dab the back of each piece with icing and affix a piece to each elephant's head as an ear.

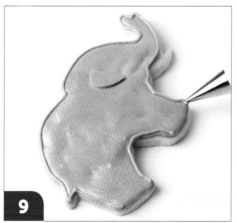

9

Transfer reserved blue icing to a pastry bag fitted with a #2 tip. ■ Pipe a border around each elephant.

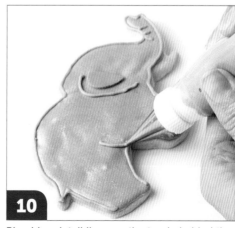

10

Pipe blue detail lines on the trunk, behind the ear and as the upper leg on each elephant, as shown.

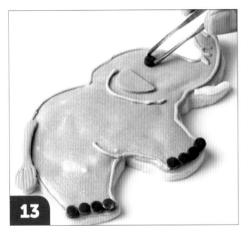

11 Transfer black and white icing to pastry bags fitted with #1 tips. ■ Use white icing to pipe a tusk on each elephant.

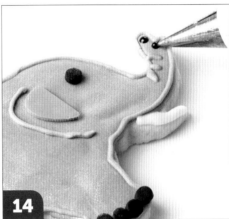

12 Dab the top back of each fondant tail with icing and affix a tail to each elephant's rump.

13 Dab the back of each fondant circle with icing and, using tweezers, affix 4 circles to each foot on each elephant, as toes. ■ Affix 1 circle as an eye on each elephant.

14 Using black icing, pipe 2 nostrils at the tip of each elephant's trunk. ■ Let cookies dry for at least 6 hours before serving.

Tips

When cutting out fondant circles with the decorating tip, prevent sticking by dipping the tip in cornstarch between cuts or spraying the inside lightly with nonstick spray.

When applying luster dust, make sure the paintbrush you use is dry; otherwise, the dust will clump rather than covering the surface in a light, even layer.

Adding embellishments, such as the fondant pieces, is easier if you use a pair of tweezers. Buy an extra pair and keep them handy with your decorating supplies.

Mr. and Mrs. Monkey

Like the Chilly Penguins (page 144), monkeys always seem to be having a pretty good time, whether they're swinging from the trees or snacking or making faces at each other. This cute couple would fit right in! **Makes about 30.**

What You Need

- 1 recipe cookie dough (pages 36–46)
- Monkey face cookie cutter
- 1 recipe Classic Royal Icing (page 47)
- Black gel paste
- Pink gel paste
- Brown gel paste
- 3 squeeze bottles
- 2 disposable pastry bags
- 2 couplers
- 2 #1 round decorating tips
- Tweezers
- White edible pearls

Techniques Used

- Tinting icing (page 22)
- Filling a squeeze bottle (page 24)
- Piping (page 27)
- Flooding (page 28)
- Filling a pastry bag (page 24)
- Adding embellishments (page 31)

Getting Started

Bake cookies: Roll out dough and cut cookies with the monkey face cookie cutter. Bake according to recipe directions. Let cool completely before decorating.

Tint and thin icing: Place $\frac{3}{4}$ cup (175 mL) icing in a bowl and tint it black. Place $\frac{1}{4}$ cup (60 mL) icing in a bowl and tint it pink. Cover both bowls tightly and set aside. Divide remaining icing among three bowls; tint one portion dark brown, one light brown and one very light brown (see tip). Thin all three to two-step icing consistency (page 24) and transfer to squeeze bottles.

1

Using dark brown icing, outline and flood the top portion of each monkey's face as shown, leaving space for the inner ears and the eye area.

2

Using light brown icing, outline and flood the bottom portion of each monkey's face and its inner ears.

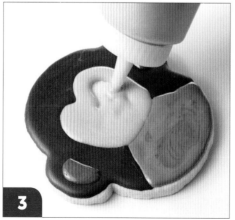

3

Using very light brown icing, flood the eye area of each monkey's face. ■ Let icing set for at least 6 hours or overnight.

4

Transfer black and pink icing to pastry bags fitted with #1 tips. ■ Use black icing to pipe a nose, nostrils and a smile on each monkey.

5 Pipe black oval eyes in the eye area of each monkey's face. ■ On half of the cookies (Mrs. Monkey!) pipe 4 eyelashes above each eye.

6 Working with one Mrs. Monkey cookie at a time, use pink icing to pipe a small bow at the top of her head.

7 Using tweezers, immediately place an edible pearl in the center of the bow. ■ Repeat steps 6 and 7 for all Mrs. Monkey cookies.

8 Using dark brown icing, pipe a border around the eye area and between the dark brown and light brown portions of each monkey's face. ■ Let cookies dry for at least 6 hours before serving.

Tips

If you have tan-colored gel paste, you may use this for the lighter shades of brown.

Keep royal icing tightly covered when you're not using it, as it tends to dry out quickly.

Adding embellishments, such as the edible pearls, is easier if you use a pair of tweezers. Buy an extra pair and keep them handy with your decorating supplies.

Happy Turtle

What You Need

- 1 recipe cookie dough (pages 36–46)
- Turtle cookie cutter
- 1 recipe Classic Royal Icing (page 47)
- Black gel paste
- Pink gel paste
- Green gel paste
- 2 squeeze bottles
- 3 disposable pastry bags
- 3 couplers
- #2 round decorating tip
- Green sanding sugar
- Tweezers
- Royal icing eyes
- 2 #1 round decorating tips

Techniques Used

- Tinting icing (page 22)
- Filling a squeeze bottle (page 24)
- Piping (page 27)
- Flooding (page 28)
- Filling a pastry bag (page 24)
- Adding sparkle (page 28)
- Adding embellishments (page 31)

Turtles are fascinating creatures — some live for over 150 years! — but their general immobility puts them lower down on zoo-goers' priority list than the lions or monkeys. These happy guys don't seem to mind though, perhaps because they are well rested thanks to all that peace and quiet! **Makes about 30.**

Getting Started

Bake cookies: Roll out dough and cut cookies with the turtle cookie cutter. Bake according to recipe directions. Let cool completely before decorating.

Tint and thin icing: Place $\frac{1}{4}$ cup (60 mL) icing in each of two bowls; tint one portion black and one pink. Cover tightly and set aside. Divide remaining icing evenly among three bowls; tint two portions dark green and one light green. Cover one dark green portion tightly and set aside. Thin light green and remaining dark green icing to two-step icing consistency (page 24) and transfer to squeeze bottles.

1 Using light green icing, outline turtle shells as shown.

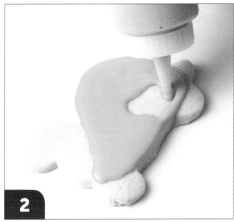

2 Flood turtle shells with light green icing.

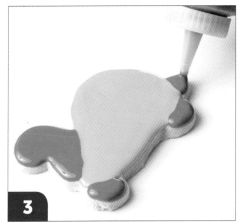

3 Using the squeeze bottle of dark green icing, outline and flood each turtle's head, feet and tail. ■ Let icing set for at least 6 hours or overnight.

4 Transfer remaining dark green icing to a pastry bag fitted with a #2 tip. ■ Working with one cookie at a time, outline the turtle shell and pipe a brick design as shown.

5

While the dark green icing is still wet, sprinkle it with sanding sugar, shaking off excess. ■ Repeat steps 4 and 5 for all cookies.

6

Using tweezers and a dab of icing on the back of each royal icing eye, place an eye at the top of each turtle's head.

7

Transfer black and pink icing to pastry bags fitted with #1 tips. ■ Use black icing to pipe a smiling mouth on each turtle.

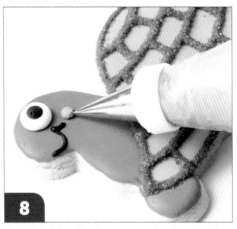

8

Use pink icing to pipe a rosy cheek on each turtle. ■ Let cookies dry for at least 4 hours before serving.

Tips

Don't be alarmed if excess sanding sugar sticks to the cookie even after you shake it. Wait until the icing dries completely, then gently brush off the unwanted sugar with a small food-safe paintbrush or a cotton swab.

Adding embellishments, such as the royal icing eyes, is easier if you use a pair of tweezers. Buy an extra pair and keep them handy with your decorating supplies.

If you don't have royal icing eyes, you can pipe your own eyes using black and white icing.

Chilly Penguin

Who doesn't love visiting the penguin habitat at the zoo, watching the cute critters play, sliding on their tummies and seemingly having a wonderful time? Unlike most of his buddies, this little guy needed some warming up, so he donned his trusty earmuffs and scarf before emerging from his igloo! **Makes about 40.**

What You Need

- 1 recipe cookie dough (pages 36–46)
- Penguin cookie cutter
- 1 recipe Classic Royal Icing (page 47)
- Orange gel paste
- Black gel paste
- 3 squeeze bottles
- Cornstarch
- Small rolling pin
- Red fondant
- Blue fondant
- X-acto knife

Techniques Used

- Tinting icing (page 22)
- Filling a squeeze bottle (page 24)
- Piping (page 27)
- Flooding (page 28)
- Working with fondant (page 30)
- Using an X-acto knife (page 31)

Getting Started

Bake cookies: Roll out dough and cut cookies with the penguin cookie cutter. Bake according to recipe directions. Let cool completely before decorating.

Thin and tint icing: Thin icing to two-step icing consistency (page 24). Place 1 cup (250 mL) icing in a bowl and tint it orange. Transfer about one-third of the remaining icing to a bowl and leave it white. Tint remaining icing black. Transfer orange, white and black icing to squeeze bottles.

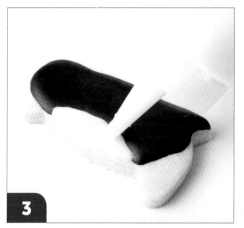

1

Using black icing, outline each penguin as shown, leaving space for the belly, feet and beak.

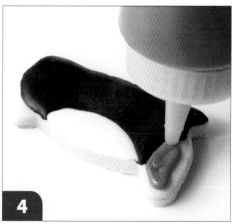

2

Flood penguins with black icing.

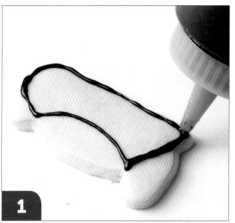

3

Using white icing, outline and flood each penguin's belly.

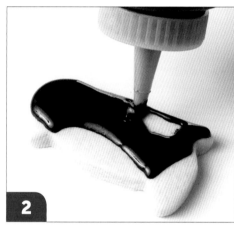

4

Using orange icing, outline and flood each penguin's feet.

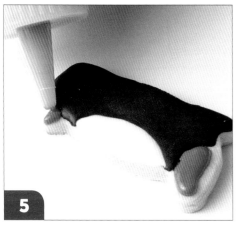

5

Pipe an orange beak on each penguin. ■ Let icing set for at least 6 hours or overnight.

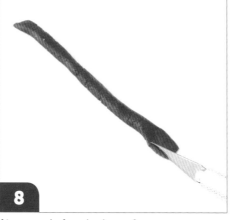

6

Roll red fondant into a rope about $\frac{1}{4}$ inch (5 mm) in diameter. ■ Cut a piece about $1\frac{1}{2}$ inches (4 cm) long and place it across a penguin's neck as the top of a scarf, pressing it into the sides of the cookie. ■ Use the X-acto knife to trim off any excess. ■ Repeat for all cookies.

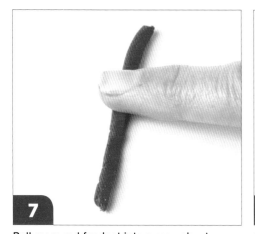

7

Roll more red fondant into a rope about $\frac{1}{4}$ inch (5 mm) in diameter. ■ Cut a piece about 2 inches (5 cm) long for each cookie.

8

At one end of each piece of rope, use the X-acto knife to gently draw lines that simulate the fringe on a scarf.

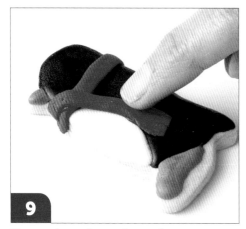

9

Place a piece of rope diagonally across each penguin as shown, overlapping the top portion of the scarf, and press to affix.

10

Roll blue fondant into a rope about $\frac{1}{4}$ inch (5 mm) in diameter. ■ Cut a piece about $\frac{3}{4}$ inch (2 cm) long for each cookie.

continued…

Tips

Sometimes air bubbles are created when you flood a cookie with icing. If this happens, use the tip of a toothpick to pop the bubbles.

For these cookies, the fondant needs to be pliable when attached, so do not prepare it in advance.

Be sure to wear disposable latex gloves when coloring fondant so the gel paste does not stain your hands.

Keep any fondant you are not presently working with tightly wrapped in plastic wrap, as it can quickly dry out, rendering it unusable.

Tips

An X-acto knife is a good investment if you plan to work with fondant often. Its blade is sharper than a paring knife, allowing for a more "x-act" cut.

Adding embellishments, such as the fondant pieces, is easier if you use a pair of tweezers. Buy an extra pair and keep them handy with your decorating supplies.

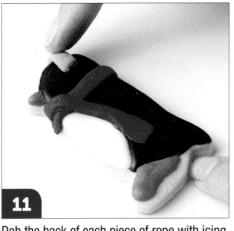

11

Dab the back of each piece of rope with icing and affix a piece to the top of each penguin's head as the headband portion of earmuffs.

12

Roll small pieces of blue fondant into balls about $\frac{1}{3}$ inch (8 mm) in diameter.

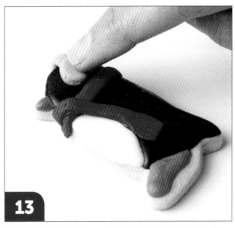

13

Dab the back of each ball with icing and affix a ball to the bottom of each headband.

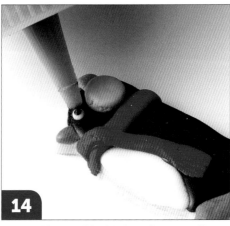

14

Using white and black icing, pipe a small eye on each penguin. ■ Let cookies dry for at least 4 hours before serving.

Purple Octopus

It's hard not to smile when you look at this happy octopus, purple limbs extending in every direction. This is another great design for beginners, using only piping, flooding and a simple brush of luster. **Makes about 30.**

Getting Started

Bake cookies: Roll out dough and cut cookies with the octopus cookie cutter. Bake according to recipe directions. Let cool completely before decorating.

Tint and thin icing: Place 1 cup (250 mL) icing in a bowl and tint it pink. Place ¼ cup (60 mL) icing in a bowl and tint it black. Cover both bowls tightly and set aside. Tint remaining icing purple, thin to two-step icing consistency (page 24) and transfer to a squeeze bottle.

What You Need

- 1 recipe cookie dough (pages 36–46)
- Octopus cookie cutter
- 1 recipe Classic Royal Icing (page 47)
- Pink, black and purple gel paste
- Squeeze bottle
- Small food-safe paintbrush
- Silver or purple luster dust
- 2 disposable pastry bags
- 2 couplers
- 2 #1 round decorating tips
- Tweezers
- Royal icing eyes

Techniques Used

- Tinting icing (page 22)
- Filling a squeeze bottle (page 24)
- Piping (page 27)
- Flooding (page 28)
- Adding sparkle (page 28)
- Filling a pastry bag (page 24)
- Adding embellishments (page 31)

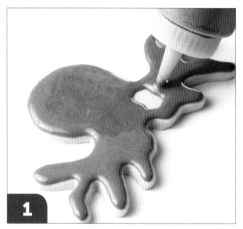

1

Using purple icing, outline and flood each octopus. ■ Let icing set for at least 6 hours or overnight.

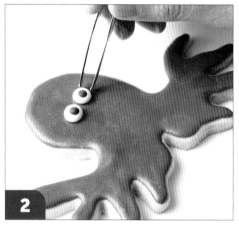

2

Using the small paintbrush, brush cookies with luster dust. ■ Using tweezers and a dab of icing on the back of each royal icing eye, place 2 eyes in the center of each octopus's head.

3

Transfer pink and black icing to pastry bags fitted with #1 tips. ■ Use pink icing to pipe small dots around each octopus's legs and on the side of its head as shown. ■ Use black icing to pipe a smile on each octopus. ■ Let cookies dry for at least 6 hours before serving.

Starfish

What You Need

- 1 recipe cookie dough (pages 36–46)
- Starfish cookie cutter
- 1 recipe Classic Royal Icing (page 47)
- Tan or brown gel paste
- Orange gel paste
- Squeeze bottle
- Small food-safe paintbrush
- Orange or gold luster dust
- Tweezers
- White edible pearls
- Disposable pastry bag
- Coupler
- #1 round decorating tip

Techniques Used

- Tinting icing (page 22)
- Filling a squeeze bottle (page 24)
- Piping (page 27)
- Flooding (page 28)
- Adding sparkle (page 28)
- Adding embellishments (page 31)
- Filling a pastry bag (page 24)

Starfish are such beautiful creatures. I love to look for them when I am snorkeling (I'm not much of a scuba diver, so snorkeling is about as close as I get). For these cookies, I tried to recreate the pattern on a starfish using a combination of piped dots and edible pearls. Yes, the process takes a bit of time, but the results are pretty spectacular! **Makes about 36.**

Getting Started

Bake cookies: Roll out dough and cut cookies with the starfish cookie cutter. Bake according to recipe directions. Let cool completely before decorating.

Tint and thin icing: Place 1 cup (250 mL) icing in a bowl and tint it tan (or light brown). Cover tightly and set aside. Tint remaining icing orange, thin to two-step icing consistency (page 24) and transfer to a squeeze bottle.

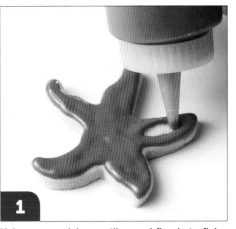

1 Using orange icing, outline and flood starfish. ■ Let icing set for at least 6 hours or overnight.

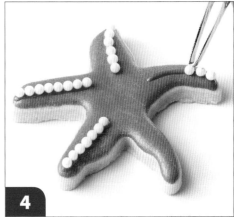

2 Using the small paintbrush, brush starfish with luster dust.

3 Working with one cookie at a time, use orange icing to pipe a thin line down the center of one starfish leg.

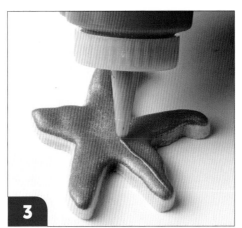

4 While the orange icing is still wet, use tweezers to place a line of edible pearls on the icing, so that they run down the center of the leg. ■ Repeat steps 3 and 4 with the other 4 legs.

5 Pipe an orange dot in the center of the starfish.

6 Using tweezers, place a ring of 5 pearls on the center dot. ■ Repeat steps 3 to 6 for all cookies.

7 Transfer tan icing to a pastry bag fitted with a #1 tip. ■ Pipe a dot in the center of each ring of pearls.

8 Using tan icing, pipe a pattern of small dots on each starfish's legs, around the lines of pearls. ■ Do not pipe dots in the center of the starfish. ■ Let cookies dry for at least 4 hours before serving.

Tips

When applying luster dust, make sure the paintbrush you use is dry; otherwise, the dust will clump rather than covering the surface in a light, even layer.

Adding embellishments, such as the edible pearls, is easier if you use a pair of tweezers. Buy an extra pair and keep them handy with your decorating supplies.

In addition to the other water creatures, you could pair these cookies with Flip-flops (page 68) and Bikini cookies (page 65) for a beach theme!

Dolphin

The inspiration for these cookies was a shiny blue dolphin sailing smoothly through the water with his friends, jumping and making happy sounds, just like Flipper. You might pair them with some drop-shaped cookies, like the ones made for the Umbrella and Raindrops cookies (page 58), or fondant raindrops, like the ones made for the Whale cookies (page 152), to simulate a big splash. **Makes about 36.**

What You Need

- 1 recipe cookie dough (pages 36–46)
- Dolphin cookie cutter
- 1 recipe Classic Royal Icing (page 47)
- Black gel paste
- Royal blue gel paste
- 2 squeeze bottles
- Blue disco dust
- Disposable pastry bag
- Coupler
- #1 round decorating tip

Techniques Used

- Tinting icing (page 22)
- Filling a squeeze bottle (page 24)
- Piping (page 27)
- Flooding (page 28)
- Adding sparkle (page 28)

Getting Started

Bake cookies: Roll out dough and cut cookies with the dolphin cookie cutter. Bake according to recipe directions. Let cool completely before decorating.

Tint and thin icing: Place 1/4 cup (60 mL) icing in a bowl and tint it black. Cover tightly and set aside. Divide remaining icing evenly between two bowls; tint one portion royal blue and leave one white. Thin blue and white icing to two-step icing consistency (page 24) and transfer to squeeze bottles.

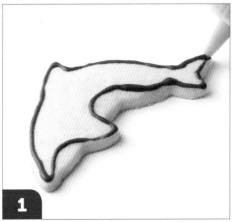

1

Working with one cookie at a time, use blue icing to outline a dolphin as shown, leaving space for the 2 belly sections.

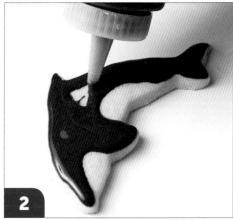

2

Flood the dolphin with blue icing.

3

While the blue icing is still wet, sprinkle it with disco dust, shaking off excess. ■ Repeat steps 1 to 3 for all cookies.

4

Using white icing, outline and flood belly sections of dolphins. ■ Let icing set for at least 6 hours or overnight.

5

Using blue icing, pipe a border around the blue section of each dolphin. ■ Pipe a small divider line on each tail fin.

6

Using white icing, pipe an eye on each dolphin.

7

Transfer black icing to a pastry bag fitted with a #1 tip. ■ Pipe a pupil in each eye.

8

Pipe a black nostril at the end of each dolphin's snout. ■ Let cookies dry for at least 4 hours before serving.

Tips

Keep royal icing tightly covered when you're not using it, as it tends to dry out quickly.

Sometimes air bubbles are created when you flood a cookie with icing. If this happens, use the tip of a toothpick to pop the bubbles.

When working with disco dust, shake excess off onto a sheet of parchment paper, which you can use to funnel it back into the jar. This helps to eliminate waste.

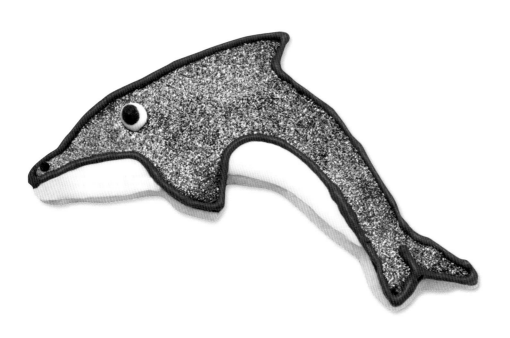

Whale

When my husband and I vacationed in Mexico, we were spoiled by the number of whales we saw. It was as if the hotel had called them in from central casting just for us! On any given day, we would see three or four at a time, bounding out of the water over and over again. I think they were showing off. **Makes about 30.**

What You Need

- 1 recipe cookie dough (pages 36–46)
- Whale cookie cutter
- 1 recipe Classic Royal Icing (page 47)
- Teal gel paste
- 2 squeeze bottles
- Blue disco dust
- Cornstarch
- Small rolling pin
- White fondant
- Raindrop cutter
- Tweezers
- Royal icing eyes

Techniques Used

- Tinting icing (page 22)
- Filling a squeeze bottle (page 24)
- Piping (page 27)
- Flooding (page 28)
- Adding sparkle (page 28)
- Working with fondant (page 30)
- Adding embellishments (page 31)

Getting Started

Bake cookies: Roll out dough and cut cookies with the whale cookie cutter. Bake according to recipe directions. Let cool completely before decorating.

Thin and tint icing: Thin icing to two-step icing consistency (page 24). Place 1½ cups (60 mL) icing in a bowl and leave it white. Tint remaining icing teal. Transfer white and teal icing to squeeze bottles.

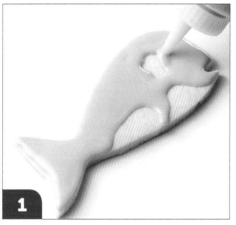

1 Working with one cookie at a time, use teal icing to outline and flood a whale as shown, leaving space for the 2 belly sections.

2 While the teal icing is still wet, sprinkle the tail with disco dust, shaking off excess. ■ Repeat steps 1 and 2 for all cookies.

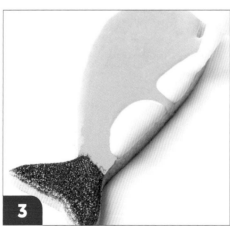

3 Using white icing, outline and flood belly sections of whales. ■ Let icing set for at least 6 hours or overnight.

4 Meanwhile, on a work surface lightly dusted with cornstarch, roll out fondant to ⅛ inch (3 mm) thick. ■ Using the raindrop cutter, cut out about 10 raindrops per cookie. ■ Place raindrops on a cookie sheet and let dry for at least 4 hours or overnight.

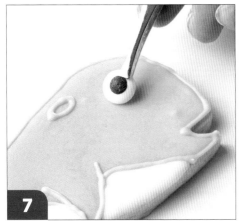

5 Using teal icing, pipe a border around the teal section of each whale.

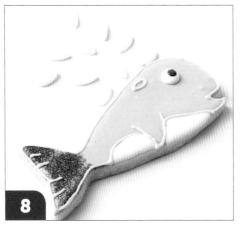

6 Pipe teal detail lines on each whale's tail fin and side fin as shown. ■ Pipe a small round spout on top of each whale's head.

7 Using tweezers and a dab of icing on the back of each royal icing eye, place an eye on each whale, positioning it so it is looking upward. ■ Let cookies dry for at least 4 hours or overnight.

8 When presenting the cookies, arrange fondant raindrops over each whale to look like a spout of water.

Tips

If all the teal icing does not fit in your squeeze bottle, cover the remaining icing tightly and refill the bottle as needed.

Don't be alarmed if excess disco dust sticks to the cookie even after you shake it. Wait until the icing dries completely, then gently brush off the unwanted dust with a small food-safe paintbrush or a cotton swab.

If you don't have royal icing eyes on hand, pipe simple eyes using black icing and a pastry bag fitted with a #2 round decorating tip.

Tennis Racquet

I used to be a pretty good tennis player. My secret weapon was my dangerous backhand. Creating these cookies has inspired me to get back onto the court very soon, although I am prepared to swallow my pride as I work on my technique. "Serve" these cookies alongside the Say It with L-O-V-E cookies (page 206) as a creative treat for someone special. **Makes about 30.**

What You Need

- 1 recipe cookie dough (pages 36–46)
- Tennis racquet cookie cutter
- 1 recipe Classic Royal Icing (page 47)
- Black gel paste
- Red gel paste
- 3 disposable pastry bags
- 3 couplers
- 2 #2 round decorating tips
- #1 round decorating tip
- Squeeze bottle
- Yellow fondant
- #1 round decorating tip

Techniques Used

- Tinting icing (page 22)
- Filling a pastry bag (page 24)
- Filling a squeeze bottle (page 24)
- Piping (page 27)
- Flooding (page 28)
- Working with fondant (page 30)

Getting Started

Bake cookies: Roll out dough and cut cookies with the tennis racquet cookie cutter. Bake according to recipe directions. Let cool completely before decorating.

Tint and thin icing: Place 1½ cups (375 mL) icing in a bowl and tint it black. Place 1 cup (250 mL) icing in a bowl and tint it red. Transfer black and red icing to pastry bags fitted with #2 tips. Place ¼ cup (60 mL) white icing in a bowl, cover tightly and set aside. Thin remaining white icing to two-step icing consistency (page 24) and transfer to a squeeze bottle.

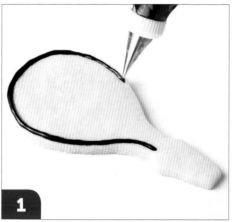

1

Using black icing, pipe a border around the head of each tennis racquet.

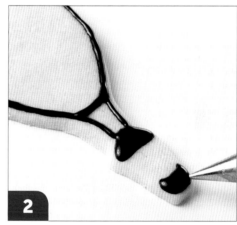

2

Pipe a black border around the neck on each racquet. ■ Pipe a thick black line at the top and bottom of each handle.

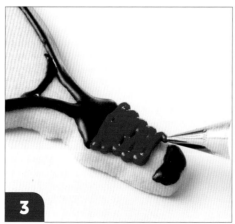

3

Using red icing, fill in the center of each handle, piping in a tight S pattern to create texture.

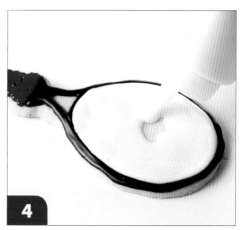

4

Using the squeeze bottle of white icing, flood the center of each racquet head. ■ Let icing set for at least 6 hours or overnight.

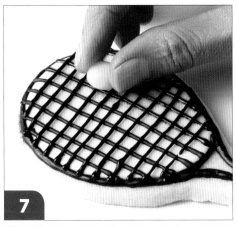

5 Meanwhile, roll 1 to 2 tsp (5 to 10 mL) fondant into a small ball. ■ Make 1 ball per cookie. ■ Place balls on a cookie sheet and let dry for at least 4 hours or overnight.

6 Change tip on black icing to a #1 tip. ■ Working with one cookie at a time, pipe strings on a racquet (see tip).

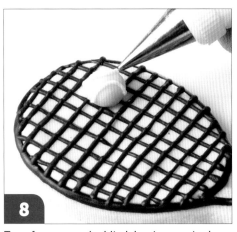

7 While the black icing is still wet, place a ball on the racquet. ■ Repeat steps 6 and 7 for all cookies.

8 Transfer reserved white icing to a pastry bag fitted with a #1 tip. ■ Pipe curved lines on each tennis ball. ■ Let cookies dry for at least 4 hours before serving.

Tips

If all the white icing does not fit in your squeeze bottle, cover the remaining icing tightly and refill the bottle as needed.

When you're piping the strings in step 6, a ruler and an X-acto knife will help you create a template for piping straight, even lines.

Pair these cookies with the Tennis Ball cookies (page 156.)

Tennis Ball

These bright tennis balls are perfect for beginning decorators or those who have a limited cutter collection. Pair them with other sports balls (pages 157–162) or serve them with Tennis Racquet cookies (page 154.) **Makes about 40.**

What You Need

- 1 recipe cookie dough (pages 36–46)
- 3-inch (7.5 cm) round cookie cutter
- 1 recipe Classic Royal Icing (page 47)
- Yellow gel paste
- Squeeze bottle
- Small food-safe paintbrush (optional)
- Gold luster dust (optional)
- Disposable pastry bag
- Coupler
- #2 round decorating tip
- Fine white sanding sugar (optional)

Techniques Used

- Tinting icing (page 22)
- Filling a squeeze bottle (page 24)
- Piping (page 27)
- Flooding (page 28)
- Adding sparkle (page 28)
- Filling a pastry bag (page 24)

Tip

For perfectly rounded white lines, use the round cutter to create a guide for your piping. Place the cutter so it overlaps the cookie and lightly trace around the edge with an X-acto knife. Repeat on the other side of the cookie. Pipe the icing over the traced lines.

Getting Started

Bake cookies: Roll out dough and cut cookies with the round cookie cutter. Bake according to recipe directions. Let cool completely before decorating.

Tint and thin icing: Place 1 cup (250 mL) icing in a bowl and leave it white. Cover tightly and set aside. Tint remaining icing yellow, thin to two-step icing consistency (page 24) and transfer to a squeeze bottle (cover any remaining yellow icing tightly and refill the bottle as needed).

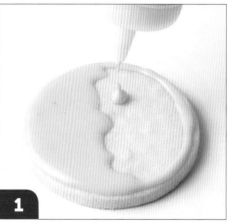

1

Using yellow icing, outline and flood cookies. ■ Let icing set for at least 6 hours or overnight.

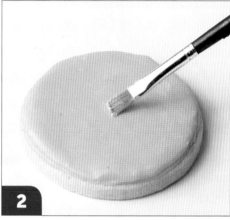

2

If desired, use the small paintbrush to brush cookies lightly with luster dust.

3

Transfer white icing to a pastry bag fitted with a #2 tip. ■ Working with one cookie at a time, pipe 2 curved lines across the ball (see tip). ■ If desired, immediately sprinkle white icing with sanding sugar, shaking off excess. ■ Repeat for all cookies. ■ Let cookies dry for at least 4 hours before serving.

"Batter Up" Baseball

Like the Tennis Ball cookies (page 156) and Slam-Dunk Basketball cookies (page 162), this is a great design to make if you are stepping up to bat for the first or second time. The detailed red stitching is good practice for perfecting steady piping. Bring your finished products to celebrate a big win… or to console a painful loss. **Makes about 40.**

Getting Started

Bake cookies: Roll out dough and cut cookies with the round cookie cutter. Bake according to recipe directions. Let cool completely before decorating.

Tint and thin icing: Place 1½ cups (375 mL) icing in a bowl and tint it red. Cover tightly and set aside. Thin remaining white icing to two-step icing consistency (page 24) and transfer to a squeeze bottle (cover any remaining white icing tightly and refill the bottle as needed).

What You Need

- 1 recipe cookie dough (pages 36–46)
- 3-inch (7.5 cm) round cookie cutter
- 1 recipe Classic Royal Icing (page 47)
- Red gel paste
- Squeeze bottle
- Disposable pastry bag
- Coupler
- #1 round decorating tip

Techniques Used

- Tinting icing (page 22)
- Filling a squeeze bottle (page 24)
- Piping (page 27)
- Flooding (page 28)
- Filling a pastry bag (page 24)

Tip

For perfectly rounded red lines, use the round cutter to create a guide for your piping. Place the cutter so it overlaps the cookie and lightly trace around the edge with an X-acto knife. Repeat on the other side of the cookie. Pipe the icing over the traced lines.

Variation

To add a nice sheen to these cookies, brush them with a thin, even layer of white or silver luster dust at the beginning of step 2.

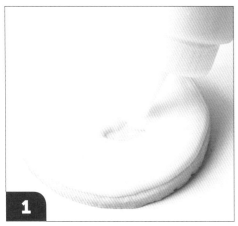

1 Using white icing, outline and flood cookies. ■ Let icing set for at least 6 hours or overnight.

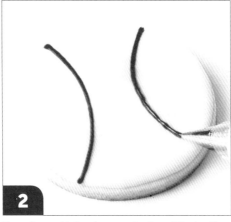

2 Transfer red icing to a pastry bag fitted with a #1 tip. ■ Pipe 2 curved lines across each ball (see tip).

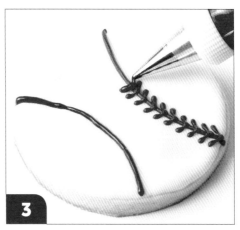

3 Pipe wide red V shapes down the length of each curved line, spacing them close together. ■ Let cookies dry for at least 6 hours before serving.

Soccer Ball

What You Need

- 1 recipe cookie dough (pages 36–46)
- 3 to 3½ inch (7.5 to 9 cm) round cookie cutter
- 1 recipe Classic Royal Icing (page 47)
- Black gel paste
- Disposable pastry bag
- Coupler
- #2 round decorating tip
- 2 squeeze bottles
- Pentagon template (page 252)
- X-acto knife or edible marker
- Ruler

Techniques Used

- Tinting icing (page 22)
- Filling a pastry bag (page 24)
- Filling a squeeze bottle (page 24)
- Working with templates (page 32)
- Using an X-acto knife (page 31)
- Piping (page 27)
- Flooding (page 28)

Of all the sports ball cookies in this book, these are the most advanced, thanks to the black pentagon/white hexagon design. Allow yourself a few extra practice balls when decorating — I like to think that "mistake" cookies are calorie-free. **Makes about 40.**

Getting Started

Bake cookies: Roll out dough and cut cookies with the round cookie cutter. Bake according to recipe directions. Let cool completely before decorating.

Tint and thin icing: Divide icing evenly between two bowls; tint one portion black and leave one white. Transfer half the black icing to a pastry bag fitted with a #2 tip. Thin white and remaining black icing to two-step icing consistency (page 24) and transfer to squeeze bottles.

1 Place the pentagon template in the center of each cookie and lightly trace around it with the X-acto knife or edible marker.

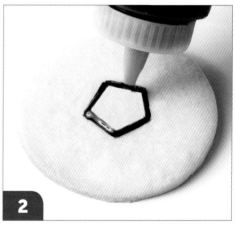

2 Using the squeeze bottle of black icing, outline the pentagon on each cookie.

3 Flood pentagons with black icing.

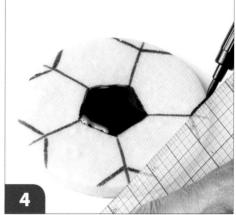

4 With the ruler as a guide, use the X-acto knife or edible marker to lightly trace 5 triangles around the border of each cookie, lining up the tip of each triangle with a corner of the pentagon.

5 Using the squeeze bottle of black icing, outline each cookie.

6 Outline and flood the triangles with black icing.

7 Using the pastry bag of black icing, pipe lines connecting the corners of the pentagon to the tips of the triangles on each cookie. ■ Let icing set for about 15 minutes.

8 Using white icing, flood the un-iced sections of each cookie ■ Let cookies dry for at least 6 hours before serving.

Tips

If you have filled a pastry bag with icing but are not using it right away, set it upright in a tall drinking glass until you're ready for it.

Sometimes air bubbles are created when you flood a cookie with icing. If this happens, use the tip of a toothpick to pop the bubbles.

Football

What You Need

- 1 recipe cookie dough (pages 36–46)
- Football cookie cutter
- 1 recipe Classic Royal Icing (page 47)
- Brown gel paste
- Squeeze bottle
- Cornstarch
- Small rolling pin
- White fondant
- 2 round cutters, one slightly larger than the other (see tip)
- Disposable pastry bag
- Coupler
- #1 round decorating tip

Techniques Used

- Tinting icing (page 22)
- Filling a squeeze bottle (page 24)
- Piping (page 27)
- Flooding (page 28)
- Working with fondant (page 30)
- Filling a pastry bag (page 24)

I went to high school in Texas, where football is not just a sport, it's practically a religion. Everyone comes out for the Friday night games, and the best players often turn into local celebrities. Come to think of it, I could probably make a fortune if I opened up a Texas bakery that only sells these football cookies! **Makes about 36.**

Getting Started

Bake cookies: Roll out dough and cut cookies with the football cookie cutter. Bake according to recipe directions. Let cool completely before decorating.

Tint and thin icing: Place 1 cup (250 mL) icing in a bowl and leave it white. Cover tightly and set aside. Tint remaining icing brown, thin to two-step icing consistency (page 24) and transfer to a squeeze bottle.

1 Using brown icing, outline footballs.

2 Flood footballs with brown icing. ■ Let icing set for at least 6 hours or overnight.

3 Meanwhile, on a work surface lightly dusted with cornstarch, roll out fondant to $\frac{1}{8}$ inch (3 mm) thick. ■ Using the larger round cutter, cut out a circle. ■ Center the smaller cutter inside the circle and cut out another circle, leaving you with a circular band.

4 Place the circular band near one end of a football and trim it so that the ends will align with the edges of the cookie. ■ Use this curved strip as a template and make 2 strips per cookie. ■ Place strips on a cookie sheet and let dry for at least 4 hours or overnight.

5

Using brown icing, pipe a seam line connecting the two end points of each football, curving slightly downward.

6

Dab the back of each fondant strip with icing and affix 2 strips to each football, one near each end, lining up the edges of the strips with the edges of the cookie.

7

Transfer white icing to a pastry bag fitted with a #1 tip. ■ Pipe a curved line across the top of each football, between the fondant strips.

8

Pipe several short white lines across the curved line, to simulate laces. ■ Let cookies dry for at least 4 hours before serving.

Tips

The size of the cutters you use to make the white fondant strips will depend on the size of your cookie. I used a 2½-inch (6 cm) cutter and a 1¾-inch (4.5 cm) cutter for my 3¼-inch (8 cm) wide football cookie.

If all the brown icing does not fit in your squeeze bottle, cover the remaining icing tightly and refill the bottle as needed.

Variation

Add a bit of sheen by brushing the footballs with a thin, even layer of brown luster dust at the beginning of step 5.

Slam-Dunk Basketball

What You Need

- 1 recipe cookie dough (pages 36–46)
- 3-inch (7.5 cm) round cookie cutter
- 1 recipe Classic Royal Icing (page 47)
- Black gel paste
- Orange gel paste
- Squeeze bottle
- Disposable pastry bag
- Coupler
- #2 round decorating tip

Techniques Used

- Tinting icing (page 22)
- Filling a squeeze bottle (page 24)
- Piping (page 27)
- Flooding (page 28)
- Filling a pastry bag (page 24)

I make these easy cookies every year during the NCAA Tournament, and they are always a hit. **Makes about 40.**

Getting Started

Bake cookies: Roll out dough and cut cookies with the round cookie cutter. Bake according to recipe directions. Let cool completely before decorating.

Tint and thin icing: Place 1 cup (250 mL) icing in a bowl and tint it black. Cover tightly and set aside. Tint remaining icing orange, thin to two-step icing consistency (page 24) and transfer to a squeeze bottle.

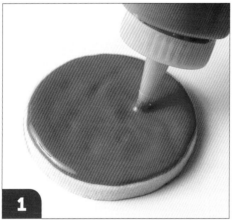

1 Using orange icing, outline and flood cookies. ■ Let icing set for at least 6 hours or overnight.

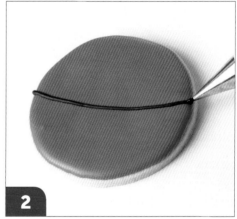

2 Transfer black icing to a pastry bag fitted with a #2 tip. ■ Pipe a horizontal line across the center of each ball, curving slightly downward.

3 Pipe 3 black lines across each cookie's center line: one near the right side curving slightly to the right; one just right of center curving slightly to the left; and one at the center curving deeply to the left. ■ Let cookies dry for at least 4 hours before serving.

Cheerleader

This adorable cheerleader is one of my favorites, mostly because of the pompoms. While trying to figure out a creative way to make them, I rummaged through my kitchen drawers, searching for inspiration. When I saw my new garlic press, I had a *eureka!* moment. **Makes about 30.**

Getting Started

Bake cookies: Roll out dough and cut cookies with the gingerbread girl cookie cutter. Bake according to recipe directions. Let cool completely before decorating.

Tint and thin icing: Place 1 cup (250 mL) icing in a bowl and tint it yellow. Place ½ cup (125 mL) icing in a bowl and tint it black. Cover both bowls tightly and set aside. Divide remaining icing evenly between two bowls; tint one portion red and leave one white. Place ¾ cup (175 mL) of the red icing in another bowl, cover tightly and set aside. Thin white and remaining red icing to two-step icing consistency (page 24) and transfer to squeeze bottles. ■

What You Need

- 1 recipe cookie dough (pages 36–46)
- Gingerbread girl cookie cutter
- 1 recipe Classic Royal Icing (page 47)
- Yellow gel paste
- Black gel paste
- Red gel paste
- 2 squeeze bottles
- Cornstarch
- Small rolling pin
- Red fondant
- Mini bow cutter
- Garlic press (see tip, page 164)
- X-acto knife
- 3 disposable pastry bags
- 3 couplers
- #2 round decorating tip
- #3 round decorating tip
- #1 round decorating tip
- Red disco dust
- Tweezers

Techniques Used

- Tinting icing (page 22)
- Filling a squeeze bottle (page 24)
- Piping (page 27)
- Flooding (page 28)
- Working with fondant (page 30)
- Filling a pastry bag (page 24)
- Adding sparkle (page 28)

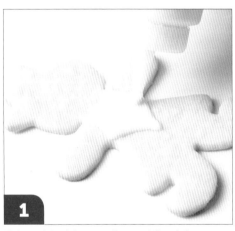

1

Using white icing, outline and flood the top portion of each cheerleader's dress as shown, scooping at the neck and coming to a point at the bottom.

2

Outline and flood shoes for each cheerleader with white icing.

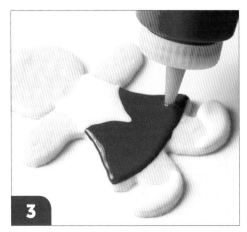

3

Using the squeeze bottle of red icing, outline and flood the skirt of each dress.

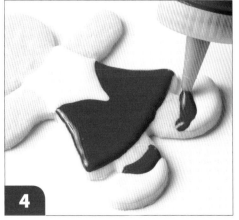

4

Outline and flood socks for each cheerleader with red icing. ■ Let icing set for at least 6 hours or overnight.

continued...

Tips

Make sure to use a new garlic press that has never been used to press garlic. Even a small trace of garlic residue would add an unpleasant taste to the cookies!

A ricer can be used in place of the garlic press.

Be sure to wear disposable latex gloves when coloring fondant so the gel paste does not stain your hands.

Keep any fondant you are not presently working with tightly wrapped in plastic wrap, as it can quickly dry out, rendering it unusable.

If you don't have an X-acto knife, any small, sharp knife will work fine.

5 Meanwhile, on a work surface lightly dusted with cornstarch, roll out fondant to $\frac{1}{16}$ inch (2 mm) thick. ■ Using the bow cutter, cut out 1 bow per cookie.

6 Roll 1 tbsp (15 mL) fondant into a ball and press it through the garlic press, creating strands for pompoms.

7 Run the X-acto knife along the surface of the garlic press to remove the strands. ■ Bunch the strands together at the base to form a pompom shape. ■ Make 2 pompoms per cookie. ■ Place bows and pompoms on a cookie sheet and let dry for at least 4 hours or overnight.

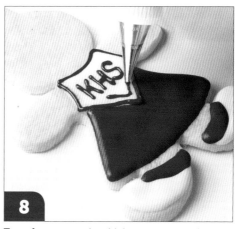

8 Transfer reserved red icing to a pastry bag fitted with a #2 tip. ■ Pipe a border around the top portion of each dress. ■ Pipe school initials in the center of the white icing and a V shape under the initials.

9 Using white icing, pipe 2 wavy border lines along the bottom of each dress.

10 Brush fondant bows lightly with water, then sprinkle with disco dust, shaking off excess.

11

Transfer yellow icing to a pastry bag fitted with a #3 tip. ■ Working with one cookie at a time, pipe hair on a cheerleader, including three individual strands on either side of the face.

12

While the yellow icing is still wet, use tweezers to place a bow at the top of the hair, angling it to the left. ■ Repeat steps 11 and 12 for all cookies.

13

Transfer black icing to a pastry bag fitted with a #1 tip. ■ Pipe eyes, a nose and a smiling mouth on each cheerleader.

14

Dab the base of each pompom with icing and affix 2 pompoms to each cheerleader, one on each hand. ■ Let cookies dry for at least 6 hours before serving.

Tips

When working with disco dust, shake excess off onto a sheet of parchment paper, which you can use to funnel it back into the jar. This helps to eliminate waste.

Match the hair colors on your cookies to those of the members of your favorite squad. For red or auburn hair, use a blend of red and brown gel paste.

Variation

If you don't have a mini bow cutter, simply cut one freehand with an X-acto knife. Alternatively, pipe a bow onto each cookie using red icing in a pastry bag fitted with a #2 tip. Make sure the rest of the cookie has dried before you pipe the bow, so that the disco dust sticks only to the bow.

Megaphone

Cheerleaders may remain on the sidelines for most of the game, but that doesn't make them any less important to a team's success. Yelling cheers helps to motivate fans, who in turn help to motivate the team. Thank your favorite cheer crew with these sparkly megaphone cookies. Pair them with Cheerleader cookies (page 163) for treats worthy of backflips! **Makes about 36.**

What You Need

- 1 recipe cookie dough (pages 36–46)
- Megaphone cookie cutter
- 1 recipe Classic Royal Icing (page 47)
- Black gel paste
- Red gel paste
- Squeeze bottle
- Red disco dust
- Cornstarch
- Small rolling pin
- Black fondant
- #10 round decorating tip (see tips)
- Disposable pastry bag
- Coupler
- #1 round decorating tip

Techniques Used

- Tinting icing (page 22)
- Filling a squeeze bottle (page 24)
- Piping (page 27)
- Flooding (page 28)
- Adding sparkle (page 28)
- Working with fondant (page 30)
- Filling a pastry bag (page 24)

Getting Started

Bake cookies: Roll out dough and cut cookies with the megaphone cookie cutter. Bake according to recipe directions. Let cool completely before decorating.

Tint and thin icing: Place 1 cup (250 mL) icing in a bowl and tint it black. Cover tightly and set aside. Tint remaining icing red, thin to two-step icing consistency (page 24) and transfer to a squeeze bottle.

3 Meanwhile, on a work surface lightly dusted with cornstarch, roll out fondant to ⅛ inch (3 mm) thick. ■ Using the round back side of the #10 tip, cut out 1 circle per cookie.

1 Working with one cookie at a time, use red icing to outline and flood a megaphone, leaving space for the handle.

4 Using the front side of the #10 piping tip, cut out 4 circles per cookie. ■ Place all circles on a cookie sheet and let dry for at least 4 hours or overnight.

2 While the red icing is still wet, sprinkle the megaphone with disco dust, shaking off excess. ■ Repeat steps 1 and 2 for all cookies. ■ Let icing set for at least 6 hours or overnight.

5

Transfer black icing to a pastry bag fitted with a #1 tip. ■ Pipe a border around each megaphone and a handle at the bottom.

6

Using black icing, pipe curved vertical lines inside both ends of each megaphone, following the contour of the outline.

7

Pipe black school initials near the left side of each megaphone, increasing the size of the letters to fit the increasing height of the megaphone as you move to the right.

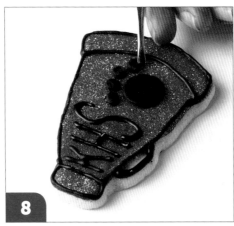

8

Dab the back of each large fondant circle with icing and affix a circle near the right side of each megaphone, slightly below center. ■ Dab the back of each small circle with icing and affix 4 circles as toes above each large circle paw. ■ Let cookies dry for at least 4 hours before serving.

Tips

If all the red icing does not fit in your squeeze bottle, cover the remaining icing tightly and refill the bottle as needed.

If you don't have a #10 decorating tip, use the back side of another decorating tip to cut the circles in step 3, and use the end of a drinking straw to cut the circles in step 4.

When cutting out fondant circles with the decorating tip, prevent sticking by dipping the tip in cornstarch between cuts or spraying the inside lightly with nonstick spray.

Adding embellishments, such as the fondant circles, is easier if you use a pair of tweezers. Buy an extra pair and keep them handy with your decorating supplies.

Variation

Customize the megaphones to match your school initials, colors and mascot. Or simply pipe "RAH!" on the side.

Stand-Out Running Shoes

What You Need

- 1 recipe cookie dough (pages 36–46)
- Running shoe cookie cutters
- 1 recipe Classic Royal Icing (page 47)
- Hot pink gel paste
- Black gel paste
- Orange gel paste
- 2 squeeze bottles
- 2 disposable pastry bags
- 2 couplers
- 2 #2 round decorating tips
- Hot pink sanding sugar

Techniques Used

- Tinting icing (page 22)
- Filling a squeeze bottle (page 24)
- Piping (page 27)
- Flooding (page 28)
- Filling a pastry bag (page 24)
- Adding sparkle (page 28)

My husband and I go through several pairs of running shoes a year. I always look for the brightest and most colorful pair on the market. For some reason, the cheery colors help motivate me. Later, I might reward my hard work with one of these equally bright cookies. **Makes about 30.**

Getting Started

Bake cookies: Roll out dough and cut cookies with the running shoe cookie cutter. Bake according to recipe directions. Let cool completely before decorating.

Tint and thin icing: Place 1 cup (250 mL) in a bowl and tint it hot pink. Place $\frac{1}{2}$ cup (125 mL) icing in a bowl and leave it white. Cover both bowls tightly and set aside. Place $1\frac{1}{2}$ cups (375 mL) icing in a bowl and tint it gray. Tint remaining icing orange. Thin gray and orange icing to two-step icing consistency (page 24) and transfer to squeeze bottles.

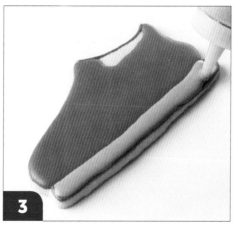

1 Using orange icing, outline the body, sole and interior section of each shoe as shown.

2 Flood the body of each shoe with orange icing.

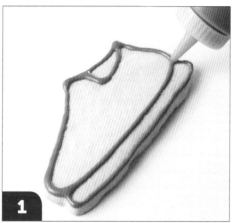

3 Using gray icing, flood the sole of each shoe.

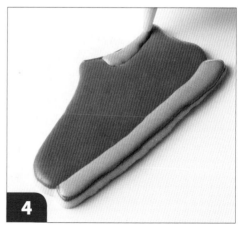

4 Flood the interior section of each shoe with gray icing. ■ Let icing set for at least 6 hours or overnight.

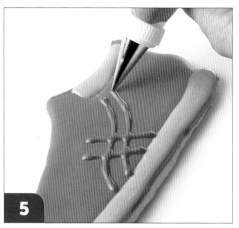

5

Transfer hot pink and white icing to pastry bags fitted with #2 tips. ■ Working with one cookie at a time, pipe hot pink detail on the side of a shoe as shown (or create your own design).

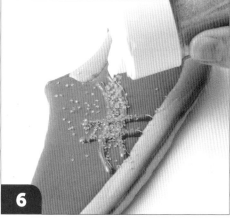

6

While the hot pink icing is still wet, sprinkle it with sanding sugar, shaking off excess. ■ Repeat steps 5 and 6 for all cookies.

Tips

To tint icing gray, mix in black gel paste a tiny dab at a time until you reach the desired shade.

If all the orange icing does not fit in your squeeze bottle, cover the remaining icing tightly and refill the bottle as needed.

When working with sanding sugar, shake excess off onto a sheet of parchment paper, which you can use to funnel it back into the jar. This helps to eliminate waste.

Make these cookies for a school sporting event, a neighborhood 5K or to tell a sick friend they will be "back on their feet" in no time!

Variation

While I love shoes in bright colors, you may have a different preference. Change the colors to match your own favorite pair.

7

Using orange icing, pipe a border around each shoe, sole, interior section and tongue area.

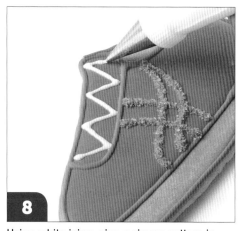

8

Using white icing, pipe a zigzag pattern in each shoe's tongue area to represent laces. ■ Let cookies dry for at least 6 hours before serving.

Pool Balls

This fun design was inspired by a similar one I did for cupcakes a few years ago. My creation took top prize in a contest, so I thought it would go over just as well for cookies! **Makes 48 individual "balls," or three sets of cookies.**

What You Need

- 1 recipe cookie dough (pages 36–46)
- 3 inch (7.5 cm) round cookie cutter
- 1 recipe Classic Royal Icing (page 47)
- Green gel paste
- Red gel paste
- Blue gel paste
- Purple gel paste
- Orange gel paste
- Yellow gel paste
- Burgundy gel paste
- Black gel paste
- 9 squeeze bottles
- Ruler
- X-acto knife or edible marker
- Cornstarch
- Small rolling pin
- White fondant
- Disposable pastry bag
- Coupler
- #1 round decorating tip

Techniques Used

- Tinting icing (page 22)
- Filling a squeeze bottle (page 24)
- Piping (page 27)
- Flooding (page 28)
- Using an X-acto knife (page 31)
- Working with fondant (page 30)
- Filling a pastry bag (page 24)

Getting Started

Bake cookies: Roll out dough and cut cookies with the round cookie cutter. Bake according to recipe directions. Let cool completely before decorating.

Tint and thin icing: Divide icing evenly among nine bowls; tint one portion green, one red, one blue, one purple, one orange, one yellow, one burgundy and one black, and leave one white. Place half the black icing in another bowl, cover tightly and set aside. Thin all remaining icings to two-step icing consistency (page 24) and transfer to squeeze bottles.

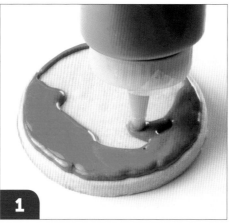

1 Using green icing, outline and flood 3 cookies. ■ Do the same with red, blue, purple, orange, yellow, burgundy and white icing. ■ Let icing set for at least 6 hours or overnight.

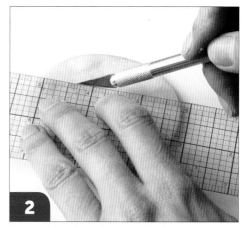

2 Meanwhile, place the ruler in the center of an un-iced cookie and use the X-acto knife or edible marker to lightly trace lines on either side of the ruler.

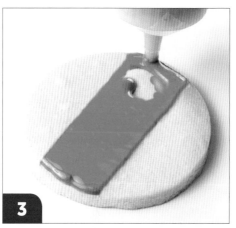

3 Using green icing, outline and flood the center stripe on the cookie, using the traced outline as a guide. ■ Repeat steps 2 and 3 with 2 more un-iced cookies.

4 Repeat steps 2 and 3 with red, blue, purple, orange, yellow and burgundy icing.

5

After all stripes have been outlined and flooded, use white icing to outline and flood the remaining sections of each striped cookie. ■ Let icing set for at least 6 hours or overnight.

6

Meanwhile, on a work surface lightly dusted with cornstarch, roll out fondant to $1/16$ inch (2 mm) thick. ■ Using the back side of a decorating tip, cut out 45 circles. ■ Place circles on a cookie sheet and let dry for at least 2 hours or overnight.

7

Dab the back of each fondant circle with icing and affix a circle to the center of each cookie except the solid white cue balls.

8

Transfer reserved black icing to a pastry bag fitted with a #1 tip. ■ Pipe a number on the circle in each pool ball (see tip). ■ Let cookies dry for at least 4 hours before racking the balls!

Tips

Because this design deals with so many colors, you might want to make $1\frac{1}{2}$ batches of icing.

Although piping may seem easier, using fondant to create the circles for the center of each cookie results in a neater, more uniform finish.

When cutting out fondant circles with the decorating tip, prevent sticking by dipping the tip in cornstarch between cuts or spraying the inside lightly with nonstick spray.

Here are the standard color/number combinations for pool balls: *Solids:* yellow=1, blue=2, red=3, purple=4, orange=5, green=6 (pipe a line under the number), burgundy=7, black=8; *Stripes:* yellow=9 (pipe a line under the number), blue=10, red=11, purple=12, orange=13, green=14, burgundy=15.

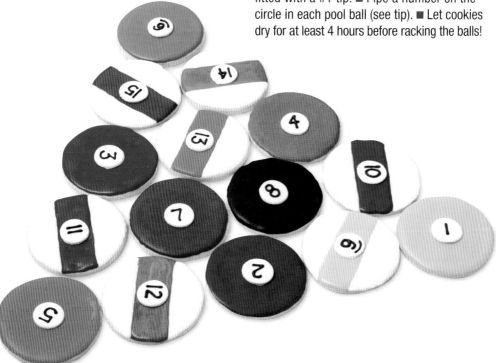

Little Red Schoolhouse

What You Need

- 1 recipe cookie dough (pages 36–46)
- Church cookie cutter (see tip)
- 1 recipe Classic Royal Icing (page 47)
- Blue gel paste
- Black gel paste
- Yellow gel paste
- Green gel paste
- Red gel paste
- 3 disposable pastry bags
- 3 couplers
- 2 #2 round decorating tips
- #1 round decorating tip
- 2 squeeze bottles
- Cornstarch
- Small rolling pin
- Beige fondant
- Ruler
- X-acto knife

Techniques Used

- Tinting icing (page 22)
- Filling a pastry bag (page 24)
- Filling a squeeze bottle (page 24)
- Piping (page 27)
- Flooding (page 28)
- Working with fondant (page 30)
- Using an X-acto knife (page 31)

From the bright yellow bell to the welcoming blue doors, these charming cookies will definitely ease any first-day-of-school jitters. Pack a few of these treats in your child's lunchbox and he or she will be the most popular student in the cafeteria! Even better, ask your child to help you with the decorating. **Makes about 24.**

Getting Started

Bake cookies: Roll out dough and cut cookies with the church cookie cutter. Bake according to recipe directions. Let cool completely before decorating.

Tint and thin icing: Place 1¼ cups (300 mL) icing in a bowl and tint it blue. Transfer ¼ cup (60 mL) of the blue icing to another bowl, cover tightly and set aside. Place 1 cup (250 mL) icing in each of two bowls; tint one portion black and one yellow. Transfer black icing to a pastry bag fitted with a #2 tip. Place ½ cup (125 mL) icing in a bowl and tint it green; cover tightly and set aside. Tint remaining icing red. Thin red, yellow and remaining 1 cup (250 mL) blue icing to two-step icing consistency (page 24) and transfer to squeeze bottles.

1

Using black icing, pipe borders on the upper and lower roofs of each schoolhouse. ∎ Pipe outlines for double front doors and for 2 windows in the schoolhouse, including panes (see tip).

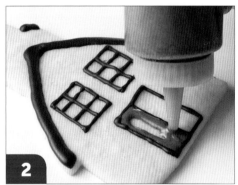

2

Using the squeeze bottle of blue icing, flood the front doors.

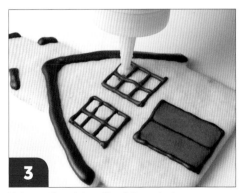

3

Using yellow icing, flood the window panes.

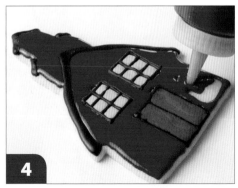

4

Using red icing, outline and flood the remaining sections of each schoolhouse. ∎ Let icing set for at least 6 hours or overnight.

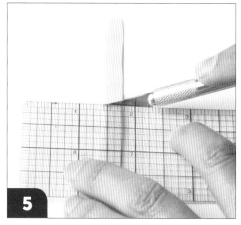

5

Meanwhile, on a work surface lightly dusted with cornstarch, roll out fondant to 1/16 inch (2 mm) thick. ■ With the ruler as a guide, use the X-acto knife to cut strips about 1/2 inch (1 cm) wide and 1 1/2 inches (4 cm) long. ■ Make 1 strip per cookie. ■ Place strips on a cookie sheet and let dry for at least 4 hours or overnight.

7

Using yellow icing, pipe knobs on the doors and a bell at the top of each schoolhouse. ■ Transfer reserved blue icing to a pastry bag fitted with a #1 tip. ■ Pipe a clapper in each bell. ■ Using black icing, pipe a window near the top of each door.

6

Transfer green icing to a pastry bag fitted with a #2 tip. ■ Pipe grass at the bottom of each schoolhouse, on either side of the doors.

8

Dab the back of each fondant strip with icing and attach a strip to each schoolhouse, centering it just above the windows. ■ Use blue icing to pipe "SCHOOL" on each strip. ■ Let cookies dry for at least 6 hours before serving.

Tips

If you don't have a church cookie cutter, a house-shaped cutter will work. Simply pipe the bell at the top of the roof.

When you're piping the doors and windows in step 1, a ruler and an X-acto knife will help you create a template for piping straight, even lines.

After rolling out fondant, let it rest for about 15 minutes (but not much longer!) before cutting out shapes. This allows it to harden a bit, making for cleaner cuts.

Variation

If you don't have fondant, pipe a strip for the "SCHOOL" sign directly onto the house using beige icing in a pastry bag fitted with a #2 round decorating tip.

Chalkboard

These miniature chalkboards even include an eraser, chalk and an apple for the teacher! **Makes about 30.**

What You Need

- 1 recipe cookie dough (pages 36–46)
- Rectangle cookie cutter
- 1 recipe Classic Royal Icing (page 47)
- Green gel paste
- Brown gel paste
- Black gel paste
- 2 squeeze bottles
- White fondant
- Black fondant
- Red fondant
- Brown fondant
- 2 disposable pastry bags
- 2 couplers
- 2 #2 round decorating tips

Techniques Used

- Tinting icing (page 22)
- Filling a squeeze bottle (page 24)
- Piping (page 27)
- Flooding (page 28)
- Working with fondant (page 30)
- Filling a pastry bag (page 24)

Getting Started

Bake cookies: Roll out dough and cut cookies with the rectangle cookie cutter. Bake according to recipe directions. Let cool completely before decorating.

Tint and thin icing: Place 1 cup (250 mL) icing in a bowl and leave it white. Place ¼ cup (60 mL) icing in a bowl and tint it green. Cover both bowls tightly and set aside. Place 1½ cups (375 mL) icing in a bowl and tint it brown. Tint remaining icing black. Thin brown and black icing to two-step icing consistency (page 24) and transfer to squeeze bottles.

1

Using black icing, outline and flood rectangles. ■ Let icing set for at least 6 hours or overnight.

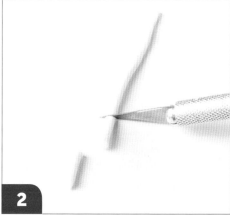

2

Meanwhile, roll white fondant into a thin rope about ⅛ inch (3 mm) in diameter. ■ Cut a piece about ½ inch (1 cm) long, to serve as a piece of chalk. ■ Make 1 piece per cookie.

3

Mold 2 tsp (10 mL) black fondant into a thick rectangle about ¼ inch (5 mm) wide and ¾ inch (2 cm) long, to serve as an eraser. ■ Make 1 eraser per cookie.

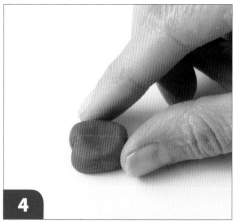

4

Mold 2 tsp (10 mL) red fondant into an apple shape. ■ Flatten the back so the apple will lie flat.

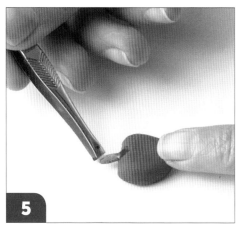

5

Mold a tiny bit of brown fondant into a stem for the apple. ■ Dab the end of the stem with water and press it lightly against the top of the apple to affix. ■ Make 1 apple per cookie. ■ Place all fondant pieces on a cookie sheet and let dry for at least 4 hours or overnight.

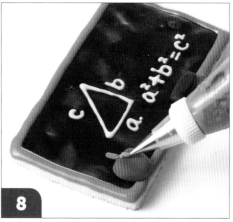

6

Transfer white and green icing to pastry bags fitted with #2 tips. ■ Using white icing, pipe a math formula on each blackboard.

7

Working with one cookie at a time, use brown icing to pipe and fill a thick border around the edge of a blackboard.

8

While the brown icing is still wet, place an apple, a piece of chalk and an eraser on the bottom border. ■ Use green icing to pipe a small leaf on the apple. ■ Repeat steps 7 and 8 for all cookies. ■ Let cookies dry for at least 6 hours before serving.

Tips

Be sure to wear disposable latex gloves when coloring fondant so the gel paste does not stain your hands.

Keep any fondant you are not presently working with tightly wrapped in plastic wrap, as it can quickly dry out, rendering it unusable.

Variation

Put your own spin on what you write on the board. If the cookies are a gift for a kindergarten teacher, decorate them with "ABCs" or pipe the teacher's name.

Colored Crayons

This fun design would make a perfect gift for an art teacher, or even a creative art class project! **Makes about 40.**

What You Need

- 1 recipe cookie dough (pages 36–46)
- Crayon cookie cutter
- 1 recipe Classic Royal Icing (page 47)
- Red gel paste
- Yellow gel paste
- Blue gel paste
- Purple gel paste
- Teal or green gel paste
- Black gel paste
- 5 squeeze bottles
- Cornstarch
- Small rolling pin
- Black fondant
- Ruler
- X-acto knife
- Oval template (page 251)
- 7 disposable pastry bags
- 7 couplers
- 6 #1 round decorating tips
- #2 round decorating tip

Techniques Used

- Tinting icing (page 22)
- Filling a squeeze bottle (page 24)
- Piping (page 27)
- Flooding (page 28)
- Working with fondant (page 30)
- Working with templates (page 32)
- Filling a pastry bag (page 24)

Getting Started

Bake cookies: Roll out dough and cut cookies with the crayon cookie cutter. Bake according to recipe directions. Let cool completely before decorating.

Tint and thin icing: Place $\frac{1}{3}$ cup (75 mL) icing in each of seven bowls; tint one portion red, one yellow, one blue, one purple, one teal and one black, and leave one white. Cover tightly and set aside. Divide remaining icing evenly among five bowls; tint one portion red, one yellow, one blue, one purple and one teal. Thin these icings to two-step icing consistency (page 24) and transfer to squeeze bottles.

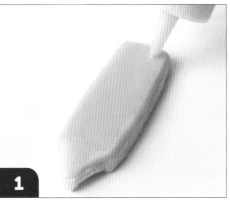

1 Using the squeeze bottles, outline and flood an even number of red, yellow, blue, purple and teal crayons. ■ Let icing set for at least 6 hours or overnight.

2 Meanwhile, on a work surface lightly dusted with cornstarch, roll out fondant to $\frac{1}{16}$ inch (2 mm) thick. ■ Using the X-acto knife and oval template, cut out ovals about 1 inch (2.5 cm) long and $\frac{1}{2}$ inch (1 cm) wide. ■ Make 1 oval per cookie.

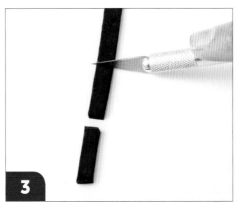

3 With the ruler as a guide, use the X-acto knife to cut strips about $\frac{1}{4}$ inch (5 mm) wide and long enough to span the width of a crayon. ■ Make 2 strips per cookie. ■ Place ovals and strips on a cookie sheet and let dry for at least 4 hours or overnight.

4 Dab the back of each oval with icing and affix an oval in the center of each crayon.

5

Dab the back of each fondant strip with icing and affix 2 strips to each crayon, on either side of the oval.

6

Transfer reserved red, yellow, blue, purple, teal and black icing to pastry bags fitted with #1 tips. ■ Pipe the name of the crayon color (e.g., "Yellow") on each oval, using the corresponding icing.

7

Using the same color, pipe a squiggly line on each strip.

8

Transfer white icing to a pastry bag fitted with a #2 tip. ■ Pipe 2 small accent lines on the point of each crayon as shown. ■ Use black icing to draw a narrow border across the crayon at the outer end of each strip. ■ Let cookies dry for at least 4 hours before serving.

Tips

If you decide to make your crayons in just one color, you will only need 1 squeeze bottle, 3 pastry bags and 1 color of gel paste (in addition to black).

An X-acto knife is a good investment if you plan to work with fondant often. Its blade is sharper than a paring knife, allowing for a more "x-act" cut.

Variation

Instead of printing the names of the colors on the fondant ovals, print the names of party guests and use the crayons as place cards.

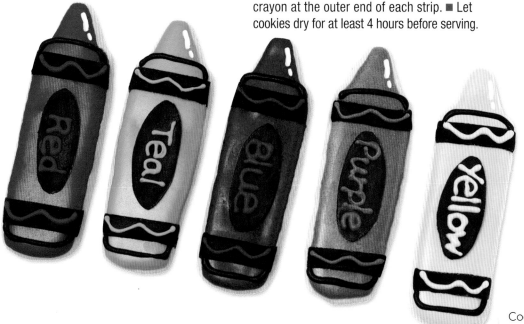

Textbook

There are countless ways to decorate book cookies. This version would make a creative gift for a favorite science teacher. See the variations for several other ideas. **Makes about 36.**

What You Need

- 1 recipe cookie dough (pages 36–46)
- Book cookie cutter
- 1 recipe Classic Royal Icing (page 47)
- Red gel paste
- Blue gel paste
- Black gel paste
- Orange gel paste
- 2 squeeze bottles
- Cornstarch
- Small rolling pin
- Yellow fondant
- Small butterfly cutter
- 4 disposable pastry bags
- 4 couplers
- 3 #1 round decorating tips
- #2 round decorating tip

Techniques Used

- Tinting icing (page 22)
- Filling a squeeze bottle (page 24)
- Piping (page 27)
- Flooding (page 28)
- Working with fondant (page 30)
- Filling a pastry bag (page 24)

Getting Started

Bake cookies: Roll out dough and cut cookies with the book cookie cutter. Bake according to recipe directions. Let cool completely before decorating.

Tint and thin icing: Place ¾ cup (175 mL) icing in each of two bowls; tint one portion red and one blue. Place ½ cup (125 mL) icing in each of two bowls; tint one portion black and one orange. Cover all bowls tightly and set aside. Place ¾ cup (175 mL) icing in a bowl and leave it white. Tint remaining icing red. Thin white and red icing to two-step icing consistency (page 24) and transfer to squeeze bottles.

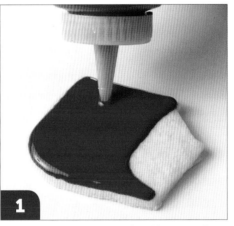

Using the squeeze bottle of red icing, outline and flood a book shape on each cookie, leaving space for white pages (see tip).

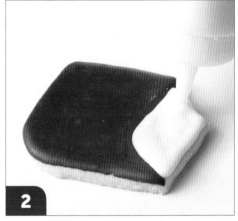

Using white icing, outline and flood the pages section of each book. ■ Let icing set for at least 6 hours or overnight.

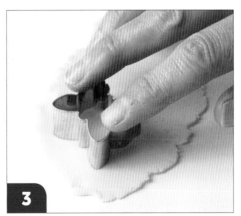

Meanwhile, on a work surface lightly dusted with cornstarch, roll out fondant to ¹⁄₁₆ inch (2 mm) thick. ■ Using the butterfly cutter, cut out 1 butterfly per cookie. ■ Place butterflies on a cookie sheet and let dry for at least 4 hours or overnight.

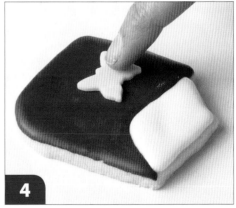

Dab each fondant butterfly with icing and affix a butterfly to the center of each book cover.

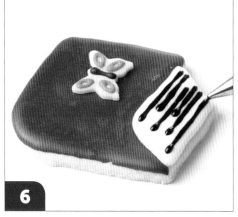

5

Transfer blue, black and orange icing to pastry bags fitted with #1 tips. ■ Use black icing to pipe a body on each butterfly. ■ Use orange icing to pipe a design on the butterfly's wings.

6

Using black icing, pipe lines across the white section of each book, to represent pages.

7

Using blue icing, pipe "SCIENCE" along each book's spine and across the top of each book cover.

8

Transfer reserved red icing to a pastry bag fitted with a #2 tip. ■ Pipe a border around the edges of each book. ■ Let cookies dry for at least 4 hours before serving.

Tip

I keep a ruler on hand when decorating cookies so that I can trace perfectly straight lines to guide my piping. Use an X-acto knife or edible marker to trace the lines, then pipe over them.

Variations

Create a cover design for the books based on your child's favorite subject.

There are many occasions for which the book cutter can be used. Pipe a specific book title for your book club party, create mini cookbooks for a budding chef, replicate a book cover for a first-time author, make a baby book to accompany other shower-themed cookies (pages 208–212) or make mini ledger cookies for an accountant (come tax season, they will be very grateful!).

Milk Carton

What You Need

- 1 recipe cookie dough (pages 36–46)
- Milk carton cookie cutter
- 1 recipe Classic Royal Icing (page 47)
- Blue gel paste
- Red gel paste
- 2 squeeze bottles
- 2-inch (5 cm) round cutter
- X-acto knife
- Red fondant
- White fondant
- Disposable pastry bag
- Coupler
- #1 round decorating tip

Techniques Used

- Tinting icing (page 22)
- Filling a squeeze bottle (page 24)
- Using an X-acto knife (page 31)
- Piping (page 27)
- Flooding (page 28)
- Working with fondant (page 30)
- Filling a pastry bag (page 24)

When I was in elementary school, a carton of milk cost about 25 cents. It sure would have been nice if that 25 cents also bought us one of these cookies! **Makes about 30.**

Getting Started

Bake cookies: Roll out dough and cut cookies with the milk carton cookie cutter. Bake according to recipe directions. Let cool completely before decorating.

Tint and thin icing: Place 1 cup (250 mL) icing in a bowl and tint it blue. Cover tightly and set aside. Divide remaining icing evenly between two bowls; tint one portion red and leave one white. Thin red and white icing to two-step icing consistency (page 24) and transfer to squeeze bottles.

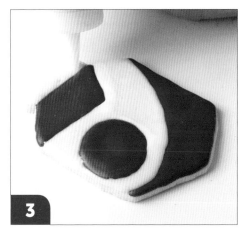

1 Place the round cutter in the center of the front section of each milk carton and lightly trace around it with the X-acto knife. ■ Use red icing to outline and flood each circle.

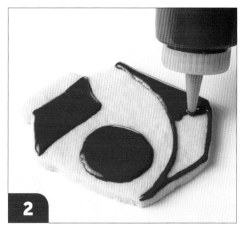

2 Using red icing, outline and flood the top rectangular section and the bottom of each carton as shown.

3 Using white icing, outline and flood the remaining sections of each carton. ■ Let icing set for at least 6 hours or overnight.

4 Meanwhile, roll red and white fondant into long ropes about $\frac{1}{8}$ inch (3 mm) in diameter. ■ Place ropes side by side and press them gently together. ■ Holding the ropes at the top and bottom, twist them until you have what resembles a spiral straw.

5

Cut spiraled ropes into 1½-inch (4 cm) long pieces. ■ Flatten one end of each piece so it will lie flat. ■ Make 1 straw per cookie. ■ Place straws on a cookie sheet and let dry for at least 4 hours or overnight.

6

Transfer blue icing to a pastry bag fitted with a #1 tip. ■ Pipe "MILK" in the top rectangular section, "GRADE A" in the circle on the front and "Farm Fresh!" on the bottom side of each carton.

7

Use red icing to pipe borders around the red sections of each carton. ■ Use white icing to pipe borders around the white sections of each carton.

8

Dab the front of the flat part of each straw with icing and affix a straw to the back of each cookie so that it appears to be coming out of the milk carton. ■ Let cookies dry for at least 6 hours before serving.

Tips

If you don't have an X-acto knife, you can use an edible marker to trace the outlines in step 1.

Sometimes air bubbles are created when you flood a cookie with icing. If this happens, use the tip of a toothpick to pop the bubbles.

Variations

Make chocolate milk cartons by replacing the red icing with brown. Pipe "CHOCOLATE MILK" instead of "MILK."

Personalize the cookies for the kids in your child's class by piping a name on each carton.

School Bus

What You Need

- 1 recipe cookie dough (pages 36–46)
- Bus cookie cutter
- 1 recipe Classic Royal Icing (page 47)
- Black gel paste
- Red gel paste
- Yellow gel paste
- 2 squeeze bottles
- Cornstarch
- Small rolling pin
- Black fondant
- Red fondant
- 1-inch (2.5 cm) round cutter
- X-acto knife
- Stop sign template (page 251)
- 3 disposable pastry bags
- 3 couplers
- 2 #2 round decorating tips
- #1 round decorating tip

Techniques Used

- Tinting icing (page 22)
- Filling a squeeze bottle (page 24)
- Piping (page 27)
- Flooding (page 28)
- Working with fondant (page 30)
- Working with templates (page 32)
- Filling a pastry bag (page 24)

Give some of these cookies to your favorite school bus driver as a thank you. **Makes about 30.**

Getting Started

Bake cookies: Roll out dough and cut cookies with the school bus cookie cutter. Bake according to recipe directions. Let cool completely before decorating.

Tint and thin icing: Place 1 cup (250 mL) icing in a bowl and tint it black. Place ½ cup (125 mL) icing in a bowl and tint it red. Place ¼ cup (60 mL) icing in a bowl and leave it white. Cover all bowls tightly and set aside. Place 1½ cups (375 mL) icing in a bowl and leave it white. Tint remaining icing yellow. Thin both icings to two-step icing consistency (page 24) and transfer to squeeze bottles.

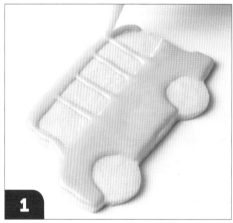

1 Using yellow icing, outline and flood each bus as shown, leaving spaces for the windows and wheels.

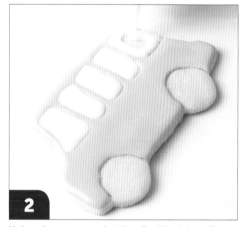

2 Using the squeeze bottle of white icing, flood the windows. ■ Let icing set for at least 6 hours or overnight.

3 Meanwhile, on a work surface lightly dusted with cornstarch, roll out black fondant to ¹⁄₁₆ inch (2 mm) thick. ■ Using the round cutter, cut out 2 black circles for each cookie.

4 Dust work surface with cornstarch and roll out red fondant to ¹⁄₁₆ inch (2 mm) thick. ■ Using the X-acto knife and stop sign template, cut out 1 hexagon per cookie. ■ Place circles and hexagons on a cookie sheet and let dry for at least 4 hours or overnight.

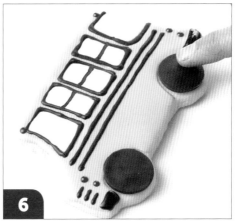

5

Transfer red and black icing to pastry bags fitted with #2 tips. ■ Pipe details including lights, window borders, siding and bumpers, as shown.

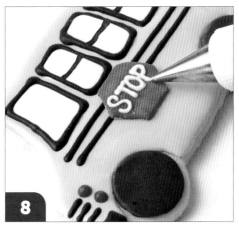

6

Dab each fondant circle with icing and affix 2 circles to each bus, one on each wheel.

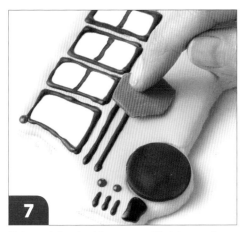

7

Dab each fondant hexagon with icing and affix a hexagon to the side of each bus, just below a window near the front of the bus.

8

Transfer reserved white icing to a pastry bag fitted with a #1 tip. ■ Pipe "STOP" on each hexagon. ■ Let cookies dry for at least 4 hours before serving.

Tips

I keep a ruler on hand when decorating cookies so that I can trace perfectly straight lines to guide my piping. Use an X-acto knife or edible marker to trace the lines, then pipe over them.

Keep any fondant you are not presently working with tightly wrapped in plastic wrap, as it can quickly dry out, rendering it unusable.

Variation

Instead of using fondant, pipe the wheels with black icing and the "STOP" sign with red icing. Let the red icing dry completely before adding the lettering.

A-B-C Cookie Pops

I can't think of a more fun way to teach your kids their ABCs or simple spelling than with cookies on a stick! But first, have them help you with the decorating. **Makes 30.**

What You Need

- 1 recipe cookie dough (pages 36–46)
- A, B and C cookie cutters
- 30 cookie pop sticks
- 1 recipe Classic Royal Icing (page 47)
- Yellow gel paste
- Red gel paste
- Blue gel paste
- 3 squeeze bottles

Techniques Used

- Tinting icing (page 22)
- Filling a squeeze bottle (page 24)
- Piping (page 27)
- Flooding (page 28)

Tip

Cookie pop sticks can be found in the baking aisle of craft stores and some well-stocked grocery stores.

Variations

Use numbers to teach children simple addition or multiplication!

Top a birthday cake with letter cookie pops that spell out a child's name.

Getting Started

Bake cookies: Roll out dough and cut cookies with the letter cookie cutters so that you have an even number of A, B and C cookies. Push a cookie pop stick into each letter, pressing it through the dough to about halfway up the height of the cookie. Bake according to recipe directions. Let cool completely before decorating.

Tint and thin icing: Divide icing evenly among three bowls; tint one portion yellow, one red and one blue. Thin all icings to two-step icing consistency (page 24) and transfer to squeeze bottles.

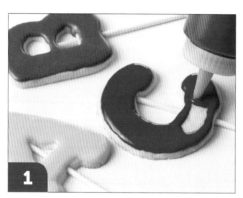

1

Using yellow icing, outline and flood all A cookies. ■ Using blue icing, outline and flood all B cookies. ■ Using red icing, outline and flood all C cookies. ■ Let icing set for at least 6 hours or overnight.

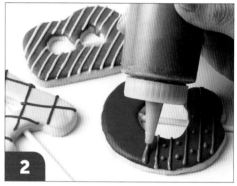

2

Using red icing, pipe a crisscross pattern on each A, spacing the lines evenly in both directions. ■ Using yellow icing, pipe diagonal lines across each B, spacing the lines evenly. ■ Using blue icing, pipe horizontal lines across each C, then pipe dots between each line. ■ Let cookies dry for at least 6 hours before serving.

5

Party Cookies

Designer Jeans

Buying a pair of designer jeans is never easy. Finding your ideal fit, style and color can involve trying on upwards of 20 pairs, leaving you exhausted (and hungry)! Fortunately, these stylish cookies come in a convenient "one size fits all" package — a perfect fit for everyone's palate. **Makes about 36.**

What You Need

- 1 recipe cookie dough (pages 36–46)
- Pants cookie cutter
- 1 recipe Classic Royal Icing (page 47)
- Brown gel paste
- Orange gel paste
- Blue gel paste
- Squeeze bottle
- 4 disposable pastry bags
- 4 couplers
- 2 #1 round decorating tips
- 2 #2 round decorating tips
- Tweezers
- Silver dragées

Techniques Used

- Tinting icing (page 22)
- Filling a squeeze bottle (page 24)
- Piping (page 27)
- Flooding (page 28)
- Filling a pastry bag (page 24)
- Adding embellishments (page 31)

Getting Started

Bake cookies: Roll out dough and cut cookies with the pants cookie cutter. Bake according to recipe directions. Let cool completely before decorating.

Tint and thin icing: Place ¾ cup (175 mL) icing in each of two bowls; tint one portion brown and leave one white. Place ½ cup (125 mL) icing in each of two bowls; tint one portion orange and one blue. Cover all bowls tightly and set aside. Tint remaining icing blue, thin to two-step icing consistency (page 24) and transfer to a squeeze bottle.

1 Using the squeeze bottle of blue icing, outline jeans.

2 Flood jeans with blue icing. ■ Let icing set for at least 6 hours or overnight.

3 Transfer white and reserved blue icing to pastry bags fitted with #1 tips. ■ Use white icing to pipe stitching around jeans as shown.

4 Add white stitching along the zipper line and to mark out the outer edge of the front pockets.

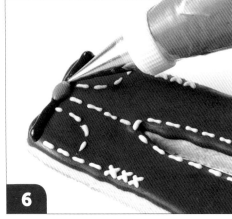

5

Transfer brown and orange icing to pastry bags fitted with #2 tips. ■ Use brown icing to pipe a belt across the top of each cookie.

6

Using orange icing, pipe a round buckle in the center of each belt.

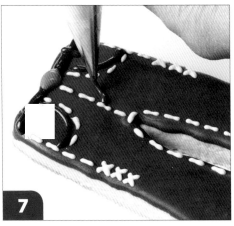

7

Working with one cookie at a time, use the pastry bag of blue icing to pipe pocket, belt loop and zipper flap details on jeans as shown.

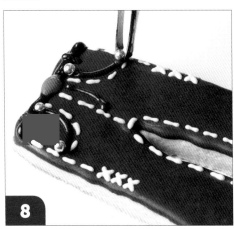

8

While the blue icing is still wet, use tweezers to apply silver dragées to jeans on both ends of pockets. ■ Repeat steps 7 and 8 for all cookies. ■ Let cookies dry for at least 4 hours before serving.

Girls' Night Out

Tips

If all the blue icing does not fit in your squeeze bottle, cover the remaining icing tightly and refill the bottle as needed.

Adding embellishments, such as the silver dragées, is easier if you use a pair of tweezers. Buy an extra pair and keep them handy with your decorating supplies.

Variation

Decorate the jeans to show the back instead of the front, piping square back pockets with a decorative design.

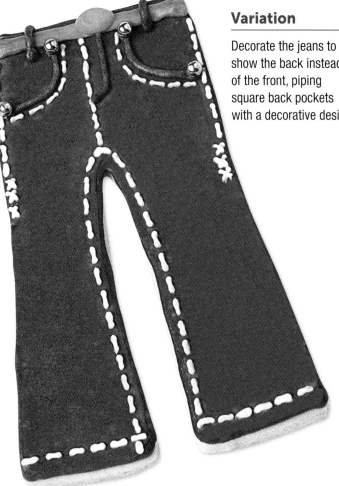

Little Black Dress

Every woman needs the perfect little black dress in her closet, which she can turn into a dozen different outfits depending on her accessories. Accented with a fondant leopard-print belt and elegant pearls, this chic "LBD" cookie will be a hit at any girlfriends' get-together! **Makes about 30.**

What You Need

- 1 recipe cookie dough (pages 36–46)
- Dress cookie cutter
- 1 recipe Classic Royal Icing (page 47)
- Brown gel paste
- Black gel paste
- Squeeze bottle
- Cornstarch
- Small rolling pin
- Light brown fondant
- Ruler
- X-acto knife
- 2 disposable pastry bags
- 2 couplers
- 2 #1 round decorating tips
- Tweezers
- White edible pearls

Techniques Used

- Tinting icing (page 22)
- Filling a squeeze bottle (page 24)
- Piping (page 27)
- Flooding (page 28)
- Working with fondant (page 30)
- Filling a pastry bag (page 24)
- Adding embellishments

Getting Started

Bake cookies: Roll out dough and cut cookies with the dress cookie cutter. Bake according to recipe directions. Let cool completely before decorating.

Tint and thin icing: Place 1/2 cup (125 mL) icing in each of two bowls; tint one portion light brown and one black. Cover tightly and set aside. Tint remaining icing black, thin to two-step icing consistency (page 24) and transfer to a squeeze bottle.

1

Using the squeeze bottle of black icing, outline dresses.

2

Flood dresses with black icing. ■ Let icing set for at least 6 hours or overnight.

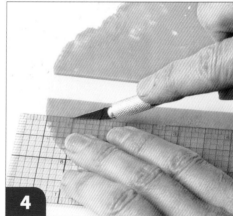

3

Meanwhile, on a work surface lightly dusted with cornstarch, roll out brown fondant to 1/16 inch (2 mm) thick.

4

With the ruler as a guide, use the X-acto knife to cut fondant strips about 1/2 inch (1 cm) wide and long enough to fit the waistline of each dress. ■ Make 1 strip per cookie. ■ Place strips on a cookie sheet and let dry for at least 4 hours or overnight.

5 Transfer brown and reserved black icing to pastry bags fitted with #1 tips. ■ Working with one cookie at a time, use black icing to pipe a necklace shape around the collar of the dress.

6 While the black icing is still wet, use tweezers to place edible pearls on icing, creating a pearl necklace. ■ Repeat steps 5 and 6 for all cookies.

7 Dab the back of each fondant strip with icing and affix a strip to the waistline of each dress.

8 Use black and brown icing to pipe a leopard print onto belts, using the picture on page 27 as a guide. ■ Let cookies dry for at least 3 hours before serving.

Tips

If all the black icing does not fit in your squeeze bottle, cover the remaining icing tightly and refill the bottle as needed.

After rolling out fondant, let it rest for about 15 minutes (but not much longer!) before cutting out shapes. This allows it to harden a bit, making for cleaner cuts.

The ruler will help you cut straight lines when you're cutting the fondant belts.

If you don't have an X-acto knife, a sharp paring knife will work fine.

Instead of using edible pearls, you can pipe a pearl necklace onto each dress using white icing in a pastry bag fitted with a #1 tip.

Leopard-Print Purse

What You Need

- 1 recipe cookie dough (pages 36–46)
- Purse cookie cutter
- 1 recipe Classic Royal Icing (page 47)
- Brown gel paste
- Black gel paste
- Squeeze bottle
- 2 disposable pastry bags
- 2 couplers
- #2 round decorating tip
- Gold disco dust
- #1 round decorating tip

Techniques Used

- Tinting icing (page 22)
- Filling a squeeze bottle (page 24)
- Piping (page 27)
- Flooding (page 28)
- Filling a pastry bag (page 24)
- Adding sparkle (page 28)

This chic purse coordinates with the Little Black Dress (page 188) and the Leopard-Print Pumps (page 192) to make a complete stylish ensemble. Make them as a set for your next girls' get-together, or as birthday party favors for a budding fashionista! **Makes about 36.**

Getting Started

Bake cookies: Roll out dough and cut cookies with the purse cookie cutter. Bake according to recipe directions. Let cool completely before decorating.

Tint and thin icing: Place 1¼ cups (300 mL) icing in a bowl and tint it dark brown. Place ¾ cup (175 mL) icing in a bowl and tint it black. Cover both bowls tightly and set aside. Tint remaining icing light brown, thin to two-step icing consistency (page 24) and transfer to a squeeze bottle.

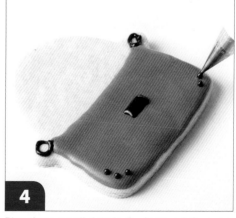

1

Using light brown icing, outline and flood the bag portion of each purse. ■ Let icing set for at least 6 hours or overnight.

2

Transfer dark brown icing to a pastry bag fitted with a #2 tip. ■ Working with one cookie at a time, pipe a small ring at the top left corner and top right corner of the bag.

3

Pipe a fastener in the center of the purse.

4

Pipe three small dots in the bottom left corner and three small dots in the bottom right corner of the purse.

5

While the dark brown icing is still wet, sprinkle rings, fastener and dots with gold disco dust, shaking off excess. ■ Repeat steps 2 to 5 for all cookies.

6

Using dark brown icing, pipe a border around the bag portion of each purse and pipe a slightly curved line that runs horizontally across the center of the purse, passing just underneath the fastener, to represent the flap.

7

Pipe a purse strap running from the top of one "metal" ring to the top of the other.

8

Transfer black icing to a pastry bag fitted with a #1 tip. ■ Use black and dark brown icing to pipe a leopard print onto purses, using the picture on page 27 as a guide. ■ Let cookies dry for at least 6 hours before serving.

Tips

If all the light brown icing does not fit in your squeeze bottle, cover the remaining icing tightly and refill the bottle as needed.

Don't be alarmed if excess disco dust sticks to the cookie even after you shake it. Wait until the icing dries completely, then gently brush off the unwanted dust with a small food-safe paintbrush or a cotton swab.

Don't worry if your version of leopard print doesn't look exactly like mine. You might want to practice the print on parchment paper before applying it to the cookies.

Leopard-Print Pumps

The red soles on these sassy designer pumps add an unexpected pop of color. Match them with the Little Black Dress (page 188) and Leopard-Print Purse (page 190) for a complete set! **Makes about 28.**

What You Need

- 1 recipe cookie dough (pages 36–46)
- High heel cookie cutter
- 1 recipe Classic Royal Icing (page 47)
- Ivory gel paste
- Black gel paste
- Red gel paste
- Brown gel paste
- 3 disposable pastry bags
- 3 couplers
- 2 #1 round decorating tips
- 2 #2 round decorating tips
- 2 squeeze bottles

Techniques Used

- Tinting icing (page 22)
- Filling a pastry bag (page 24)
- Filling a squeeze bottle (page 24)
- Piping (page 27)
- Flooding (page 28)

Variation

Have fun customizing the design of these shoes to match your favorite pair, whether they are covered in glittery red sequins or are sleek black patent leather.

Getting Started

Bake cookies: Roll out dough and cut cookies with the high heel cookie cutter. Bake according to recipe directions. Let cool completely before decorating.

Tint and thin icing: Place 1 cup (250 mL) icing in each of two bowls; tint one portion ivory and one black. Place ¾ cup (175 mL) icing in each of two bowls; tint one portion red and one dark brown. Transfer dark brown icing to a pastry bag fitted with a #1 tip. Transfer black and red icing to pastry bags fitted with #2 tips. Tint remaining icing light brown. Thin ivory and light brown icing to two-step icing consistency (page 24) and transfer to squeeze bottles.

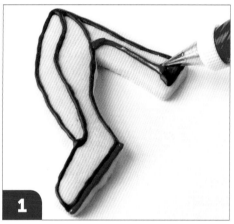

1 Using black icing, outline shoes as shown, leaving space at the ball of the foot and the interior of the heel. ■ Pipe red icing at ball of foot and in interior of heel.

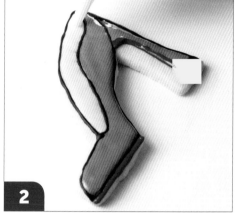

2 Flood the exterior of each shoe and heel with light brown icing and the interior of each shoe with ivory icing. ■ Let icing set for at least 6 hours or overnight.

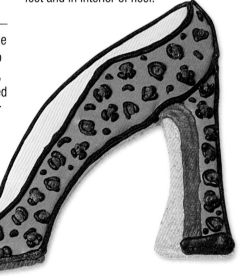

3 Change tip on black icing to a #1 tip. ■ Use black and dark brown icing to pipe a leopard print onto exterior of each shoe and heel, using the picture on page 27 as a guide. ■ Let cookies dry for at least 6 hours before serving.

Bride

Whether she's a bride-to-be at her shower or a newlywed at her wedding reception, she's guaranteed to absolutely adore these sweet designs. You could even pair this cookie with the Groom (page 196) and make a unique custom topper for the wedding cake! **Makes about 30.**

Getting Started

Bake cookies: Roll out dough and cut cookies with the gingerbread girl cookie cutter. Bake according to recipe directions. Let cool completely before decorating.

Tint and thin icing: Place 1 cup (250 mL) icing in a bowl and tint it brown. Place ¾ cup (175 mL) icing in a bowl and tint it green. Place ½ cup (125 mL) icing in each of two bowls; tint one portion black and one red. Cover all bowls tightly and set aside. Thin remaining white icing to two-step icing consistency (page 24) and transfer to a squeeze bottle.

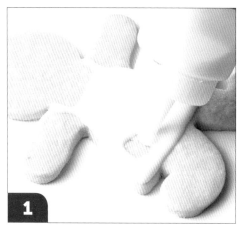

Using white icing, outline and flood each bride's dress as shown, including straps.

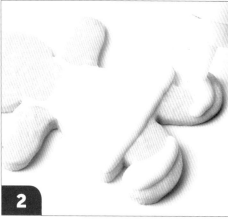

Outline and flood each bride's shoes. ■ Let icing set for at least 6 hours or overnight.

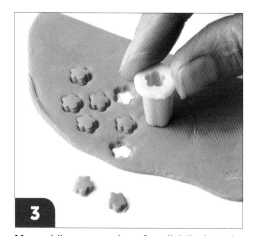

Meanwhile, on a work surface lightly dusted with cornstarch, roll out pink fondant to ⅛ inch (3 mm) thick. ■ Using the flower cutter, cut out 7 to 8 flowers per cookie. ■ Place flowers on a cookie sheet and let dry for at least 4 hours or overnight.

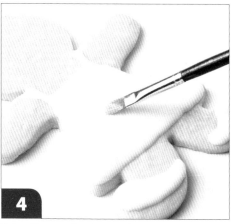

Using the small paintbrush, brush each dress lightly with luster dust.

What You Need

- 1 recipe cookie dough (pages 36–46)
- Gingerbread girl cookie cutter
- 1 recipe Classic Royal Icing (page 47)
- Brown gel paste
- Green gel paste
- Black gel paste
- Red gel paste
- Squeeze bottle
- Cornstarch
- Small rolling pin
- Pink fondant
- Small flower cutter
- Small food-safe paintbrush
- White luster dust
- White sanding sugar
- 4 disposable pastry bags
- 4 couplers
- #2 round decorating tip
- 3 #1 round decorating tips
- Brown fondant
- Tweezers
- White edible pearls

Techniques Used

- Tinting icing (page 22)
- Filling a squeeze bottle (page 24)
- Piping (page 27)
- Flooding (page 28)
- Working with fondant (page 30)
- Adding sparkle (page 28)
- Filling a pastry bag (page 24)
- Adding embellishments (page 31)

continued… Party Cookies **193**

Tips

Match the color of the cookie bride's hair to the color of the real bride's hair. If the bride has blond or red hair, you will need an extra pastry bag, as brown and black are used for all cookies regardless of hair color. Make red or auburn hair by mixing brown and red gels.

Don't be alarmed if excess sanding sugar sticks to the cookie even after you shake it. Wait until the icing dries completely, then gently brush off the unwanted sugar with a small food-safe paintbrush or a cotton swab.

Be sure to wear disposable latex gloves when coloring fondant so the gel paste does not stain your hands.

Keep any fondant you are not presently working with tightly wrapped in plastic wrap, as it can quickly dry out, rendering it unusable.

Adding embellishments, such as edible pearls, is easier if you use a pair of tweezers. Buy an extra pair and keep them handy with your decorating supplies.

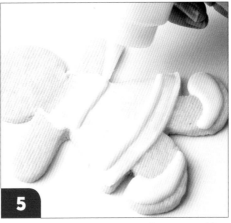

5

Working with one cookie at a time, use white icing to pipe two border lines across the bottom of each dress and one line across the waist.

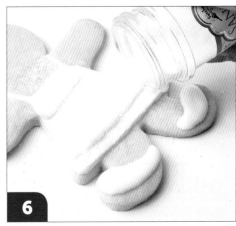

6

While the white icing is still wet, sprinkle the lines with sanding sugar, shaking off excess. ■ Repeat steps 5 and 6 for all cookies.

7

Transfer brown icing to a pastry bag fitted with a #2 tip. ■ Pipe each bride's hair, first outlining the shape, then piping lines to mimic the texture of hair.

8

Create each bride's bun by molding a piece of brown fondant into the desired shape. ■ Flatten the back of the bun so it will lie flat.

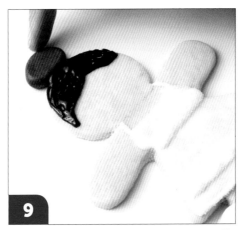

9

Dab the bottom of the bun with icing and affix it to the top of the bride's head.

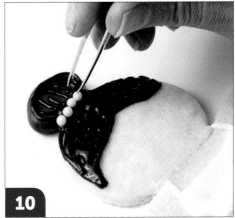

10

Using brown icing, pipe an outline around the bun, then pipe lines inside the bun to mimic the texture of hair. ■ Using tweezers and a dab of icing on the back of each pearl, place a row of edible pearls along the seam where the bun meets the head.

11

Place edible pearls along the neckline to create a necklace, and place one pearl just below the hairline on each side to create earrings.

12

Transfer black, red and green icing to pastry bags fitted with #1 tips. ■ Pipe each bride's eyes and eyebrows with black icing, nose with brown icing and smile with red icing.

Variations

Instead of making fondant flowers, pipe flowers freehand using pink icing and a pastry bag fitted with a #1 tip.

Surprise your wedding party with custom bridesmaid cookies! Color the dresses to match the bridesmaid dresses and customize their hair colors too.

13

Place fondant flowers in a bunch on one hand, affixing them with dabs of icing. ■ Pipe a white dot in the center of each flower.

14

Using green icing, pipe stems coming from each flower. ■ Carefully transfer cookies to a flat surface (so that the fondant buns stay attached to the brides' heads) and let dry for at least 8 hours or overnight.

Groom

This is one smartly dressed groom, complete with a red boutonniere and freshly shined shoes! Pair these husbands-to-be with their blushing Brides (page 193) and package them as memorable favors (page 33) for your lucky wedding guests! **Makes about 30.**

What You Need

- 1 recipe cookie dough (pages 36–46)
- Gingerbread man cookie cutter
- 1 recipe Classic Royal Icing (page 47)
- Brown gel paste
- Black gel paste
- Red gel paste
- Pink gel paste
- 2 squeeze bottles
- Small food-safe paintbrush
- Black or silver luster dust
- 4 disposable pastry bags
- 4 couplers
- #2 round decorating tip
- 3 #1 round decorating tips

Techniques Used

- Tinting icing (page 22)
- Filling a squeeze bottle (page 24)
- Piping (page 27)
- Flooding (page 28)
- Adding sparkle (page 28)
- Filling a pastry bag (page 24)

Getting Started

Bake cookies: Roll out dough and cut cookies with the gingerbread man cookie cutter. Bake according to recipe directions. Let cool completely before decorating.

Tint and thin icing: Place 1 cup (250 mL) icing in a bowl and tint it brown. Place $\frac{3}{4}$ cup (175 mL) icing in a bowl and tint it black. Place $\frac{1}{4}$ cup (60 mL) icing in each of two bowls; tint one portion red and one pink. Cover all bowls tightly and set aside. Place 1 cup (250 mL) icing in a bowl and leave it white. Tint remaining icing black. Thin both icings to two-step icing consistency (page 24) and transfer to squeeze bottles.

1 Using the squeeze bottle of black icing, outline and flood each groom's tuxedo jacket and pants as shown, leaving space for a white shirt and white cuffs.

2 Outline and flood each groom's shoes.

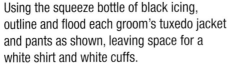

3 Using white icing, outline and flood each groom's shirt and cuffs. ■ Let icing set for at least 6 hours or overnight.

4 Using the small paintbrush, brush each groom's shoes lightly with luster dust to give them a nice shine.

5

Transfer brown icing to a pastry bag fitted with a #2 tip. ■ Pipe each groom's hair, first outlining the shape, then piping lines to mimic the texture of hair.

6

Transfer black, red and pink icing to pastry bags fitted with #1 tips. ■ Use black icing to pipe a border around the tuxedo jacket and pants. ■ Add details including cummerbund, lapels, bowtie, shirt buttons, cuff buttons and shoe laces. ■ Pipe eyes and eyebrows.

7

Pipe each groom's nose with brown icing and mouth with pink icing.

8

Using red icing, pipe a small flower on each groom's lapel. ■ Let cookies dry for at least 6 hours before serving.

Wedding Reception

Tips

Match the color of the cookie groom's hair to the color of the real groom's hair. If the groom has blond or red hair, you will need an extra pastry bag, as brown and black are used for all cookies regardless of hair color. Make red or auburn hair by mixing brown and red gels.

When applying luster dust, make sure the paintbrush you use is dry; otherwise, the dust will clump rather than covering the surface in a light, even layer.

Variation

Add a little extra pizzazz to the groom's tuxedo by decorating the pants with a white pinstripe design. Apply thin rows of vertical white stripes using a pastry bag fitted with a #1 tip.

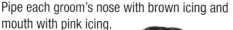

Champagne Glass

These bubbly glasses of champagne would be perfect to serve guests along with the customary toast, or wrap them in cellophane bags with a simple ribbon for a special take-home favor. You could also pair them with Bottles of Champagne (page 236) for any celebratory occasion! **Makes about 30.**

What You Need

- 1 recipe cookie dough (pages 36–46)
- Champagne glass cookie cutter
- 1 recipe Classic Royal Icing (page 47)
- Black gel paste
- Disposable pastry bag
- Coupler
- #2 round decorating tip
- 2 squeeze bottles
- Silver luster dust
- Vodka or lemon juice
- 2 small food-safe paintbrushes
- Gold luster dust
- White edible pearls
- Tweezers

Techniques Used

- Tinting icing (page 22)
- Filling a pastry bag (page 24)
- Filling a squeeze bottle (page 24)
- Piping (page 27)
- Flooding (page 28)
- Adding sparkle (page 28)
- Adding embellishments (page 31)

Getting Started

Bake cookies: Roll out dough and cut cookies with the champagne glass cookie cutter. Bake according to recipe directions. Let cool completely before decorating.

Tint and thin icing: Divide icing evenly among three bowls; tint two portions light gray (see tip) and leave one white. Transfer one portion of gray icing to a pastry bag fitted with a #2 tip. Thin white and remaining gray icing to two-step icing consistency (page 24) and transfer to squeeze bottles.

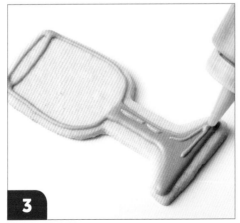

1 Using the pastry bag of gray icing, outline the bowl of each champagne glass and add a circular rim.

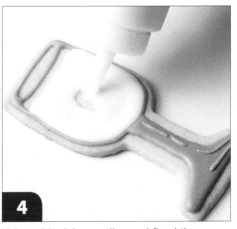

2 Using the squeeze bottle of gray icing, outline and flood the stem of each champagne glass. ■ Let dry for 10 minutes.

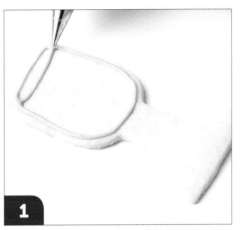

3 Using the squeeze bottle of gray icing, pipe detail lines on the stem of each glass as shown.

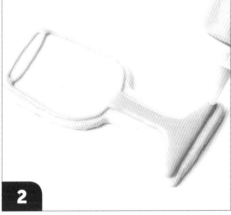

4 Using white icing, outline and flood the "champagne" section of each glass, leaving a small space at the top between the champagne and the rim. ■ Let icing set for at least 6 hours or overnight.

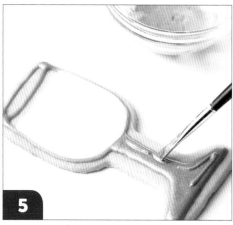

5

Place about ½ tsp (2 mL) silver luster dust in a small bowl. ■ Add a few drops of vodka and mix with a paintbrush until well blended but not runny. ■ Use the paintbrush to coat the stem, edges and rim of each champagne glass with the luster mixture.

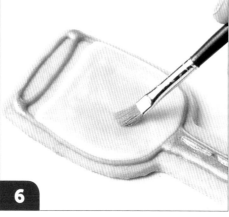

6

Using a dry paintbrush, brush the white icing lightly with gold luster dust.

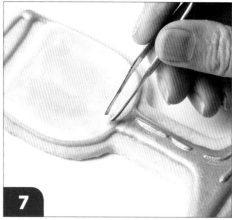

7

Dab the back of an edible pearl with icing and, using tweezers, place it at the bottom of the champagne section of the glass, as a bubble.

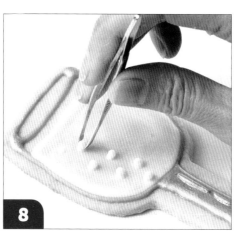

8

Continue to add edible pearl bubbles, rising to the top of the glass as shown. ■ Let cookies dry for at least 6 hours before serving.

Tips

To tint icing light gray, mix in black gel paste a tiny dab at a time until you reach the desired shade.

Vodka is the best choice to mix with luster dust for a metallic finish because it evaporates quickly and won't change the flavor of the icing. But if you prefer not to use alcohol, lemon juice is a good substitute.

When applying luster dust to the champagne, make sure to use a dry paintbrush; otherwise, the dust will clump rather than covering the surface in a light, even layer.

Variation

Instead of using luster dust to create a metallic finish, you can make the glasses really sparkle by using gold or silver disco dust. Apply it when the icing is wet, shaking off excess.

Wedding Cake

These elegant cookies are guaranteed to make that special day even more special! Although the design looks very intricate, it is actually quite easy to make with the help of a wedding cake texture set (see tip). If you don't have one of these sets, you can still make beautiful cookies (see variation, page 202). **Makes about 30.**

What You Need

- 1 recipe cookie dough (pages 36–46)
- Tiered wedding cake cookie cutter
- Cornstarch
- Small rolling pin
- Dark pink fondant
- White fondant
- Light pink fondant
- Wedding cake texture set
- Nonstick baking spray
- X-acto knife
- Offset spatula
- 1 recipe Classic Royal Icing (page 47)
- Small food-safe paintbrush
- Pink luster dust
- Silver or white luster dust
- Disposable pastry bag
- Coupler
- #1 round decorating tip
- Tweezers
- White edible pearls

Techniques Used

- Working with fondant (page 30)
- Using an X-acto knife (page 31)
- Filling a pastry bag (page 24)
- Piping (page 27)
- Adding embellishments (page 31)

Getting Started

Bake cookies: Roll out dough and cut cookies with the wedding cake cookie cutter. Bake according to recipe directions. Let cool completely before decorating.

1

On a work surface lightly dusted with cornstarch, roll out dark pink fondant to 1/8 inch (3 mm) thick. ■ Lightly mist inside of wedding cake texture piece with baking spray. ■ Place texture piece on fondant and use a rolling pin to gently roll over the bottom section so that the pattern is transferred to the fondant.

2

Carefully peel away texture piece and, using an X-acto knife, trim fondant so you are left with a piece that will fit the bottom tier of the cake. ■ Repeat to make 1 bottom piece per cookie.

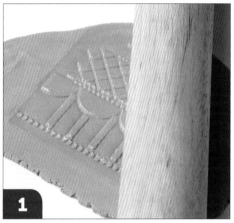

3

Repeat steps 1 and 2 using white fondant and the center section of the texture piece for the center tier of the cake. ■ Make 1 center piece per cookie.

4

Repeat steps 1 and 2 using light pink fondant and the top section of the texture piece for the top tier of the cake. ■ Make 1 top piece per cookie.

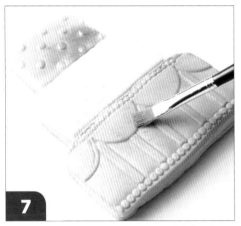

5

Working with one cookie at a time, use an offset spatula to spread a thin layer of icing over a cookie.

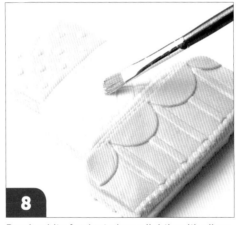

6

Carefully place one bottom, one center and one top tier fondant piece on the cookie, positioning to fit as neatly as possible. ■ Repeat steps 5 and 6 with remaining cookies.

7

Using a small paintbrush, brush pink fondant pieces lightly with pink luster dust.

8

Brush white fondant pieces lightly with silver or white luster dust.

9

Transfer remaining icing to a pastry bag fitted with a #1 tip. ■ Working with one cookie at a time, pipe a line along the bottom border of each cake.

10

While the icing is still wet, use tweezers to position a line of edible pearls along the border.

continued…

Wedding Reception

Tips

A texture set allows you to imprint a pattern onto fondant using gentle pressure from a rolling pin, resulting in an elegant and impressive finish. Look for these sets in the baking supply aisle of well-stocked craft stores or check the Source Guide (page 253) for other vendors.

Be sure to wear disposable latex gloves when coloring fondant so the gel paste does not stain your hands.

Keep any fondant you are not presently working with tightly wrapped in plastic wrap, as it can quickly dry out, rendering it unusable.

After rolling out fondant, let it rest for about 15 minutes (but not much longer!) before cutting out shapes. This allows it to harden a bit, making for cleaner cuts.

If you don't have an X-acto knife, any small, sharp knife will work fine.

Tip

Adding embellishments, such as the edible pearls, is easier if you use a pair of tweezers. Buy an extra pair and keep them handy with your decorating supplies.

Variation

No texture set? No problem! The possibilities for these cookies are endless. If you can get a picture of the bride and groom's cake from the bakery, use it as inspiration for the cookies and use basic piping and flooding techniques to mimic it. Embellish dried icing with dragées and luster dust.

Pipe a line along the bottom of the middle cake tier and position a line of edible pearls along it.

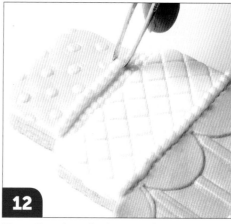

Pipe a line along the bottom of the top cake tier and position a line of edible pearls along it.

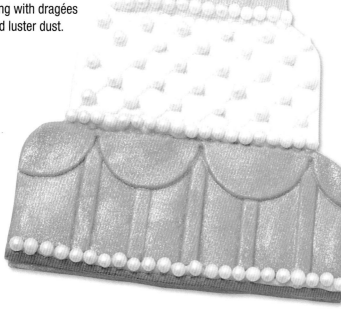

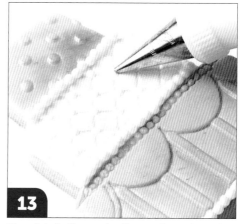

Pipe dots in the center tier section where the crisscross lines meet.

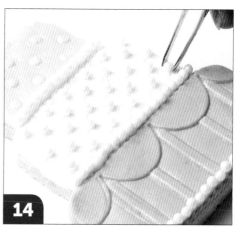

Place an edible pearl on each dot of icing so that you have a nice even pattern. ■ Repeat steps 9 to 14 for all cookies. ■ Let cookies dry for at least 6 hours before serving.

"Just Married" Car

Send your wedding guests off with a special custom favor. These whimsical car cookies, complete with a fondant banner waving in the wind, make the perfect sweet treat for the ride home. **Makes about 30.**

Getting Started

Bake cookies: Roll out dough and cut cookies with the car cookie cutter. Bake according to recipe directions. Let cool completely before decorating.

Tint and thin icing: Place 1¼ cups (300 mL) icing in a bowl and tint it black. Place 1 cup (250 mL) icing in each of two bowls; tint one portion red and leave one white. Place ½ cup (125 mL) icing in each of two bowls; tint one portion blue and one pink. Transfer red, blue and pink icing to pastry bags fitted with #2 tips. Transfer ½ cup (125 mL) black icing to a pastry bag fitted with a #1 tip. Tint remaining icing red. Thin this red icing, along with white and remaining black icing, to two-step icing consistency (page 24) and transfer to squeeze bottles.

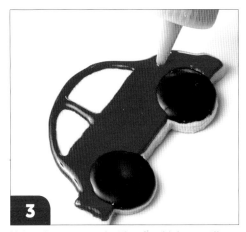

Using the X-acto knife, lightly trace around the outside of the larger round cutter (see tips, page 204) to mark the outline for each car's front wheel. ■ Repeat for the back wheel.

Use the squeeze bottle of black icing to outline and flood the wheels, using the traced outline as a guide.

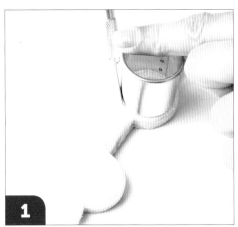

Using the squeeze bottle of red icing, outline and flood cars, leaving space for front and rear windows.

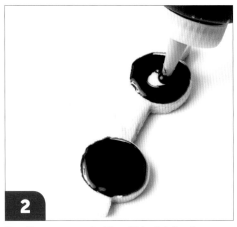

Working with one cookie at a time, use white icing to flood windows.

continued…

What You Need

- 1 recipe cookie dough (pages 36–46)
- Car cookie cutter
- 1 recipe Classic Royal Icing (page 47)
- Black, red, blue and pink gel paste
- 4 disposable pastry bags
- 4 couplers
- 3 #2 round decorating tips
- #1 round decorating tip
- 3 squeeze bottles
- X-acto knife
- 2 small round cutters, one slightly larger than the other
- Cornstarch
- Small rolling pin
- White fondant
- "Just Married" banner template (page 251)
- Small food-safe paintbrush
- Red or pink luster dust
- Red or silver disco dust (optional)

Techniques Used

- Tinting icing (page 22)
- Filling a pastry bag (page 24)
- Filling a squeeze bottle (page 24)
- Using an X-acto knife (page 31)
- Piping (page 27)
- Flooding (page 28)
- Working with fondant (page 30)
- Working with templates (page 32)
- Adding sparkle (page 28)

Tips

These cookies will look more finished if the wheels are perfectly round. For the larger round cutter, choose one the size of your desired wheel.

If you have filled a pastry bag with icing but are not using it for a while, set it upright in a tall drinking glass until you're ready for it.

If you don't have an X-acto knife, you can use an edible marker to trace the outlines in step 1, and a sharp paring knife to cut out the template in step 7.

Keep any fondant you are not presently working with tightly wrapped in plastic wrap, as it can quickly dry out, rendering it unusable.

When applying luster dust, make sure the paintbrush you use is dry; otherwise, the dust will clump rather than covering the surface in a light, even layer.

5

While the white icing is still wet, use blue icing to pipe a small accent mark on each window. ■ Repeat steps 4 and 5 for all cookies. ■ Let icing set for at least 6 hours or overnight.

6

Meanwhile, on a work surface lightly dusted with cornstarch, roll out fondant to ⅛ inch (3 mm) thick. ■ Using the smaller round cutter, cut out 2 circles per car.

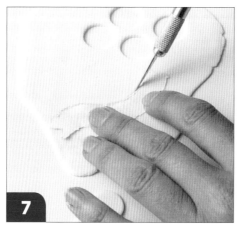

7

Using the X-acto knife and "Just Married" banner template, cut out 1 banner per car.

8

Using the pastry bag of black icing, pipe "Just Married" on each banner. ■ Place fondant wheels and banners on a cookie sheet and let dry for at least 4 hours or overnight.

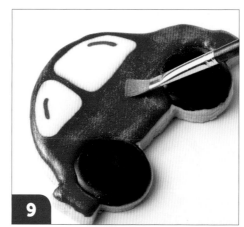

9

Using the small paintbrush, brush each car lightly with luster dust.

10

Using the pastry bag of red icing, outline each car and its windows, outline a door, and pipe a door handle and front and rear bumpers.

11 If desired, while red icing is still wet, sprinkle rear bumper with disco dust, shaking off excess.

12 Using pink icing, pipe small hearts on the side of each car.

13 Dab the back of each fondant circle with icing and affix a circle to the center of each wheel.

14 Use a dab of icing to affix a banner to the back of each car. ■ Let cookies dry for at least 6 hours before serving.

Tip

Don't be alarmed if excess disco dust sticks to the cookie even after you shake it. Wait until the icing dries completely, then gently brush off the unwanted dust with a small food-safe paintbrush or a cotton swab.

Variation

Use these cutters to make race car cookie pops for birthday party favors. (See page 184 for information on how to make cookie pops.) Omit the hearts and the "Just Married" banner. Pipe a number (such as the age of the birthday boy) in the center of the car, then sprinkle the wet icing with sanding sugar, shaking off excess, for a little extra sparkle.

Say It with L-O-V-E

These colorful cookies are a great example of how you can turn a basic rectangle into a spectacular decorated treat. They are perfect for a wedding dessert table, a romantic Valentine's Day dinner for two or any occasion when you want to send your sweetie an extra-special message. **Makes about 30.**

What You Need

- 1 recipe cookie dough (pages 36–46)
- Rectangle cookie cutter
- 1 recipe Classic Royal Icing (page 47)
- Red gel paste
- Purple gel paste
- Pink gel paste
- Disposable pastry bag
- Coupler
- #2 round decorating tip
- 4 squeeze bottles
- Edible marker
- Red disco dust

Techniques Used

- Tinting icing (page 22)
- Filling a pastry bag (page 24)
- Filling a squeeze bottle (page 24)
- Piping (page 27)
- Flooding (page 28)
- Adding sparkle (page 28)

Getting Started

Bake cookies: Roll out dough and cut cookies with the rectangle cookie cutter. Bake according to recipe directions. Let cool completely before decorating.

Tint and thin icing: Divide icing evenly among four bowls; tint one portion red, one purple and one pink, and leave one white. Place ¼ cup (60 mL) red icing in a pastry bag fitted with a #2 tip. Thin purple, pink, white and remaining red icing to two-step icing consistency (page 24) and transfer to squeeze bottles.

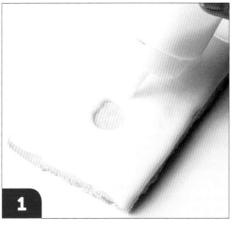

1

Using white icing, outline and flood rectangles. ■ Let icing set for at least 6 hours or overnight.

2

Using the edible marker, write "L-O-V-E" in large decorative letters across each cookie, replacing the "O" with a heart shape, if desired.

3

Working with one cookie at a time, use the squeeze bottle of red icing to outline the "O" (or heart) and flood it generously enough that the letter poofs up a bit, creating texture.

4

While the red icing is still wet, sprinkle the "O" with disco dust, shaking off excess. ■ Repeat steps 3 and 4 for all cookies.

5

Outline and generously flood each "L" with pink icing.

6

Outline and generously flood each "V" with purple icing.

7

Outline and generously flood each "E" with red icing.

8

Using the pastry bag of red icing, pipe a few small hearts in empty spaces on each cookie. ■ Pipe varied sizes of pink and purple dots in other empty spaces. ■ Let cookies dry for at least 6 hours before serving.

Tips

Look for edible markers in the baking supply aisle of your craft store or in the baking aisle of well-stocked grocery stores.

Don't try too hard to make "perfect" letters. Mismatched spacing and sizes make these cookies more fun and whimsical!

Variations

Use fine red sanding sugar in place of the disco dust.

Change the colors of the letters to match the wedding colors.

Baby Onesie

You can tailor these cookies to fit any shower theme or color, and they will always impress. This variation, featuring a sweet little duck, is a great way to get your feet wet experimenting with fondant. **Makes about 30.**

What You Need

- 1 recipe cookie dough (pages 36–46)
- Onesie cookie cutter
- 1 recipe Classic Royal Icing (page 47)
- Black gel paste
- Green gel paste
- 2 squeeze bottles
- Yellow fondant
- Orange fondant
- Tweezers (optional)
- White edible pearls (optional)
- Disposable pastry bag
- Coupler
- #1 round decorating tip

Techniques Used

- Tinting icing (page 22)
- Filling a squeeze bottle (page 24)
- Piping (page 27)
- Flooding (page 28)
- Working with fondant (page 30)
- Adding embellishments (page 31)
- Filling a pastry bag (page 24)

Getting Started

Bake cookies: Roll out dough and cut cookies with the onesie cookie cutter. Bake according to recipe directions. Let cool completely before decorating.

Tint and thin icing: Place $\frac{1}{4}$ cup (60 mL) icing in a bowl and tint it black. Cover tightly and set aside. Place 1 cup (250 mL) icing in a bowl and leave it white. Tint remaining icing light green. Thin white and green icing to two-step icing consistency (page 24) and transfer to squeeze bottles.

1 Using green icing, outline and flood onesies, leaving space for the sleeves. ■ Using white icing, outline and flood sleeves. ■ Let icing set for at least 6 hours or overnight.

2 Meanwhile, use yellow fondant to make duck decorations, rolling a small ball for the head and a larger ball for the body. ■ Shape a tail by pinching the back of the body. ■ Flatten the back of the head and body so that the duck will lie flat against the onesie when attached.

3 Use a small triangle of orange fondant to create a beak. ■ Use a dab of water or icing to attach the beak to the head, and another to attach the head to the body, pressing to adhere. ■ Repeat steps 2 and 3 to make 1 duck per onesie. ■ Place ducks on a cookie sheet and let dry for at least 3 hours or overnight.

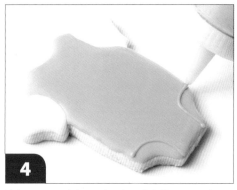

4 Using green icing, pipe leg detail on onesies.

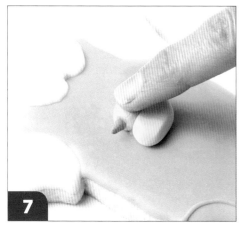

5 Using white icing, pipe collars on onesies.

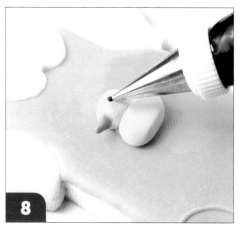

6 If desired, affix edible pearls to the center of the collar and at the bottom of each onesie for buttons, using dabs of icing as needed.

7 Dab the back of each fondant duck with icing and affix a duck to each onesie.

8 Transfer black icing to a pastry bag fitted with a #1 tip. ■ Pipe a tiny eye on each duck. ■ Let cookies dry for at least 6 hours before serving.

Tips

If all the light green icing does not fit in your squeeze bottle, cover the remaining icing tightly and refill the bottle as needed.

Be sure to wear disposable latex gloves when coloring fondant so the gel paste does not stain your hands.

Keep any fondant you are not presently working with tightly wrapped in plastic wrap, as it can quickly dry out, rendering it unusable.

Edible pearls can be found in the baking aisle of most well-stocked grocery stores or in craft stores.

Baby Bib

These sweet baby bibs make an adorable complement to the Baby Onesie cookies (page 208) and Baby Block cookies (page 212) for a customized baby shower cookie tray. Match the colors of the bibs to the color scheme of the baby shower. The design is quite simple, perfect for anyone just getting started on decorating cookies. **Makes about 36.**

What You Need

- 1 recipe cookie dough (pages 36–46)
- Baby bib cookie cutter
- 1 recipe Classic Royal Icing (page 47)
- Pink gel paste
- Green gel paste
- Purple gel paste
- Yellow gel paste
- Squeeze bottle
- 3 disposable pastry bags
- 3 couplers
- 3 #2 round decorating tips

Techniques Used

- Tinting icing (page 22)
- Filling a squeeze bottle (page 24)
- Piping (page 27)
- Flooding (page 28)
- Filling a pastry bag (page 24)

Getting Started

Bake cookies: Roll out dough and cut cookies with the baby bib cookie cutter. Bake according to recipe directions. Let cool completely before decorating.

Tint and thin icing: Place 1 cup (250 mL) icing in a bowl and tint it pink. Place ¾ cup (175 mL) icing in each of two bowls; tint one portion light green and one purple. Cover all bowls tightly and set aside. Tint remaining icing yellow, thin to two-step icing consistency (page 24) and transfer to a squeeze bottle.

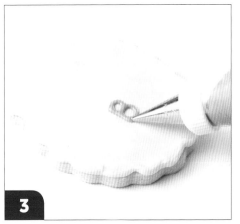

1. Using yellow icing, outline bibs.

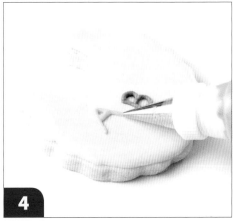

2. Flood bibs with yellow icing. ■ Let icing set for at least 6 hours or overnight.

3. Transfer pink, green and purple icing to pastry bags fitted with #2 tips. ■ Use purple icing to pipe a small "B" in the center of each bib.

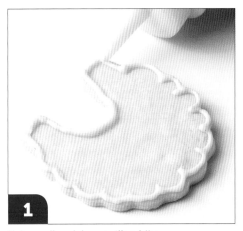

4. Using green icing, pipe a small "A" to the left of and slightly higher than the "B."

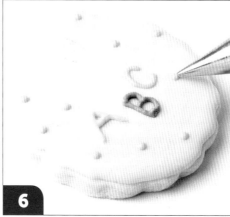

5

Using pink icing, pipe a small "C" to right of and slightly higher than the "B."

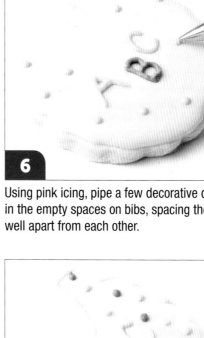

6

Using pink icing, pipe a few decorative dots in the empty spaces on bibs, spacing them well apart from each other.

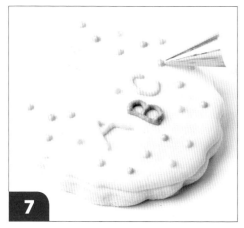

7

Continue adding decorative dots with green and purple icing, making an attractive pattern on each bib.

8

Using pink icing, pipe a border around bibs.
■ Let cookies dry for at least 4 hours before serving.

Tips

If all the yellow icing does not fit in your squeeze bottle, cover the remaining icing tightly and refill the bottle as needed.

Most craft stores carry clear cellophane favor bags, which are perfect for wrapping cookies for gifts and party favors. Finish the look by tying the bags with matching ribbon.

Variation

Instead of the "ABC" design, match the design on the Baby Onesie cookies (page 208).

Baby Block

While the design of these blocks is fairly simple, they will still result in adoring "oohs" and "aahs" from baby shower guests. **Makes about 36.**

What You Need

- 1 recipe cookie dough (pages 36–46)
- Cube cookie cutter
- 1 recipe Classic Royal Icing (page 47)
- Pink gel paste
- Yellow gel paste
- Blue gel paste
- 3 squeeze bottles
- Ruler
- X-acto knife or edible marker
- Disposable pastry bag
- Coupler
- #2 round decorating tip

Techniques Used

- Tinting icing (page 22)
- Filling a squeeze bottle (page 24)
- Using an X-acto knife (page 31)
- Piping (page 27)
- Flooding (page 28)
- Filling a pastry bag (page 24)

Getting Started

Bake cookies: Roll out dough and cut cookies with the cube cookie cutter. Bake according to recipe directions. Let cool completely before decorating.

Tint and thin icing: Divide icing evenly among three bowls; tint one portion light pink, one light yellow and one light blue. Place half the blue icing in another bowl, cover tightly and set aside. Thin pink, yellow and remaining blue icing to two-step icing consistency (page 24) and transfer to squeeze bottles.

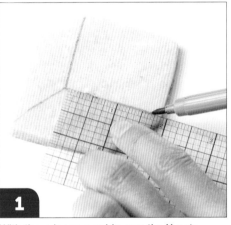

1

With the ruler as a guide, use the X-acto knife or edible marker to lightly trace lines separating each block into three separate faces.

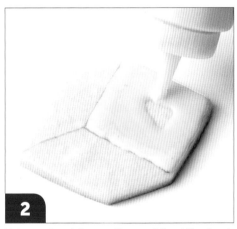

2

Using yellow icing, outline and flood the front face of each block.

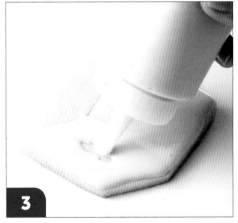

3

Using the squeeze bottle of blue icing, outline and flood the side face of each block.

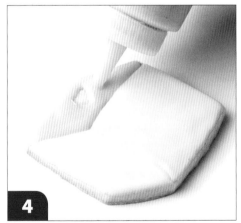

4

Using pink icing, outline and flood the top face of each block. ∎ Let icing set for at least 6 hours or overnight.

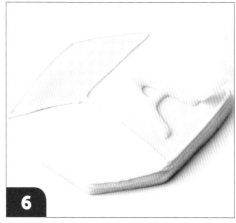

5

Transfer reserved blue icing to a pastry bag fitted with a #2 tip. ■ Pipe a border around each face of the blocks.

6

Using pink icing, outline and flood a block letter "A" on the front face of each block (see tip).

7

Using yellow icing, outline and flood a block letter "B" on the side face of each block.

8

Using the squeeze bottle of blue icing, outline and flood a block letter "C" on the top face of each block. ■ Let cookies dry for at least 6 hours before serving.

Tips

I like to use a ruler as a guide to help me make straight lines when piping. First, lightly trace your lines with an X-acto knife or edible marker, then pipe over the traced lines with icing.

If you draw the letters with an X-acto knife or edible marker before piping them with icing, it is easier to shape them correctly.

You can use the same cookie cutter to make Lucky Dice (page 242) for another occasion, giving you more bang for your cookie cutter buck!

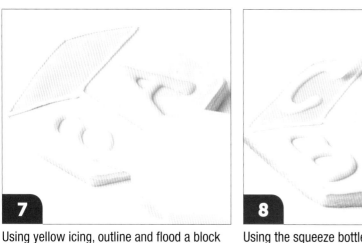

Lobster

The first time I tried lobster, I was in Maine on vacation, so the bar was set quite high. Aside from a special occasion or a beach vacation, if I'm eating lobster it's more likely to be one of these bright red cookies than the more expensive kind in a shell! **Makes about 24.**

What You Need

- 1 recipe cookie dough (pages 36–46)
- Lobster cookie cutter
- 1 recipe Classic Royal Icing (page 47)
- Red gel paste
- Squeeze bottle
- Red fondant
- Black fondant
- Small food-safe paintbrush
- Red luster dust
- Disposable pastry bag
- Coupler
- #2 round decorating tip
- Tweezers

Techniques Used

- Tinting icing (page 22)
- Filling a squeeze bottle (page 24)
- Piping (page 27)
- Flooding (page 28)
- Working with fondant (page 30)
- Adding sparkle (page 28)
- Filling a pastry bag (page 24)

Getting Started

Bake cookies: Roll out dough and cut cookies with the lobster cookie cutter. Bake according to recipe directions. Let cool completely before decorating.

Tint and thin icing: Tint icing red. Place 1 cup (250 mL) icing in a bowl, cover tightly and set aside. Thin remaining icing to two-step icing consistency (page 24) and transfer to a squeeze bottle.

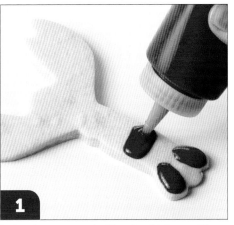

Using the squeeze bottle of red icing, outline and flood every other section of lobsters, using the completed example on page 215 as a guide. ■ Let icing set for 15 minutes.

Outline and flood remaining sections of lobsters. ■ Let icing set for at least 6 hours or overnight.

Meanwhile, roll red fondant into very thin ropes. ■ Cut ropes into 1-inch (2.5 cm) pieces. ■ Make 2 antennae per cookie.

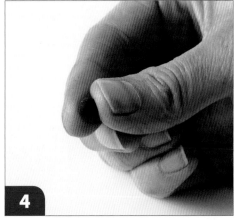

Roll black fondant into very small balls, about the size of a peppercorn. ■ Make 2 eyes per cookie. ■ Place all fondant pieces on a cookie sheet and let dry for at least 1 hour or overnight.

5 Using the small paintbrush, brush lobsters lightly with luster dust.

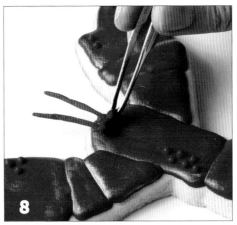

6 Transfer reserved red icing to a pastry bag fitted with a #2 tip. ■ Pipe dot detail onto lobsters, using the completed example below as a guide.

7 Using tweezers and small dabs of icing, affix 2 red fondant antennae to each lobster's head.

8 Affix 2 black fondant eyes to each lobster. ■ Let cookies dry for at least 4 hours before serving.

Tips

If all the icing does not fit in your squeeze bottle, cover the remaining icing tightly and refill the bottle as needed.

By outlining and flooding the lobster in sections, you create texture on the cookies.

For an "Under the Sea" theme party, pair these lobsters with other ocean creatures (pages 147–152).

Variation

Instead of creating eyes out of fondant, you can simply pipe them on using black icing and a pastry bag with a #2 tip.

Slice of Lemon

Some people drench their lobster in butter, but I prefer to squeeze lemon juice over the meat. Make these cookies using Lemon Royal Icing (variation, page 47) for authentic flavor! **Makes about 36.**

What You Need

- 1 recipe cookie dough (pages 36–46)
- 3-inch (7.5 cm) round cookie cutter
- 1 recipe Classic Royal Icing (page 47)
- Disposable pastry bag
- Coupler
- #2 round decorating tip
- Yellow gel paste
- 2 squeeze bottles
- Toothpick

Techniques Used

- Tinting icing (page 22)
- Filling a pastry bag (page 24)
- Filling a squeeze bottle (page 24)
- Piping (page 27)
- Flooding (page 28)

Tip

Don't be overly generous when flooding the cookies with yellow icing, or the icing might overflow when you add the white icing.

Variation

Instead of piping seeds with icing, add white chocolate–covered sunflower seeds while the icing is wet, pointed tips facing the center.

Getting Started

Bake cookies: Roll out dough and cut cookies with the round cookie cutter. Bake according to recipe directions. Let cool completely before decorating.

Tint and thin icing: Transfer 1/2 cup (125 mL) white icing to a pastry bag fitted with a #2 tip. Transfer one-third of remaining icing to a bowl and leave it white. Tint remaining icing yellow. Thin both icings to two-step icing consistency (page 24) and transfer to squeeze bottles (cover any remaining yellow icing tightly and refill the bottle as needed).

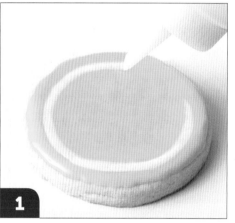

1

Working with one cookie at a time, use yellow icing to outline and flood the cookie. ■ While the yellow icing is still wet, use the squeeze bottle of white icing to pipe a smaller circle inside the yellow circle.

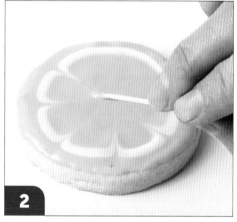

2

Immediately use the end of a toothpick to create 8 lemon sections, starting at the outer edge of the white circle and dragging the toothpick in toward the center at equal intervals around the circle.

3

Using the pastry bag of white icing, pipe 8 seeds in the center of each cookie, 1 per section. ■ Repeat steps 1 to 3 for all cookies. ■ Let cookies dry for at least 6 hours before serving.

Watermelon

I never worry about getting my recommended daily dose of fruit during the summer, mostly because I eat so much juicy, sweet watermelon! Serve these bright cookies alongside a hollowed-out half watermelon filled with fruit salad for a perfectly balanced (and colorful!) dessert. **Makes about 24.**

Getting Started

Bake cookies: Roll out dough and cut cookies with the watermelon cookie cutter. Bake according to recipe directions. Let cool completely before decorating.

Tint and thin icing: Place 1 cup (250 mL) icing in each of two bowls; tint one portion green and leave one white. Transfer to pastry bags fitted with #2 tips. Place ½ cup (125 mL) icing in a bowl and tint it black. Transfer to a pastry bag fitted with a #1 tip. Tint remaining icing hot pink, thin to two-step icing consistency (page 24) and transfer to squeeze bottle.

What You Need

- 1 recipe cookie dough (pages 36–46)
- Watermelon cookie cutter
- 1 recipe Classic Royal Icing (page 47)
- Green gel paste
- Black gel paste
- Hot pink gel paste
- 3 disposable pastry bags
- 3 couplers
- 2 #2 round decorating tips
- #1 round decorating tip
- Squeeze bottle

Techniques Used

- Tinting icing (page 22)
- Filling a pastry bag (page 24)
- Filling a squeeze bottle (page 24)
- Piping (page 27)
- Flooding (page 28)

Tips

To create seed shapes, angle the pastry bag at about 45 degrees and place the tip on the piping surface. Apply light pressure as you pull the tip away, creating a narrow end and a wider end.

If you don't have a watermelon cookie cutter, cut circles using a 4-inch (10 cm) round cutter, then cut a flat top using a ruler as a guide. Create a bite mark by cutting a section out with a small fluted round cutter.

Using green icing, pipe a thick border along lower edge of watermelon. ■ Using white icing, pipe a second thick layer just inside green layer.

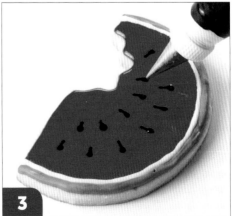

Working with one cookie at a time, use hot pink icing to outline and flood the remaining portion of the cookie.

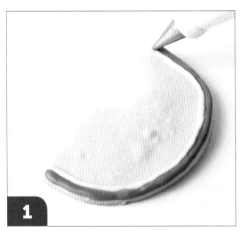

While the hot pink icing is still wet, use black icing to pipe several seeds in the watermelon (see tip). ■ Repeat steps 2 and 3 for all cookies. ■ Let cookies dry for at least 6 hours before serving.

Corn on the Cob

These cookies have extra pizzazz in the form of a fondant pat of butter and some sanding sugar "salt"! **Makes about 24.**

What You Need

- 1 recipe cookie dough (pages 36–46)
- Corn on the cob cookie cutter
- 1 recipe Classic Royal Icing (page 47)
- Light yellow gel paste (see tip)
- Dark yellow gel paste
- Brown gel paste
- 4 squeeze bottles
- Ivory fondant
- Small food-safe paintbrush
- White sanding sugar

Techniques Used

- Tinting icing (page 22)
- Filling a pastry bag (page 24)
- Filling a squeeze bottle (page 24)
- Working with fondant (page 30)
- Piping (page 27)
- Adding sparkle (page 28)

Getting Started

Bake cookies: Roll out dough and cut cookies with the corn on the cob cookie cutter. Bake according to recipe directions. Let cool completely before decorating.

Tint and thin icing: Place $1\frac{1}{2}$ cups (375 mL) icing in a bowl and tint it light yellow. Place $\frac{1}{2}$ cup (125 mL) icing in each of two bowls; tint one portion light brown and leave one white. Tint remaining icing dark yellow. Thin all icings to two-step icing consistency (page 24) and transfer to squeeze bottles.

1 Using light brown icing, outline and flood stems. ■ Using dark yellow icing, outline and flood corn cobs. ■ Let icing set for at least 6 hours or overnight.

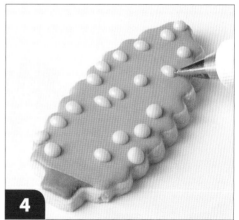

2 Meanwhile, mold 2 tsp (10 mL) fondant into a flat square shape about $\frac{3}{4}$ inch (2 cm) square and $\frac{1}{8}$ inch (3 mm) thick. ■ Make 1 "pat of butter" per cookie.

3 Using the small paintbrush, brush the top of each fondant piece lightly with water. ■ Using your fingers, sprinkle lightly with sanding sugar to mimic grains of salt. ■ Place on a cookie sheet and let dry for at least 4 hours or overnight.

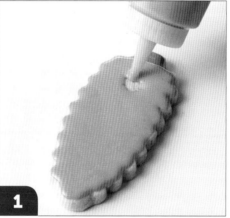

4 Using light yellow icing, pipe individual small oval kernels on each cob, leaving space around each kernel (see tip).

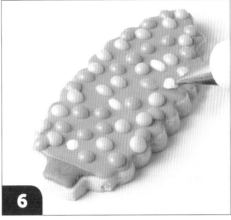

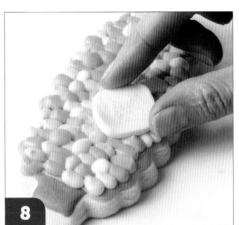

Using dark yellow icing, add more kernels, still leaving space around each kernel.

Using white icing, add a few white kernels, leaving space around each kernel. ■ Let icing set for 15 minutes.

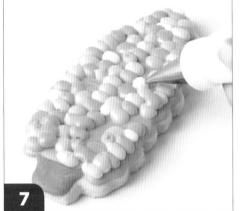

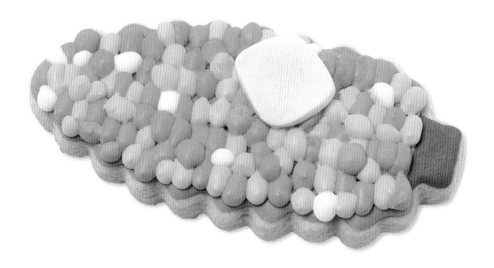

Repeat steps 4 to 6 until all spaces on cobs are filled with kernels. ■ Let cookies set for at least 3 hours.

Dab the back of each fondant piece with icing and affix a pat of butter to each corn cob. ■ Let cookies dry for at least 3 hours before serving.

Tips

If you don't have two shades of yellow in your supply kit, create the different hues by using a little bit of yellow gel paste for one and a larger amount for the other.

If all the dark yellow icing does not fit in your squeeze bottle, cover the remaining icing tightly and refill the bottle as needed.

Allow each kernel to set before piping another next to it so that each retains its individual shape.

Fresh Cherry Pie

What You Need

- 1 recipe cookie dough (pages 36–46)
- Pie cookie cutter
- 1 recipe Classic Royal Icing (page 47)
- Red gel paste
- Brown gel paste
- Blue gel paste
- 3 disposable pastry bags
- 3 couplers
- 2 #2 round decorating tips
- 2 squeeze bottles
- White sanding sugar
- #1 round decorating tip

Techniques Used

- Tinting icing (page 22)
- Filling a pastry bag (page 24)
- Filling a squeeze bottle (page 24)
- Piping (page 27)
- Flooding (page 28)
- Adding sparkle (page 28)

I am definitely a pie lover, so much so that my first cookbook (*175 Best Mini Pie Recipes*) was all about pie. I couldn't help but incorporate a pie-themed cookie into this collection! What better way to end your outdoor summer feast than with a slice of pie filled with fresh cherries? Send your guests home with these replicas as a party favor. **Makes about 30.**

Getting Started

Bake cookies: Roll out dough and cut cookies with the pie cookie cutter. Bake according to recipe directions. Let cool completely before decorating.

Tint and thin icing: Place 1$\frac{1}{4}$ cups (300 mL) icing in each of three bowls; tint two portions red and one light brown. Cover brown icing and one red portion tightly and set aside. Transfer $\frac{1}{2}$ cup (125 mL) white icing to a pastry bag fitted with a #2 tip. Tint remaining icing blue. Thin blue and remaining red icing to two-step icing consistency (page 24) and transfer to squeeze bottles.

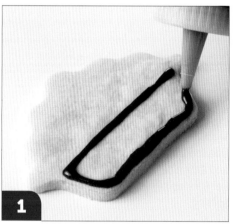

1 Working with one cookie at a time, use blue icing to outline the pie plate portion of the cookie.

2 Flood the pie plate with blue icing.

3 While the blue icing is still wet, use white icing to pipe two curved accent lines in the pie plate.

4 Using the squeeze bottle of red icing, outline the pie portion of the cookie.

5

Flood the pie portion with red icing. ■ Repeat steps 1 to 5 for all cookies. ■ Let icing set for at least 6 hours or overnight.

6

Transfer brown icing to a pastry bag fitted with a #2 tip. ■ Working with one cookie at a time, pipe crisscross detail and edging onto pie tops, using the completed example as a guide.

7

While the brown icing is still wet, sprinkle it with sanding sugar, shaking off excess. ■ Repeat steps 6 and 7 for all cookies.

8

Transfer reserved red icing to a pastry bag fitted with a #1 tip. ■ Pipe several dots inside each lattice pie crust diamond to mimic cherries. ■ Let cookies dry for at least 6 hours before serving.

Tips

Don't be alarmed if excess sanding sugar sticks to the cookie even after you shake it. Wait until the icing dries completely, then gently brush off the unwanted sugar with a small food-safe paintbrush or a cotton swab.

If you have filled a pastry bag with icing but are not using it right away, set it upright in a tall drinking glass until you're ready for it.

Variations

For blueberry pie, use red icing for the pie plate and blue icing for the filling.

This design can work just as well for fall or winter as it does for summer. For the filling, use smooth orange icing to mimic pumpkin or sweet potato pie. Use Pumpkin Spice cookie dough (page 43) to make the cookies.

Frosty Mug of Beer

Nothing complements dinner on the beach better than a mug of ice-cold beer enjoyed while watching the sun go down. These fun cookies, complete with a generous amount of froth on top, are also a great fit for a sporting event, Father's Day or a casual outdoor barbecue. **Makes about 30.**

What You Need

- 1 recipe cookie dough (pages 36–46)
- Beer mug cutter
- 1 recipe Classic Royal Icing (page 47)
- Brown gel paste
- Orange gel paste
- 2 squeeze bottles
- Small food-safe paintbrush
- Gold luster dust
- Silver luster dust
- Disposable pastry bag
- Coupler
- #2 round decorating tip

Techniques Used

- Tinting icing (page 22)
- Filling a squeeze bottle (page 24)
- Piping (page 27)
- Flooding (page 28)
- Adding sparkle (page 28)
- Filling a pastry bag (page 24)

Tips

For the orange-brown beer color, I used about 4 parts brown to 1 part orange gel paste.

When applying luster dust, make sure the paintbrush you use is dry; otherwise, the dust will clump rather than covering the surface in a light, even layer.

Getting Started

Bake cookies: Roll out dough and cut cookies with the beer mug cookie cutter. Bake according to recipe directions. Let cool completely before decorating.

Tint and thin icing: Place 1 cup (250 mL) icing in a bowl and tint it light brown. Cover tightly and set aside. Divide remaining icing evenly between two bowls; tint one bowl light brown with a slight orange hue (see tip) and leave one white. Thin orange-brown and white icing to two-step icing consistency (page 24) and transfer to squeeze bottles.

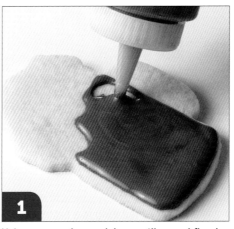

1 Using orange-brown icing, outline and flood beer mugs, leaving room at the top for foam.

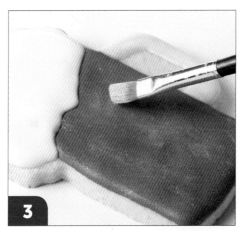

2 Using white icing, outline and flood mug handles and top portion of beer mugs. ■ Let icing set for at least 6 hours or overnight.

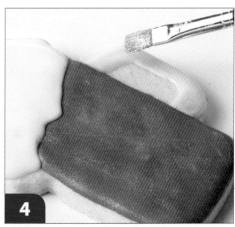

3 Using the small paintbrush, brush orange-brown portion of beer mugs lightly with gold luster dust.

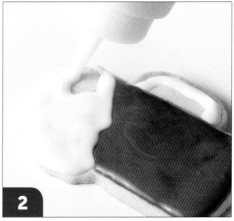

4 Brush handles with silver luster dust.

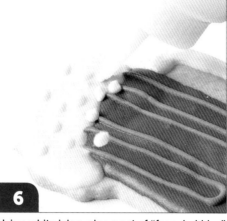

5

Transfer light brown icing to a pastry bag fitted with a #2 tip. ■ Pipe 3 rectangles onto each beer mug as shown.

6

Using white icing, pipe a set of "foam bubbles" on the top portion of each beer mug, squeezing circles of various sizes and leaving space around each circle (see tip). ■ Be sure to run some foam down the side of the mug. ■ Let icing set for 15 minutes.

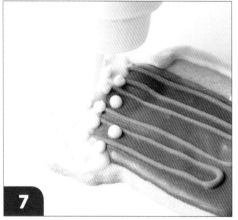

7

Pipe another set of bubbles, leaving space around each circle. ■ Let icing set for 15 minutes.

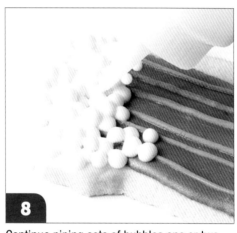

8

Continue piping sets of bubbles one or two more times, until your mugs have a nice foamy top. ■ Let cookies dry for at least 6 hours before serving.

Lobster Bake

Tip

Allow each "foam bubble" to set before piping another next to it so that each retains its individual shape.

Variation

These cutters can also be used to make "mug of root beer" cookies for the kids! Color the root beer a darker shade of brown and create a fondant straw to stick out the top!

French Flag

I am a true francophile, which I attribute to my six years of French classes in junior high and high school. One year I combined my love for baking with my love for all things *français*, baking a cake for class decorated with the *bleu, blanc et rouge* stripes of the French flag. For a budding decorator, it was an easy design, as are these sparkly flag cookies. **Makes about 30.**

What You Need

- 1 recipe cookie dough (pages 36–46)
- Flag cookie cutter
- 1 recipe Classic Royal Icing (page 47)
- Black gel paste
- Blue gel paste
- Red gel paste
- Disposable pastry bag
- Coupler
- #2 round decorating tip
- 3 squeeze bottles
- Ruler
- X-acto knife or edible marker
- Blue disco dust
- Red disco dust
- Tweezers
- Silver dragées

Techniques Used

- Tinting icing (page 22)
- Filling a pastry bag (page 24)
- Filling a squeeze bottle (page 24)
- Piping (page 27)
- Flooding (page 28)
- Using an X-acto knife (page 31)
- Adding embellishments (page 31)
- Adding sparkle (page 28)

Getting Started

Bake cookies: Roll out dough and cut cookies with the flag cookie cutter. Bake according to recipe directions. Let cool completely before decorating.

Tint and thin icing: Place 1 cup (250 mL) icing in a bowl and tint it black. Transfer to a pastry bag fitted with a #2 tip. Divide remaining icing among three bowls; tint one portion red and one blue, and leave one white. Thin red, blue and white icing to two-step icing consistency (page 24) and transfer to squeeze bottles.

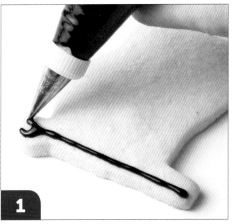

1 Using black icing, pipe a flagpole, including a round dot at the top for the finial, on the left side of each cookie.

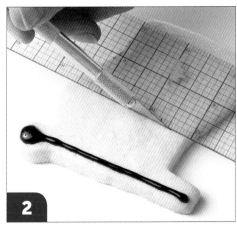

2 With the ruler as a guide, use the X-acto knife or edible marker to lightly trace vertical lines separating each cookie into three even sections (see tip).

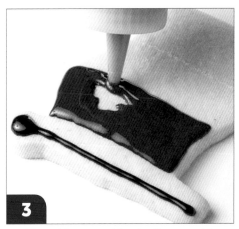

3 Working with one cookie at a time, use blue icing to outline and flood the left section.

4 While the blue icing is still wet, sprinkle it with blue disco dust, shaking off excess. ■ Repeat steps 3 and 4 for all cookies.

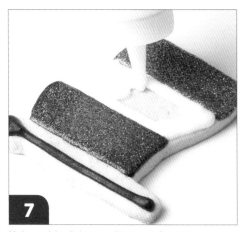

5 Working with one cookie at a time, use red icing to outline and flood the right section.

6 While the red icing is still wet, sprinkle it with red disco dust, shaking off excess. ■ Repeat steps 5 and 6 for all cookies.

7 Using white icing, outline and flood the center section of each cookie.

8 Using tweezers and small dabs of icing, affix silver dragées in three groups of two so that they connect flag and pole. ■ Let cookies dry for at least 6 hours before serving.

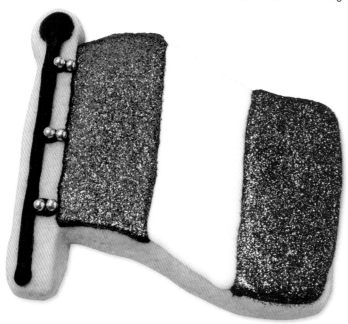

Tips

To make neat, even sections for the flag, measure the width of the flag, divide it into thirds, then trace two straight lines with the X-acto knife to mark the sections. Use the lines as guides for neat piping.

Don't be alarmed if excess disco dust sticks to the cookie even after you shake it. Wait until the icing dries completely, then gently brush off the unwanted dust with a small food-safe paintbrush or a cotton swab.

Adding embellishments, such as the silver dragées, is easier if you use a pair of tweezers. Buy an extra pair and keep them handy with your decorating supplies.

Variation

Create American flag cookies for your Fourth of July celebration or Canadian flags for Canada Day!

La Tour Eiffel

This is one cookie that needs no embellishment in terms of sparkly glitter, multiple colors or decor. The iconic architecture of La Tour Eiffel is spectacular (and detailed) enough to impress on its own. This is a great cookie to try if you want to hone your piping skills without spending too much time preparing your tools. **Makes about 30.**

What You Need

- 1 recipe cookie dough (pages 36–46)
- Eiffel Tower cookie cutter
- 1 recipe Classic Royal Icing (page 47)
- Black gel paste
- Disposable pastry bag
- Coupler
- #2 round decorating tip
- Squeeze bottle

Techniques Used

- Tinting icing (page 22)
- Filling a pastry bag (page 24)
- Filling a squeeze bottle (page 24)
- Piping (page 27)
- Flooding (page 28)

Tip

I like to use a ruler and an X-acto knife for designs requiring straight lines, as the finished product simply looks better when the lines are piped perfectly straight. Using a ruler as a guide, lightly trace a light line into the cookie. Brush away excess crumbs and pipe over the top — voila!

Getting Started

Bake cookies: Roll out dough and cut cookies with the Eiffel Tower cookie cutter. Bake according to recipe directions. Let cool completely before decorating.

Tint and thin icing: Tint icing black. Transfer half the icing to a pastry bag fitted with a #2 tip. Thin remaining icing to two-step icing consistency (page 24) and transfer to a squeeze bottle.

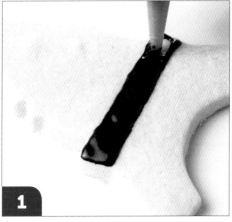

Using the squeeze bottle, outline and flood the bottom tier of each tower.

Outline and flood the top bulb of each tower.

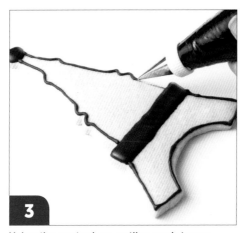

Using the pastry bag, outline each tower.

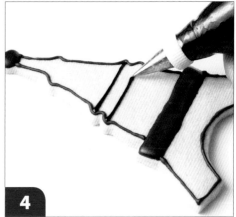

Pipe two straight lines across the top and bottom of the middle tier.

5 Pipe a single straight line across the top tier.

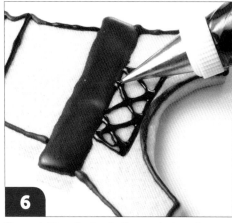

6 Pipe a lattice design in the central portion under the bottom tier.

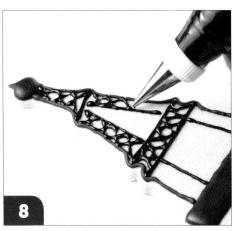

7 Pipe a lattice design in the middle tier.

8 Pipe a lattice design up the sides of each tower. ■ Let cookies dry for at least 6 hours before serving.

Variation

Use Dark Chocolate cookie dough (page 40) to make the cookies and tint the icing silver or gold for a more glitzy effect!

La Bicyclette

What You Need

- 1 recipe cookie dough (pages 36–46)
- Bicycle cookie cutter
- 1 recipe Classic Royal Icing (page 47)
- Red gel paste
- Black gel paste
- 2 disposable pastry bags
- 2 couplers
- 2 #2 round decorating tips
- Round cutter (see tip)
- X-acto knife
- #1 round decorating tip
- Tweezers
- Silver dragées
- Cornstarch
- Small rolling pin
- Pink fondant
- Small flower cutter
- Pointed fondant modeling tool
- Brown fondant

Techniques Used

- Tinting icing (page 22)
- Filling a pastry bag (page 24)
- Piping (page 27)
- Using an X-acto knife (page 31)
- Adding embellishments (page 31)
- Working with fondant (page 30)

Like many European cities, Paris is bicycle-friendly. Throughout the streets you will see Parisians pedaling with baskets full of freshly baked baguettes or an array of colorful flowers. This delightful *bicyclette rouge*, equipped with its own fondant basket, is almost too impressive to eat… almost. **Makes about 30.**

Getting Started

Bake cookies: Roll out dough and cut cookies with the bicycle cookie cutter. Bake according to recipe directions. Let cool completely before decorating.

Tint and thin icing: Divide icing evenly between two bowls; tint one portion red and one black. Transfer to pastry bags fitted with #2 tips.

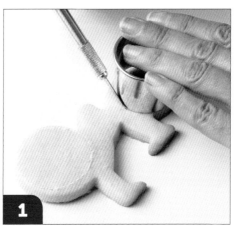

1

Place the round cutter on the front wheel of each bicycle, and use the X-acto knife to lightly trace around the outside. ■ Repeat for the back wheel.

2

Use black icing to pipe a thick circle for each bicycle wheel, using the traced outlines as guides.

3

Pipe a black seat, bottom pedal and handle on each bicycle.

4

Change tip on black icing to a #1 tip. ■ Pipe 16 black spokes coming from the center of each wheel.

5

Working with one cookie at a time, use red icing to pipe a frame for each bicycle as shown. ■ The lines should be slightly thicker than those for the wheels.

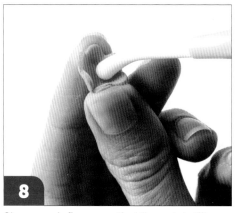

6

While the red icing is still wet, use tweezers to place a silver dragée in the center of each wheel and 3 dragées just above the pedal. ■ Repeat steps 5 and 6 for all cookies. ■ Let icing set for at least 6 hours or overnight.

7

Meanwhile, on a surface lightly dusted with cornstarch, roll out pink fondant to $\frac{1}{16}$ inch (2 mm) thick. ■ Using the flower cutter, cut out 5 to 6 flowers per cookie.

8

Shape each flower so that the petals tilt upward from the center. ■ To do so, carefully hold a flower between thumb and two forefingers and use the modeling tool to gently press the center down. ■ Place flowers on a cookie sheet and let dry for at least 4 hours or overnight.

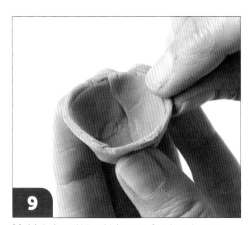

9

Mold 1 tbsp (15 mL) brown fondant into a round basket shape. ■ Make 1 basket per cookie.

10

Pipe a generous amount of icing inside each basket, so it is nearly full.

Tips

These cookies will look more finished if the wheels are perfectly round. Use a round cutter the size of your cookie's wheels.

If you don't have an X-acto knife, you can use an edible marker to trace the outlines in step 1.

Adding embellishments, such as the silver dragées, is easier if you use a pair of tweezers. Buy an extra pair and keep them handy with your decorating supplies.

Be sure to wear disposable latex gloves when coloring fondant so the gel paste does not stain your hands.

Keep any fondant you are not presently working with tightly wrapped in plastic wrap, as it can quickly dry out, rendering it unusable.

My baskets are about 1 inch (2.5 cm) in diameter and $\frac{1}{2}$ inch (1 cm) deep, but feel free to alter basket size and shape, depending on the size of your bicycles and flowers.

continued…

Tips

When you're elevating the tops of the bikes in preparation for attaching the baskets (step 12), try using a wire cooling rack, resting the top edges of each cookie (the seat and the handle) on the edge of the rack.

In addition to the "Vive La France" category, these bicycles would be a great addition to a sports theme (see pages 154–170). Omit the basket and flowers.

Variations

For an easier design, eliminate the fondant baskets.

Change the color of the bike to match the cookie recipient's bike.

11 Arrange 5 to 6 fondant flowers in each basket, using dabs of icing to secure them. ■ Place baskets on a cookie sheet and let dry for at least 4 hours or overnight.

12 Place cookies on a stable surface with the top of each bike slightly elevated (see tip), leaving room for the width of the baskets when they are attached.

13 Dab bottom and one side of each basket with icing. ■ Attach a basket to the front of each bike.

14 Anchor each basket and bike with something sturdy, such as a small drinking glass, while the icing dries, about 4 hours.

French Painter

Ooh la la! This little French painter has more paint on his coat than he has on his easel! From his signature red beret and moustache to his tiny palette, he would be right at home standing in front of the Eiffel Tower (page 226), painting the beautiful scenery. **Makes about 24.**

Getting Started

Bake cookies: Roll out dough and cut cookies with the gingerbread man cookie cutter. Bake according to recipe directions. Let cool completely before decorating.

Tint and thin icing: Place ³⁄₄ cup (175 mL) icing in each of four bowls; tint one portion blue, one brown, one black and one red. Place ¹⁄₂ cup (125 mL) icing in a bowl and leave it white. Place ¹⁄₄ cup (60 mL) icing in each of three bowls; tint one portion yellow, one green and one orange. Cover all bowls tightly except brown and blue icing and set aside. Thin blue, brown and remaining white icing to two-step icing consistency (page 24) and transfer to squeeze bottles.

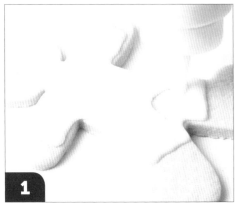

1

Use the squeeze bottle of white icing to outline and flood each painter's coat as shown.

2

Using blue icing, outline and flood each painter's pants.

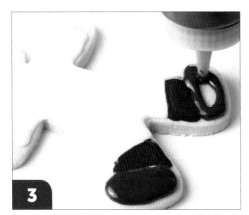

3

Using brown icing, outline and flood each painter's shoes. ■ Let icing set for at least 6 hours or overnight.

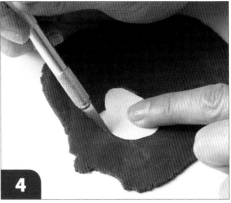

4

Meanwhile, on a work surface lightly dusted with cornstarch, roll out brown fondant to ¹⁄₁₆ inch (2 mm) thick. ■ Using the X-acto knife and mini palette template, cut out 1 palette per cookie.

continued…

Vive la France

Keep royal icing tightly covered when you're not using it, as it tends to dry out quickly.

Be sure to wear disposable latex gloves when coloring fondant so the gel paste does not stain your hands.

After rolling out fondant, let it rest for about 15 minutes (but not much longer!) before cutting out shapes. This allows it to harden a bit, making for cleaner cuts.

Keep any fondant you are not presently working with tightly wrapped in plastic wrap, as it can quickly dry out, rendering it unusable.

An X-acto knife is a good investment if you plan to work with fondant often. Its blade is sharper than a paring knife, allowing for a more "x-act" cut.

5

Mold 2 tsp (10 mL) red fondant into a beret shape, sizing it to fit the painter's head. ■ Flatten the back of the beret so it will lie flat. ■ Mold a tiny piece of red fondant into a ball. ■ Dab the ball with water and press it lightly to the top center of the beret to affix. ■ Make 1 beret per cookie. ■ Place palettes and berets on a cookie sheet and let dry for at least 4 hours or overnight.

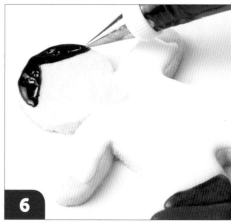

6

Transfer black, red, reserved white, yellow, green and orange icing to pastry bags fitted with #2 tips. ■ Working with one cookie at a time, use black icing to pipe hair on the painter's head.

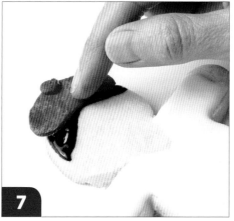

7

While the black icing is still wet, affix a beret on the painter's head. ■ Repeat steps 6 and 7 for all cookies.

8

Using the pastry bag of white icing, pipe a border around each painter's coat.

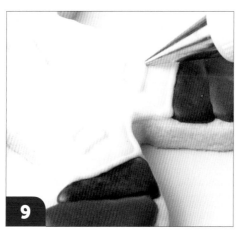

9

Pipe lapels, a center line and white pockets on each coat.

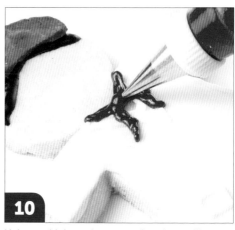

10

Using red icing, pipe a scarf and a smiling mouth on each painter.

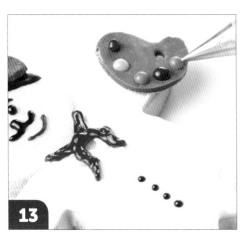

11

Using black icing, pipe eyebrows, eyes, a nose and a moustache on each painter.
■ Pipe 4 buttons down the center of the painter's coat.

12

Dab the back of each fondant palette with icing and affix a palette to each painter's right hand.

13

Pipe a dollop each of blue, red, yellow, green and orange icing on each palette.

14

Using edible markers, draw splatters of paint all over each painter's coat. ■ Let cookies dry for at least 6 hours before serving.

Tip

Look for edible markers in the baking supply aisle of your craft store or in the baking aisle of well-stocked grocery stores.

Variation

If you don't want to work with fondant, use red icing to pipe a beret onto each cookie after the black "hair" is completely dry. Instead of creating the mini palettes, serve these cookies with Painter's Palette cookies (page 234) as a set (eliminate the fondant paintbrushes).

Painter's Palette

This is a close-up of the tiny palette our French Painter (page 231) is holding, complete with a fondant brush dipped in blue paint. **Makes about 24.**

What You Need

- 1 recipe cookie dough (pages 36–46)
- X-acto knife
- Palette template (page 252)
- 1 recipe Classic Royal Icing (page 47)
- Red gel paste
- Yellow gel paste
- Purple gel paste
- Blue gel paste
- Pink gel paste
- Green gel paste
- Brown gel paste
- 7 squeeze bottles
- Brown fondant
- White fondant
- Small food-safe paintbrush
- Brown or mahogany luster dust

Techniques Used

- Using an X-acto knife (page 31)
- Working with templates (page 32)
- Tinting icing (page 22)
- Filling a squeeze bottle (page 24)
- Piping (page 27)
- Flooding (page 28)
- Working with fondant (page 30)

Getting Started

Bake cookies: Roll out dough and, using the X-acto knife and palette template, cut out cookies, rerolling scraps as necessary. Bake according to recipe directions. Let cool completely before decorating.

Thin and tint icing: Thin icing to two-step icing consistency (page 24). Place $\frac{1}{2}$ cup (125 mL) icing in each of six bowls; tint one portion red, one yellow, one purple, one blue, one pink and one green. Cover tightly and set aside. Tint remaining icing light brown and transfer to a squeeze bottle.

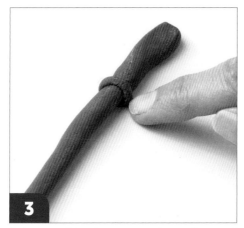

1 Using brown icing, outline and flood palettes. ■ Let icing set for at least 6 hours or overnight.

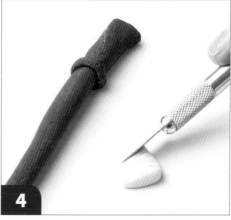

2 Meanwhile, roll a piece of brown fondant into a rope about $\frac{1}{4}$ inch (5 mm) in diameter and 4 inches (10 cm) long, tapering one end like the end of a paintbrush.

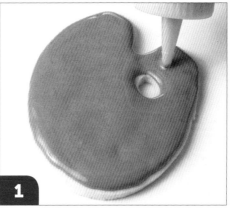

3 Roll a very thin, short rope and wrap it around the upper third of the paintbrush stem, attaching it with a dab of water.

4 To make the brush, mold a piece of white fondant into a flat square shape about $\frac{1}{2}$ inch (1 cm) square and $\frac{1}{4}$ inch (5 mm) thick. ■ Using the X-acto knife, draw lines on the square to simulate individual bristles (don't cut all the way through the fondant).

5 Use a dab of water to attach the brush to the stem of the paintbrush, pressing them lightly together.

6 Dip the tip of the brush in blue icing.

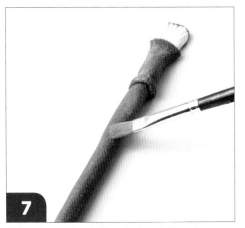

7 Using the real paintbrush, brush the stem of the fondant paintbrush lightly with luster dust. ■ Make 1 brush per cookie. ■ Place brushes on a cookie sheet and let dry for at least 6 hours or overnight.

8 Transfer red, yellow, purple, blue, pink and green icing to squeeze bottles. ■ Use alternating colors to make pools of paint around the edge of each palette. ■ Space the pools evenly, but use a slightly different shape for each color.

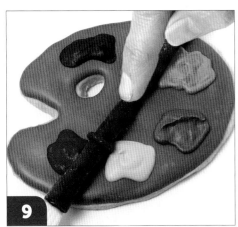

9 Dab the back of each paintbrush with icing and affix a paintbrush diagonally across each palette. ■ Let cookies dry for at least 6 hours before serving.

Vive la France

Tips

If you don't have an X-acto knife, any small, sharp knife will work fine.

Cookie dough retains its shape best when cold. If the rolled-out dough gets too warm while you're cutting shapes, carefully transfer it to a cookie sheet and place it in the refrigerator for 15 minutes before continuing.

When applying luster dust, make sure the paintbrush you use is dry; otherwise, the dust will clump rather than covering the surface in a light, even layer.

For an art theme, you could serve these palettes along with Colored Crayons (page 176).

Variations

For an easier design, eliminate the fondant paintbrush.

Bottle of Champagne

- 1 recipe cookie dough (pages 36–46)
- Wine bottle cookie cutter
- 1 recipe Classic Royal Icing (page 47)
- Black gel paste
- Yellow gel paste
- Green gel paste
- 2 squeeze bottles
- Cornstarch
- Small rolling pin
- Peach fondant
- 1-inch (2.5 cm) round cutter
- X-acto knife
- Champagne label template (page 252)
- Ruler
- Small food-safe paintbrush
- Gold luster dust
- Disposable pastry bag
- Coupler
- #2 round decorating tip

Techniques Used

- Tinting icing (page 22)
- Filling a squeeze bottle (page 24)
- Piping (page 27)
- Flooding (page 28)
- Working with fondant (page 30)
- Using an X-acto knife (page 31)
- Working with templates (page 32)
- Adding sparkle (page 28)
- Filling a pastry bag (page 24)

Paris is known for being a romantic city. What's more romantic than sharing a bottle of France's native bubbly with your loved one? These cookies are perfect for a wedding dessert table, New Year's Eve or any occasion worthy of a toast. **Makes about 30.**

Getting Started

Bake cookies: Roll out dough and cut cookies with the wine bottle cookie cutter. Bake according to recipe directions. Let cool completely before decorating.

Tint and thin icing: Place 1 cup (250 mL) icing in each of two bowls; tint one portion black and one yellow. Cover black icing tightly and set aside. Tint remaining icing green. Thin yellow and green icing to two-step icing consistency (page 24) and transfer to squeeze bottles.

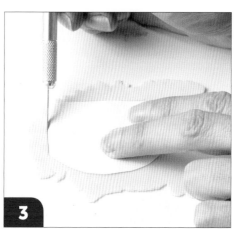

1 Using green icing, outline and flood bottom portion of champagne bottles. ■ Using yellow icing, outline and flood top portion of bottles. ■ Let icing set for at least 6 hours or overnight.

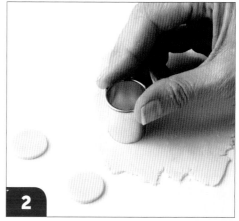

2 On a work surface lightly dusted with cornstarch, roll out fondant to $\frac{1}{16}$ inch (2 mm) thick. ■ Using the round cutter, cut out 1 circle per cookie.

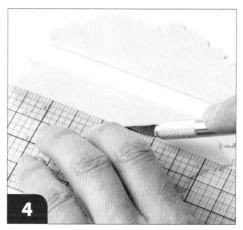

3 Using the X-acto knife and Champagne label template, cut out 1 label per cookie.

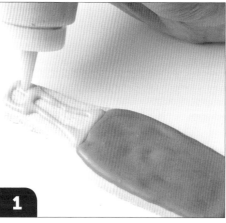

4 Using the X-acto knife and ruler, cut out a rectangle about $\frac{3}{4}$ inch (2 cm) high and the width of the bottle at the top of the green icing.

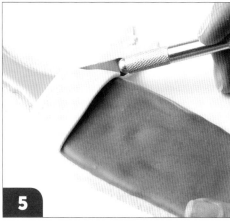

5

Place the rectangle on a cookie so that it covers the seam between yellow and green icing. ■ Trim the short edges of the rectangle so that they are flush with the cookie. ■ Make 1 piece per cookie. ■ Place all fondant pieces on a cookie sheet and let dry for at least 4 hours or overnight.

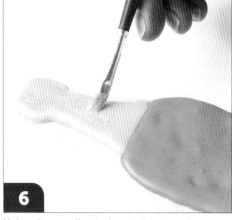

6

Using the small paintbrush, brush yellow icing lightly with luster dust.

7

Dab the back of each fondant piece with icing and affix to cookies as follows. ■ Affix a label, arched side up, near the bottom of each cookie. ■ Affix a rectangle over the seam between yellow and green icing on each cookie. ■ Affix a circle in the center of each rectangle.

8

Transfer black icing to a pastry bag fitted with a #2 tip. ■ Pipe borders inside each label, rectangle and circle as shown. ■ Pipe "Salut!" in the center of the label. ■ Let cookies dry for at least 6 hours before serving.

Tips

After rolling out fondant, let it rest for about 15 minutes (but not much longer!) before cutting out shapes. This allows it to harden a bit, making for cleaner cuts.

An X-acto knife is a good investment if you plan to work with fondant often. Its blade is sharper than a paring knife, allowing for a more "x-act" cut.

When applying luster dust, make sure the paintbrush you use is dry; otherwise, the dust will clump rather than covering the surface in a light, even layer.

Variation

Use this cookie cutter to make wine bottles that mimic your favorite varietal or label. Serve them for dessert at a cocktail party or pair them with a dessert wine at a wine-tasting.

Poker Chips

Normally, a depleting stack of poker chips would be a very bad thing. In this case, it just means everyone loves your cookies. Present these easy cookies stacked in a variety of colors for a true jackpot effect! **Makes about 36.**

What You Need

- 1 recipe cookie dough (pages 36–46)
- 2½-inch (6 cm) round cookie cutter
- 1 recipe Classic Royal Icing (page 47)
- Black gel paste
- Red gel paste
- Blue gel paste
- 2 squeeze bottles
- 1-inch (2.5 cm) round cookie cutter
- X-acto knife
- 3 disposable pastry bags
- 3 couplers
- 3 #2 round decorating tips

Techniques Used

- Tinting icing (page 22)
- Filling a squeeze bottle (page 24)
- Piping (page 27)
- Flooding (page 28)
- Using an X-acto knife (page 31)
- Filling a pastry bag (page 24)

Getting Started

Bake cookies: Roll out dough and cut cookies with the 2½-inch (6 cm) round cookie cutter. Bake according to recipe directions. Let cool completely before decorating.

Tint and thin icing: Place 1 cup (250 mL) icing in each of two bowls; tint one portion black and leave one white. Place ½ cup (125 mL) icing in a bowl and tint it red. Cover all bowls tightly and set aside. Divide remaining icing evenly between two bowls; tint one portion red and one blue. Thin this red and blue icing to two-step icing consistency (page 24) and transfer to squeeze bottles.

1 Using the squeeze bottle of red icing, outline and flood half the cookies. ■ Outline and flood the remaining cookies with blue icing. ■ Let icing set for at least 6 hours or overnight.

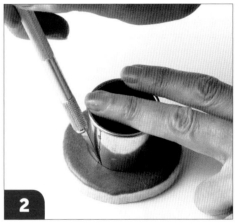

2 Center the 1-inch (2.5 cm) round cutter inside each cookie and use the X-acto knife to lightly trace around the outside.

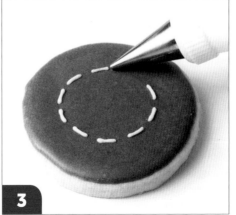

3 Transfer black, white and reserved red icing to pastry bags fitted with #2 tips. ■ Use white icing to pipe a dotted line around the traced outline on each blue poker chip.

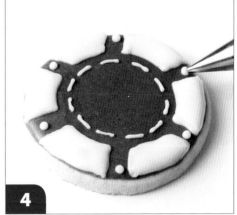

4 Pipe the remaining white details on blue poker chips as shown.

5 Using black icing, pipe a dotted line around the traced outline on each red poker chip.

6 Pipe the remaining black details on red poker chips as shown.

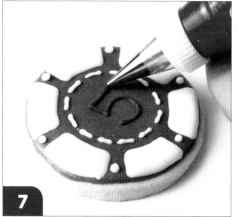

7 Using the pastry bag of red icing, pipe a "5" in the center of each blue poker chip.

8 Using black icing, pipe a "10" in the center of each red poker chip. ■ Let cookies dry for at least 3 hours before serving.

Tips

I like to use the smaller cutter as a guide for the center circle because I prefer it to be perfectly round. (I'm very picky!) Feel free to pipe the dotted lines freehand and skip step 2.

If you don't have an X-acto knife, you can use an edible marker to trace the outlines in step 2.

Winning Hand Playing Cards

What You Need

- 1 recipe cookie dough (pages 36–46)
- Hand of cards cookie cutter
- 1 recipe Classic Royal Icing (page 47)
- Black gel paste
- Red gel paste
- Squeeze bottle
- Playing card
- X-acto knife
- 2 disposable pastry bags
- 2 couplers
- 2 #2 round decorating tips

Techniques Used

- Tinting icing (page 22)
- Filling a squeeze bottle (page 24)
- Piping (page 27)
- Flooding (page 28)
- Using an X-acto knife (page 31)
- Filling a pastry bag (page 24)

There is no "luck of the draw" with these cookies. Each and every bite is 100% guaranteed to be delicious. Serve them for dessert at poker night or in between rounds during a family Go Fish tournament. Change the cards in the hand to "suit" yourself! **Makes about 30.**

Getting Started

Bake cookies: Roll out dough and cut cookies with the hand of cards cookie cutter. Bake according to recipe directions. Let cool completely before decorating.

Tint and thin icing: Place 1 cup (250 mL) icing in each of two bowls; tint one portion black and one red. Cover tightly and set aside. Thin remaining white icing to two-step icing consistency (page 24) and transfer to a squeeze bottle.

1

Using white icing, outline and flood cookies. ■ Let icing set for at least 6 hours or overnight.

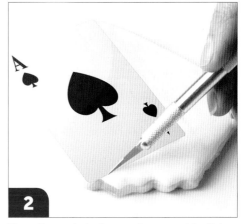

2

Place the real playing card on a cookie, lining up the edges as shown, and use the X-acto knife to lightly trace the outline of the card.

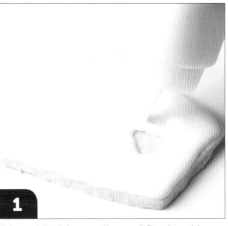

3

Gradually tilt the card, tracing borders along the way, to create traced outlines for a fanned hand of five cards. ■ Repeat steps 2 and 3 for all cookies.

4

Transfer black and red icing to pastry bags fitted with #2 tips. ■ Use black icing to pipe the borders of the playing cards, using the traced outlines as a guide.

5

Working with one cookie at a time, use red icing to pipe a "10" in the top left corner of the bottom card, a "J" in the top left corner of the next card, a "Q" on the next and a "K" on the next.

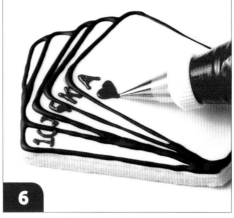

6

Pipe a red "A" in the top corner of the top card and a small heart underneath the "A."

7

Turn the cookie upside down and pipe another "A" in the opposite corner. ■ Pipe a small heart underneath the "A."

8

Turn the cookie right side up and pipe a heart in the center of the front card. ■ Repeat steps 5 to 8 for all cookies. ■ Let cookies dry for at least 3 hours before serving.

Tips

If all the white icing does not fit in your squeeze bottle, cover the remaining icing tightly and refill the bottle as needed.

If you don't have an X-acto knife, you can use an edible marker to trace the outlines in steps 2 and 3.

I often use a real example of the shape I am decorating to inspire my design. Use a real deck of cards as a reference if you decide to use different cards or suits for your cookies.

Variation

Instead of using a hand of cards cutter, use a rectangular cutter to make single cards, or use a playing card as a template.

Lucky Dice

Your friends will definitely feel like luck is on their side when they see a platter of these two-toned treats on the table. **Makes about 36.**

What You Need

- 1 recipe cookie dough (pages 36–46)
- Cube cookie cutter
- 1 recipe Classic Royal Icing (page 47)
- Black gel paste
- 2 squeeze bottles
- Cornstarch
- Small rolling pin
- White fondant
- #10 round decorating tip (see tips)
- Black fondant
- 2 disposable pastry bags
- 2 couplers
- 2 #2 round decorating tips
- X-acto knife

Techniques Used

- Tinting icing (page 22)
- Filling a squeeze bottle (page 24)
- Piping (page 27)
- Flooding (page 28)
- Working with fondant (page 30)
- Filling a pastry bag (page 24)
- Using an X-acto knife (page 31)

Getting Started

Bake cookies: Roll out dough and cut cookies with the cube cookie cutter. Bake according to recipe directions. Let cool completely before decorating.

Tint and thin icing: Place 1 cup (250 mL) icing in each of two bowls; tint one portion black and leave one white. Cover tightly and set aside. Divide remaining icing evenly between two bowls; tint one portion black and leave one white. Thin both icings to two-step icing consistency (page 24) and transfer to squeeze bottles.

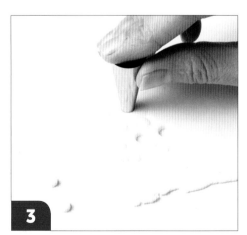

1

Using the squeeze bottle of black icing, outline and flood half the cookies.

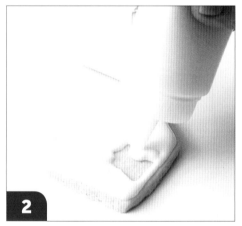

2

Using the squeeze bottle of white icing, outline and flood the remaining cookies. ■ Let icing set for at least 6 hours or overnight.

3

Meanwhile, on a work surface lightly dusted with cornstarch, roll out white fondant to $\frac{1}{16}$ inch (2 mm) thick. ■ Using the #10 tip as a cutter, cut out 10 circles per black cube.

4

Dust work surface with cornstarch and roll out black fondant to $\frac{1}{16}$ inch (2 mm) thick. ■ Using the #10 tip as a cutter, cut out 11 circles per white cube. ■ Place all circles on a cookie sheet and let dry for at least 4 hours or overnight.

5

Transfer reserved black and white icing to pastry bags fitted with #2 tips. ■ Use white icing to pipe borders dividing black dice into three faces (see tip).

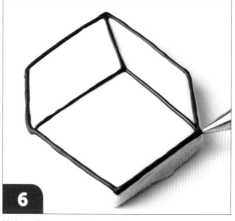

6

Using the pastry bag of black icing, pipe borders dividing white dice into three faces.

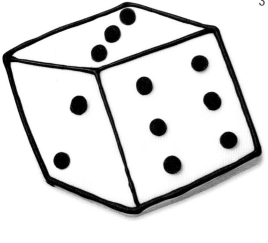

7

Working with one cookie at a time, use white icing to pipe 5 dots on the front face of each black die, 4 dots on the top face and 1 dot on the side face, as shown. ■ Place a white fondant circle on each dot. ■ Repeat for all black dice.

8

Working with one cookie at a time, use black icing to pipe 6 dots on the front face of each white die, 3 dots on the side face and 2 dots on the top face, as shown. ■ Place a black fondant circle on each dot. ■ Repeat for all white dice. ■ Let cookies dry for at least 3 hours before serving.

Tips

If you don't have a #10 decorating tip, use the end of a drinking straw as a cutter.

When cutting out fondant circles with the decorating tip, prevent sticking by dipping the tip in cornstarch between cuts or spraying the inside lightly with nonstick spray.

I like to use a ruler as a guide to help me make straight lines when piping. First, lightly trace your lines with an X-acto knife or edible marker, then pipe over the traced lines with icing.

Variations

Change up the colors of the dice and dots based on personal preference or the color scheme of your party.

Instead of using fondant dots, simply pipe the dots using pastry bags fitted with #2 tips.

Pink Martini

What You Need

- 1 recipe cookie dough (pages 36–46)
- Martini glass cookie cutter
- 1 recipe Classic Royal Icing (page 47)
- Red gel paste
- Black gel paste
- Hot pink gel paste
- 2 squeeze bottles
- Red sanding sugar
- Olive green fondant
- Disposable pastry bag
- Coupler
- #2 round decorating tip

Techniques Used

- Tinting icing (page 22)
- Filling a squeeze bottle (page 24)
- Piping (page 27)
- Flooding (page 28)
- Adding sparkle (page 28)
- Working with fondant (page 30)
- Filling a pastry bag (page 24)

Once associated with the vintage Las Vegas era that made the Rat Pack famous, martinis have made a comeback. You can now order them in every flavor and color imaginable, including shocking shades of pink. These sugar-rimmed cookies are appropriate for guests with a sweet tooth, who might prefer to pair them with ice-cold milk. **Makes about 30.**

Getting Started

Bake cookies: Roll out dough and cut cookies with the martini glass cookie cutter. Bake according to recipe directions. Let cool completely before decorating.

Tint and thin icing: Place 1/2 cup (125 mL) icing in a bowl and tint it red. Cover tightly and set aside. Divide remaining icing evenly between two bowls; tint one portion black and one hot pink. Thin black and hot pink icing to two-step icing consistency (page 24) and transfer to squeeze bottles.

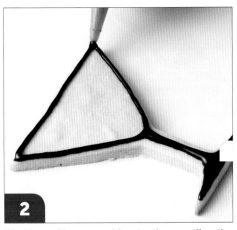

1

Using black icing, outline and flood each martini glass stem and base.

2

Working with one cookie at a time, outline the triangular portion of each martini glass.

3

While the black icing is still wet, sprinkle the rim of each glass with sanding sugar, shaking off excess. ■ Repeat steps 2 and 3 for all cookies.

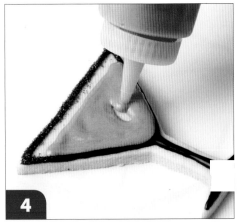

4

Using hot pink icing, outline and flood interior of martini glasses, leaving a small strip at the top un-iced. ■ Let icing set for at least 6 hours or overnight.

5

Meanwhile, mold 2 tsp (10 mL) fondant into an oval olive shape. ■ Flatten the back so the olive will lie flat. ■ Make 1 olive per cookie. ■ Place olives on a cookie sheet and let dry for at least 4 hours or overnight.

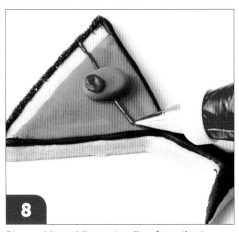

6

Dab the back of each olive with icing and affix an olive to the interior of each martini glass.

7

Transfer red icing to a pastry bag fitted with a #2 tip. ■ Pipe a small red circle on one end of each olive.

8

Pipe a thin red line extending from the top and bottom of each olive as a cocktail pick. ■ Let cookies dry for at least 3 hours before serving.

Tips

Don't be alarmed if excess sanding sugar sticks to the cookie even after you shake it. Wait until the icing dries completely, then gently brush off the unwanted sugar with a small food-safe paintbrush or a cotton swab.

Keep any fondant you are not presently working with tightly wrapped in plastic wrap, as it can quickly dry out, rendering it unusable.

Variations

Instead of making olives, float a cherry in each glass. If you have a small cherry cutter, cut cherries out of red fondant and affix one to each martini with a dab of icing. Or pipe a cherry freehand with red icing. Pipe a stem using black or brown icing.

Play around with the colors of the martini liquid and glass. Try a silver-tinted glass and a purple martini!

Elvis

These cool cookies are definitely fit for The King! From his jet black hair, dark shades and signature smirk to his famous white jumpsuit and blue suede shoes, the results are a hunka-hunka-burnin' deliciousness! **Makes about 24.**

What You Need

- 1 recipe cookie dough (pages 36–46)
- Gingerbread man cutter
- 1 recipe Classic Royal Icing (page 47)
- Red gel paste
- Black gel paste
- Yellow gel paste
- Blue gel paste
- 2 squeeze bottles
- Cornstarch
- Small rolling pin
- Blue fondant
- Ruler
- X-acto knife
- 3 disposable pastry bags
- 3 couplers
- #1 round decorating tip
- 2 #2 round decorating tips

Techniques Used

- Tinting icing (page 22)
- Filling a squeeze bottle (page 24)
- Piping (page 27)
- Flooding (page 28)
- Working with fondant (page 30)
- Using an X-acto knife (page 31)
- Filling a pastry bag (page 24)

Getting Started

Bake cookies: Roll out dough and cut cookies with the gingerbread man cookie cutter. Bake according to recipe directions. Let cool completely before decorating.

Tint and thin icing: Place ¾ cup (175 mL) icing in each of four bowls; tint one portion red, one black, one yellow and one blue. Cover red, black and yellow icing tightly and set aside. Thin blue icing and remaining white icing to two-step icing consistency (page 24) and transfer to squeeze bottles.

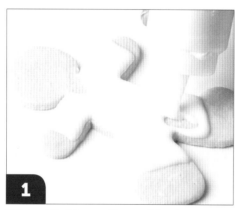

1

Using white icing, outline and flood a jumpsuit for each cookie.

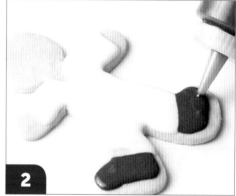

2

Using blue icing, outline and flood blue suede shoes for each cookie. ■ Let icing set for at least 6 hours or overnight.

3

Meanwhile, on a work surface lightly dusted with cornstarch, roll out blue fondant to ¹⁄₁₆ inch (2 mm) thick. ■ With the ruler as a guide, use the X-acto knife to cut strips about ½ inch (1 cm) wide and long enough to fit the waistline of each jumpsuit. ■ Make 1 strip per cookie. ■ Place strips on a cookie sheet and let dry for at least 4 hours or overnight.

4

Transfer yellow icing to a pastry bag fitted with a #1 tip. ■ Transfer red and black icing to pastry bags fitted with #2 tips. ■ Use red and yellow icing to pipe details onto each jumpsuit as shown.

5 Using black icing, pipe hair, sunglasses lenses and a nose on each cookie.

6 Using red icing, pipe a half smile on each cookie.

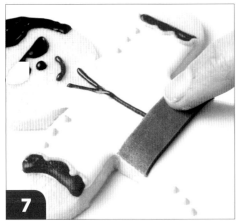

7 Dab the back of each fondant strip with icing and affix a strip to the waistline of each jumpsuit.

8 Using yellow icing, pipe a star in the center of each belt, a dot on either side of the star and the arms of the sunglasses. ■ Let cookies dry for at least 4 hours before serving.

Casino Night

Tips

Make these cookies with Peanut Butter cookie dough (page 41), one of Elvis's favorite flavors.

If all the white icing does not fit in your squeeze bottle, cover the remaining icing tightly and refill the bottle as needed.

After rolling out fondant, let it rest for about 15 minutes (but not much longer!) before cutting out shapes. This allows it to harden a bit, making for cleaner cuts.

If you don't have an X-acto knife, a sharp paring knife will work fine.

The ruler will help you cut straight lines when you're cutting the fondant belts.

Variation

Instead of creating the belts out of fondant, simply pipe them on with blue icing. Wait at least 1 hour for the belts to dry before piping the details on top.

"Welcome to Las Vegas" Sign

What You Need

- 1 recipe cookie dough (pages 36–46)
- X-acto knife
- Las Vegas sign template (page 251)
- 1 recipe Classic Royal Icing (page 47)
- Blue gel paste
- Red gel paste
- Yellow gel paste
- 4 disposable pastry bags
- 4 couplers
- 3 #2 round decorating tips
- Squeeze bottle
- Cornstarch
- Small rolling pin
- White fondant
- Red disco dust or sanding sugar
- #1 round decorating tip

Techniques Used

- Using an X-acto knife (page 31)
- Working with templates (page 32)
- Tinting icing (page 22)
- Filling a pastry bag (page 24)
- Filling a squeeze bottle (page 24)
- Piping (page 27)
- Flooding (page 28)
- Working with fondant (page 30)
- Adding sparkle (page 28)

Las Vegas is full of glitzy signs, but few are more iconic than the "Welcome to Fabulous Las Vegas" sign. These replica cookies welcome guests to a casino party, but can be adapted to suit any occasion. **Makes about 24.**

Getting Started

Bake cookies: Roll out dough and, using the X-acto knife and Las Vegas sign template, cut out cookies, rerolling scraps as necessary. Bake according to recipe directions. Let cool completely before decorating.

Tint and thin icing: Place ³⁄₄ cup (125 mL) icing in each of three bowls. Tint one portion blue, one red and one yellow. Transfer blue icing to a piping bag fitted with a #2 tip. Cover red and yellow portions tightly and set aside. Thin remaining white icing to two-step icing consistency (page 24) and transfer to a squeeze bottle.

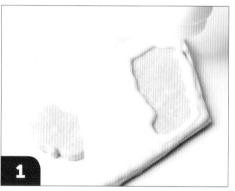

1 Using white icing, outline and flood the diamond-shaped portion of each cookie.

2 Using blue icing, pipe a square arch onto the portion of each cookie that juts out on the left side, as shown. ■ Let icing set for at least 6 hours or overnight.

3 Meanwhile, on a work surface lightly dusted with cornstarch, roll out fondant to ¹⁄₁₆ inch (2 mm) thick. ■ Using the round back side of a decorating tip, cut out 7 circles per cookie. ■ Place circles on a cookie sheet and let dry for at least 4 hours or overnight.

4 Transfer red and yellow icing to piping bags fitted with #2 tips. ■ Working with one cookie at a time, use red icing to pipe a star onto the portion of each cookie that juts out on the left side, overlapping the blue icing, as shown.

5

While the red icing is still wet, sprinkle the star with disco dust, shaking off excess. ■ Repeat steps 4 and 5 for all cookies.

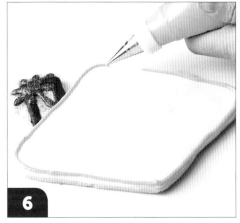

6

Using yellow icing, pipe a border around the diamond-shaped portion of each cookie.

Tips

If you don't have an X-acto knife, any small, sharp knife will work fine.

Cookie dough retains its shape best when cold. If the rolled-out dough gets too warm while you're cutting shapes, carefully transfer it to a cookie sheet and place it in the refrigerator for 15 minutes before continuing.

If you have filled a pastry bag with icing but are not using it right away, set it upright in a tall drinking glass until you're ready for it.

If all the white icing does not fit in your squeeze bottle, cover the remaining icing tightly and refill the bottle as needed.

Keep any fondant you are not presently working with tightly wrapped in plastic wrap, as it can quickly dry out, rendering it unusable.

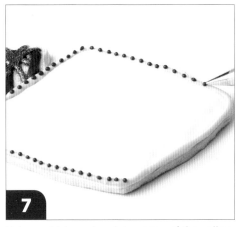

7

Using red icing, pipe dots on top of the yellow border, spacing them close together and an equal distance apart.

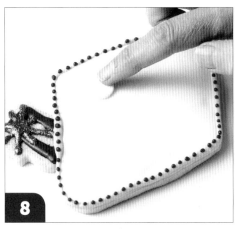

8

Working with one cookie at a time, dab the back of a fondant circle with icing and affix it near the top of the cookie, centered horizontally.

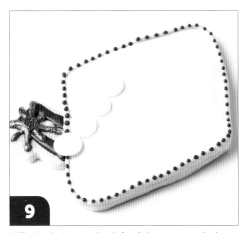

9

Affix 3 circles to the left of the center circle.

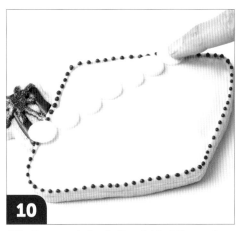

10

Affix 3 more circles to the right of the center circle, so that you end up with 7 circles in a line across the top of the cookie. ■ Repeat steps 8 to 10 for all cookies.

continued… Party Cookies **249**

Tip

I use a ruler to help me pipe words in a straight line. Lay the ruler across the part of the cookie where you intend to pipe and make subtle marks with an X-acto knife to serve as a guide for the bottom of each letter.

Variation

Change the words on the cookies to create a memorable thank-you note: "T-H-A-N-K-S-! For a fabulous weekend!"

11

Using red icing, pipe "W-E-L-C-O-M-E" across the fondant circles, centering one letter in each circle.

12

Pipe "LAS VEGAS" in red across each cookie, just below center, spacing the letters as evenly as possible.

13

Change tip on blue icing to a #1 tip. ■ Underneath the fondant circles, pipe "TO OUR FABULOUS," as shown.

14

Pipe "PARTY!" underneath "LAS VEGAS." ■ Let cookies dry for at least 4 hours before serving.

Templates

"Welcome to Fabulous Las Vegas" sign (page 248)

Colored Crayons oval (page 176)

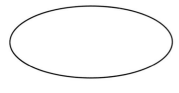

"Just Married" Car banner (page 203)

School Bus stop sign (page 182)

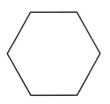

Painter's Palette (page 234)

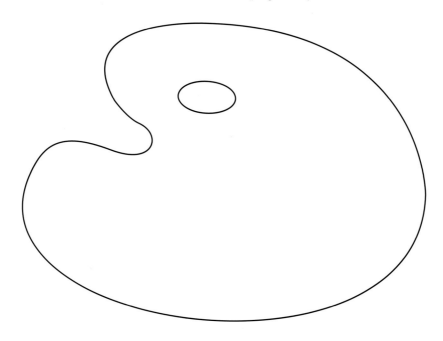

French Painter's mini palette (page 231)

Soccer Ball pentagon (page 158)

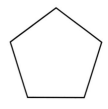

Curious Owl wing (page 126)

Bottle of Champagne label (page 236)

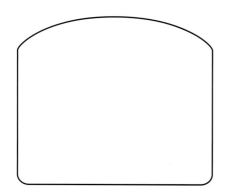

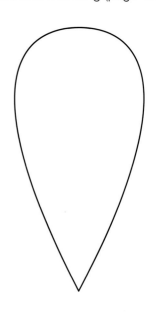

Source Guide

Cookie Cutters

Ann Clark
www.annclark.com

Cheap Cookie Cutters
www.cheapcookiecutters.com

The Cookie Cutter Shop
www.thecookiecuttershop.com

Copper Gifts
www.coppergifts.com

Off the Beaten Path
www.cookiecutter.com

Karen's Cookies
www.karenscookies.net

King Arthur Flour
www.kingarthurflour.com

N.Y. Cake
www.nycake.com

Sugarcraft
www.sugarcraft.com

Wilton
www.wilton.com

Baking and Decorating Supplies

Chicago Metallic
www.chicagometallicbakeware.com

Country Kitchen SweetArt
www.countrykitchensa.com

Fancy Flours
www.fancyflours.com

Global Sugar Art
www.globalsugarart.com

Chains/Bricks and Mortar Resources

Hobby Lobby
www.hobbylobby.com

Michaels
www.michaels.com

Sur La Table
www.surlatable.com

Williams-Sonoma
www.williams-sonoma.com

Library and Archives Canada Cataloguing in Publication

Hession, Julie Anne, author
    100 best decorated cookies : featuring 750 step-by-step photos / Julie Anne Hession.

Includes index.
ISBN 978-0-7788-0456-7 (bound)

    1. Cookies. 2. Cookbooks. I. Title. II. Title: One hundred best decorated cookies.

TX772.H48 2013   641.86'54   C2013-902264-3

Index